Development and Humanitarianism

Development and Humanitarianism: Practical Issues is based on articles
published in *Development in Practice* Volume 16, Numbers 3&4 (June 2006);
Volume 16, Number 2 (April 2006); and Volume 15, Number 6 (November 2005),
published by Routledge, Taylor & Francis Ltd.

The chapter by Martha Thompson and Deborah Eade was originally published in
Social Development Issues Volume 24, Number 3, pp. 50–58 (2002).

The chapter by Suzanne Williams originally appeared as "Conflicts of Interest:
Gender in Oxfam's Emergency Response" in Cynthia Cockburn and Dubravka
Zarkov (eds.) *The Postwar Moment: Militaries, Masculinities and International
Peacekeeping,* London: Lawrence & Wishart, 2002, pp. 85–102.

Development and Humanitarianism

Practical Issues

EDITED BY
DEBORAH EADE AND TONY VAUX

Kumarian
Press, Inc.

Development and Humanitarianism: Practical Issues

Published 2007 in the United States of America by Kumarian Press, Inc., 1294 Blue Hills Avenue, Bloomfield, CT 06002 USA

Design, production, and editorial services were provided by Publication Services, Inc., Champaign, Illinois. The text of this book is set in Adobe Times 10.5/13.

Printed in the United States on acid-free paper by Thomson-Shore.

Text printed with vegetable oil-based ink.

∞ The paper used in this publication meets the minimum requirements of the American National Standard for Information Sciences—Permanence of Paper for printed Library Materials, ANSI Z39.48-1984

Library of Congress Cataloging-in-Publication Data

Development and humanitarianism : practical issues / edited by Deborah Eade and Tony Vaux.
    p. cm.
 Includes bibliographical references and index.
 ISBN 978-1-56549-239-4 (alk. paper)
 1. Humanitarian assistance—Developing countries. 2. War relief—Developing countries. I. Eade, Deborah. II. Vaux, Tony.
 HV555.D44D48 2007
 363.34'988091724—dc22   2007026225

15   14   13   12   11   10   09   08   1   2   3   4   5   6   7   8   9

Contents

Preface

DEBORAH EADE

Breaches of human rights and humanitarian law including mutilation, rape, forced displacement, denial of the right to food and medicines, diversion of aid and attacks on medical personnel and hospitals are no longer inevitable by-products of war. They have become the means to achieve a strategic goal.

Sérgio Vieira de Mello 1999
(quoted in Frohardt, Paul and Minear 1999:65)

The Special Representative of the United Nations Secretary-General in Iraq, Sérgio Vieira de Mello, was killed along with twenty-three of his staff on August 19, 2003, in an attack on the UN compound in Baghdad. He had told the UN Security Council only the month before that the mission might become a target. Some observers suggested, however, that the true target was the political reconstruction of Iraq under conditions of occupation.

Humanitarian intervention invariably rubs shoulders with politics, albeit awkwardly and sometimes, as in this case, with tragic results. Tensions between them take many forms, ranging from different assessments of the extent or even the existence of a crisis[1] to claims that humanitarian assistance is not saving innocent lives but sustaining politico-military forces,[2] or to the conclusion that the constraints upon aid agencies compel them to withdraw from the area of operation—whether to ensure the safety of their own staff[3] or because they believe that their integrity is unacceptably compromised by staying.[4] Framing these operational issues are questions of the role of "military humanitarianism" (Slim 1995) and the political economy of "network wars" and the "securitisation of development" (Duffield 2001).

Clearly, providers of humanitarian assistance do not all share compatible mandates, analyses, priorities, or ways of working. But even similar or like-minded agencies may weigh up the situation, and their role within it, quite differently. One organization may judge that it can achieve more by closing down its mission in order to engage in "humanitarian advocacy," while another may stay because it prefers to continue providing assistance even if some of that assistance gets into the wrong hands. Or an agency may believe that simply witnessing violations of human rights may in itself offer a modicum of protection to civilians whose lives are at risk, by potentially raising the international political stakes of committing abuses. In other words, aid agencies may have equally valid justifications for choosing quite different courses of action. Since the question is usually one of judgment rather than of inviolable principle, then no single position is absolutely right.

To some extent, it may be argued that the challenges facing humanitarian agencies since the end of the Cold War, in particular since the declaration of the "global war on terror," are contemporary permutations of age-old problems—the apocalyptic predictions following the events of September 11, 2001, notwithstanding.[5] Although long-standing international covenants governing the treatment of civilians and enemy prisoners in situations of armed conflict may not be widely known or cared about, this does not in itself render them redundant. Nobody would suggest, after all, that the extensive use of torture invalidates the 1985 Convention Against Torture and Other Cruel, Inhuman or Degrading Treatment or Punishment or that because it is used in one country, that justifies its use elsewhere. The view that "humanitarianism is dead," as some "'back to basics' humanitarian Luddites" (Slim 2003: 3, his response to David Rieff on this point), seems as premature as the claim that the fall of the Berlin Wall and the breakup of the Soviet Union heralded "the end of history" (Fukuyama 1992). The phenomenal response to the 2004 Asian tsunami disaster also belies the argument that donors and the general public are suffering terminal "fatigue," although it is true that chronic tragedies—for instance, the number of lives avoidably lost each year to malaria, tuberculosis, measles, and diarrhea, let alone HIV and AIDS—fail to kindle the same spirit of compassion and global responsibility. Memories are short, a fact poignantly illustrated by Mary Kayitesi-Blewitt (2006) in relation to the international oblivion surrounding the continuing tragedy of the thousands of women and girls who were raped during the 1994 Rwanda genocide.

That having been said, the greater willingness of some Western governments to intervene with military force in situations that they deem threatening to the local population or to global security makes it increasingly difficult for humanitarian actors to avoid furthering Western political agendas, irrespective of whether they endorse them. Many humanitarian organizations, including the specialized UN agencies, agonized over whether their contingency plans for post-invasion Iraq constituted in some sense an endorsement of the US-led military intervention. Even if they eschew government funding, humanitarian agencies may find it hard to adhere to the traditional principles of independence, impartiality, and neutrality when their access to people in need is mediated by armed intervention or political violence. Moreover, conflict and catastrophe interact in ways that complicate the humanitarian terrain. Thus, when the tsunami struck areas that were already in the throes of armed conflict, such as Aceh and Sri Lanka, the issue of who should control the relief and reconstruction programs in the affected regions necessarily responded to politico-military considerations as well as to "simple" humanitarian concerns. Similar dynamics played out in the wake of Hurricane Katrina in New Orleans.

This *Reader* is based mainly on articles selected from a special issue of the international journal, *Development in Practice* (Volume 16, Numbers 3 and 4) that was guest-edited by Tony Vaux, for many years one of Oxfam GB's senior humanitarian directors and previously a development worker in India. The contributions gathered here seek to address some of these concerns and the dilemmas that they pose for aid agencies and their frontline staff in interpreting the principles of humanitarianism in contexts in which they risk being manipulated by one or another political agenda. He asks: "How should Western aid agencies manage their connections with Western governments? How should they relate to local organizations? Should they extend their functions from humanitarian relief to protection and address the political causes of conflict and disaster? If so, how will they remain independent?" (pp. 1–2).

The first section of the book looks at the politics of violent confrontation, whether this takes the form of conflict between sovereign nations, conflict between governments and opposing groups operating within national borders, or the use of troops in bilateral or multilateral "humanitarian intervention"—or, as Slim (2003:5) refers to it, "the deeply regrettable phenomenon of humanitarian invasion"—either to prevent mass killings or to enforce a peace plan, as in the cases of Bosnia, Côte d'lvoire, Haiti, Kosovo, Liberia, Sierra Leone, or Timor Leste (Roth 2004). Vanessa Pupavac sets the scene, arguing that while humanitarian advocacy has traditionally underlined the causal relationship between state policies and situations in which people's lives are endangered, the recent tendency to challenge national sovereignty helps to legitimize the erosion of equality among sovereign states and the reassertion of international inequalities. A recent report by the World Bank (World Bank 2004) reiterates the widespread belief that large commitments are made in the immediate post-conflict phase—the so-called CNN effect—soon tapering off to more "normal" levels. The report criticizes such "frontloading," claiming that it damages the prospects of the economic growth that is needed to secure peace. Astri Suhrke and Julia Buckmaster argue, however, that this analysis and the assumptions upon which it is based are critically flawed. The report, they allege, fails to distinguish between commitments and disbursements or to take sufficient account of other factors that influence aid patterns, and that it vastly overplays the importance of the link between official aid and postwar economic performance.

Drawing on the case of a group of renegade soldiers from the Democratic Republic of Congo (DRC) who claimed refugee status in Rwanda, Volker Schimmel illustrates how the artificial separation of political and humanitarian considerations, reinforced by the fact that the two areas were managed by different agencies, had the perverse (albeit unintended) effect of foreclosing on a political outcome that would have been acceptable to all parties and would have helped to consolidate the fragile DRC transition process. Furthermore, the differences of emphasis among the different types of agency, official and nongovernmental, that were focused on the humanitarian aspects of the intervention undermined the possibility their taking more robust concerted action. He calls for agencies involved in humanitarian operations to be proactive in seeking to understand and complement each other's mandates and insights, and in particular for all parties relevant to aid and postwar reconstruction to cross the political-humanitarian divide.

The second section of the book examines the issue of protection in situations of war or sustained violence, whether politically motivated or not. Andrew Bonwick challenges the widespread assumption that the "protection of civilians" depends on international intervention, arguing that humanitarian action should support and strengthen the rational decisions that people themselves take to try to ensure their own "safety"

in situations of armed conflict, rather than focusing exclusively on lobbying governments and other powers bearing a legal responsibility to protect civilians. While the protection of civilians has recently assumed prominence in the advocacy agendas of some Northern NGOs—possibly fired up by the apparent success of recent international campaigns on land mines or small arms-this approach risks casting all those living in situations of conflict as "helpless victims" rather than political and humanitarian actors in their own right. Based on their experience of working in Central America during the height of the counterinsurgency wars of the 1980s and 1990s, Martha Thompson and Deborah Eade draw out some of the lessons of policy and practice regarding security and protection from the ways in which Salvadoran peasant women developed their own "protection capacities" and leadership potential, even in the face of brutal aggression.

This theme is taken up by Gretchen Alther, who sets out how national and international agencies might best support Colombian grassroots "peace communities" in their own efforts to create nonviolent solutions to Latin America's longest contemporary armed conflict. While material assistance may help such communities to sustain themselves economically, living alongside or accompanying them and bearing witness to their struggle may be equally or more important in ensuring their survival.

The third section highlights the difficulties of providing humanitarian assistance in highly complex or contested terrains in ways that most of the parties involved agree should promise to do more good than they risk doing harm. This outcome can be equally difficult to achieve, whether the aid agency in question runs its own programs or channels its assistance through local organizations. These chapters therefore focus in particular on the relationships among the long string of agencies typically involved—from official donors to international NGOs, to national governments, to local NGOs, to the affected communities. Udan Fernando and Dorothea Hilhorst examine three types of response to the 2004 tsunami in Sri Lanka, arguing that the real way to understand humanitarian aid is to focus on what happens in practice and how those who are directly involved navigate their way through the challenges and dilemmas facing them. Jonathan Makuwira describes the problems experienced in trying to balance the accountability demands and the political and operational priorities of three "partners"—an official donor, an intermediary agency, and a local organization—in the case of postconflict and subsequent conflict prevention programs in Bougainville. He concludes that formal accountability frameworks are a poor substitute for the mutual trust that will make relationships between such partners effective. Frank James Tester describes an innovative (though problematic) project that sought to combine disarming the civilian population in Mozambique with providing them with agricultural and other tools, and using the former weapons to create artistic sculptures to highlight the proliferation of arms and munitions among civilian populations. Again, the conclusion is that well-intended programs designed by external agencies that do not match local perceptions not only risk failure but can undermine other successes. With reference to its work in Kosovo, Suzanne Williams explores the difficulties faced by Oxfam GB in integrating gender equity goals into the institutional structures and policies that govern its activities in conflict and its aftermath. Despite organizational policies that assert the universal importance of gender power relations in shaping the gendered outcomes of aid interventions, in practice many humanitarian aid workers assume that gender analysis and gender-sensitive progamming belong to the "nonconflict" field of reconstruction and development and do not fall within the scope of urgent interventions. Effectively, there are two institutional cultures, each with its own norms and values. Williams argues that addressing gender equity is in and of itself essential to overcoming these divisions.

A final section includes a brief review by Martha Thompson of recent literature on the political economy of conflict and feminist writing on women in conflict. She argues that the former tends to be gender-blind, while the latter generally fails to take the wider political issues into account. Both perspectives need to be integrated in order to understand how women and men survive conflict and the ways in which their experiences of war and the survival strategies they adopt affect subsequent gender power relations. The volume concludes with a listing of current resources selected and annotated by Deborah Eade.

Recent years have seen a proliferation of standards and systems designed to increase agencies' accountability to donors and to their intended beneficiaries. As Tony Vaux argues, the impetus for this trend was the 1994 Rwanda genocide, but the enormous expansion of the emergency relief industry had already led to concerns that the resulting competition within the sector could depress rather than raise standards. The problem with the insistence on technical and measurable standards—such as the size of food rations for refugees in enclosed camps—is that they tend to foster a "checklist" mentality that can seduce aid workers into believing that a good job is being done simply because the boxes on the form have all been completed correctly. Standards and frameworks are not, after all, political compasses or navigational tools: they will not tell you where you are, why you are there, or where you are headed. While humanitarian action is invariably political, so too is the failure to act or, more insidiously, the "'cleansing" of the humanitarian ethic from politics that wants neither humanitarian norms nor humanitarian workers in a given political arena (Slim 2003:5). As is clear from the contributions to this volume, and from the wider literature covered in the resources list, it is quite possible to do a good technical job within an overall context that is far from positive in its impact—for example by being part of a particular political or economic agenda, whether as a willing party or as a stooge. As Vaux points out, "[t]he awkward reality is that providing relief aid . . . can create new threats to human life."

NOTES

[1] The case of "famine" in North Korea is a recent example of this kind of standoff. Specialized UN agencies, such as the World Food Programme, claimed that food shortages were leading to extensive and chronic hunger and malnutrition, while the Pyongyang government initially denied that the situation was critical. A report written for the United States Institute of Peace (USIP) referred to "[a]n acrimonious policy debate . . . within humanitarian organizations about the severity of the famine—indeed, its very existence-and the role of international food assistance in ending it" (Natsios 1999:2). The report admitted that these questions were not new, but that in this case they reflected "legimate concerns about the effect of food aid to a country where those with political authority may have objectives very different from those of humanitarian agencies trying to reduce death rates" (ibid.). The interlinked nature of humanitarianism and politics was underscored by the passing of the 2004 North Korean Human Rights Act, which simultaneously provides US humanitarian assistance and allows North Koreans to be granted asylum in the USA (Amnesty International 2005).

[2] The definition of "humanitarian" aid is often bitterly contested. During the twelve-year civil war in El Salvador, for instance, the military authorities persistently maintained that any assistance to civilians in areas outside government control, including to refugees, was part of the FMLN guerrilla war effort. As Martha Thompson, who was a humanitarian worker in Central America for almost fifteen years, notes, "Counter-insurgency is about militarising politics, and politicising the military. Humanitarian aid to the war-displaced becomes a military issue. . . . In counter-insurgency, where the state must control everything, 'non-government' means 'anti-government'" (Thompson 1996:327). Meanwhile, in 1985 the Reagan Administration requested US$ 14 million in

military aid for the Nicaraguan Contras, promising to restrict this to "humanitarian" assistance if the Sandinista government agreed to a cease-fire. In 1998 a further US$ 47.9 million was granted, again for "humanitarian" purposes, despite the exposure in 1986 of the Administration's acquiescence in smuggling arms in the so-called Contragate affair.

[3] For instance, in January 2006 the International Committee of the Red Cross (ICRC) withdrew from the southern region of the Republic of Congo (RoC; Congo-Brazzaville) after threats made against its staff by so-called Ninja fighters loyal to rebel leader Frédéric Bitsangou (International Relations and Security Network 2006). In July 2004, Médecins Sans Frontières (MSF) withdrew from Afghanistan after five of its staff had been murdered while serving there. Only weeks before the killings, MSF had criticized attempts by the US-led coalition forces "to co-opt humanitarian aid," arguing that this was "endangering the lives of humanitarian volunteers and jeopardizing the aid to people in need." In particular, it condemned "the distribution of leaflets by the coalition forces in southern Afghanistan informing the population that providing information about the Taliban and al Qaeda was necessary if they wanted the delivery of aid to continue" (MSF 2004).

[4] Médecins Sans Frontières (MSF), for instance, withdrew from the Rwandan refugee camps because it judged that humanitarian assistance was doing more to strengthen the *génocidaires* than to relieve suffering. Though MSF has sometimes been accused by other humanitarian agencies of being utopian, Fiona Terry, formerly MSF's Research Director and now an ICRC delegate in Myanmar, counters that it is utopian to imagine that aid can be given without causing any harm and that such a pretense makes it harder to assess the relative good and harm of a specific humanitarian intervention and act accordingly (Terry 2002).

[5] Fiona Terry (2002) argues that too much emphasis is placed on changes in the post–Cold War context to explain the difficulties encountered in assisting victims of conflict, and that some aid agencies invoke such changes as a pretext to avoid responsibility for the consequences of their actions. The intertwining of aid and conflict has always been complex, and Terry maintains that some of the dilemmas faced in the past—for instance, the case of assistance for Cambodians along the Thai–Cambodian border and inside Cambodia in the 1980s—were probably more difficult than those being confronted today.

REFERENCES

Amnesty International (2005) *AI Report 2005*, available at http://web.amnesty.org/report2005/prk-summary-eng (retrieved January 24, 2006).

Duffield, Mark (2001) *Global Governance and the New Wars: The Merging of Development and Security*, London: Zed Books.

Frohardt, Mark, Diane Paul and Larry Minear (1999) *Protecting Human Rights: The Challenge to Humanitarian Organizations*, Occasional Paper 35, Providence, RI: Thomas J. Watson Jr Institute for International Studies.

Fukuyama, Francis (1992) *The End of History and the Last Man*, New York: Free Press.

International Relations and Security Network (2006) "ICRC Pulls Out of Republic of Congo Region," available at www.isn.ethz.ch/news/sw/details.cfm?id= 14467 (retrieved 24 January 2006).

Médecins Sans Frontières (2004) "After 24 Years of Independent Aid to the Afghan People Doctors Without Borders Withdraws from Afghanistan Following Killings, Threats, and Insecurity," press release, July 28, available at www.doctorswithoutborders.org/pr/2004/07-28-2004.cfm (retrieved January 26, 2006).

Kayitesi-Blewitt, Mary (2006) "Funding Development in Rwanda: the Survivors' Perspective," *Development in Practice* 16(3&4): 316–321.

Natsios, Andrew (1999) *The Politics of Famine in North Korea*, Special Report No. 51, Washington, DC: USIP.

Roth, Kenneth (2004) "War in Iraq: Not a Humanitarian Intervention," in *Human Rights and Armed Conflict: Human Rights Watch World Report 2004*, New York: Human Rights Watch.

Slim, Hugo (1995) "Military Humanitarianism and the New Peacekeeping: An Agenda for Peace?," *Journal of Humanitarian Assistance*, available at http://www.jha.ac/articles/a003.htm (retrieved January 27, 2006).

Slim, Hugo (2003) "Is Humanitarianism Being Politicised? A Reply to David Rieff," paper delivered at The Dutch Red Cross Symposium on Ethics in Aid, The Hague, October 8, available at http://www.hdcentre.org/datastore/ shaping%20opinion/Reply%20to%20David%20%20Rieff.pdf (retrieved November 30, 2006).

Terry, Fiona (2002) *Condemned to Repeat: The Paradox of Humanitarian Action*, Ithaca, NY: Cornell University Press.

Thompson, Martha (1996) "Empowerment and Survival: Humanitarian Work in Civil Conflict," Part One, *Development in Practice* 6(4):324–333.

World Bank (2004) *Breaking the Conflict Trap*, Washington, DC: World Bank.

ONE

Humanitarian Trends and Dilemmas

TONY VAUX

INTRODUCTION

The concept of humanitarianism is applied in two contexts: war and
general disaster. Both of these contexts are included in the scope of this
Development in Practice Reader. The idea behind humanitarianism is
that in extreme cases of human suffering external agents may offer
assistance to people in need. In doing so, the humanitarian agents
should be accorded respect—and even "rights"—while carrying out
their functions. The capacity of Western agencies to respond to crises
has increased rapidly, with greater resources, faster travel, and a general
easing of restrictions following the end of the Cold War. But so, too,
have global tensions, arising from the assertion of Western power.

Although there have always been a few agencies with an explicitly
political agenda, humanitarians have traditionally described themselves
as nonpolitical. But today humanitarians find themselves constantly
questioned about their political connections. Instead of working in
neutral territory between the two global superpowers (as in the Cold
War) humanitarianism now finds itself rubbing shoulders with a single
superpower and its allies, and it is this relationship that is a primary
cause of concern for aid workers today.

This collection presents some of these concerns in the words of
practitioners and their academic counterparts. How should Western aid
agencies manage their relations with Western governments? How should
they relate to local organizations? Should they extend their functions

1

from humanitarian relief to the protection of civilians, and address the political causes of conflict and disaster? If so, how will they remain independent?

 One of the most immediate causes for concern is that global human-itarianism is highly biased toward a few situations that interest the most powerful Western politicians, such as the invasions of Afghanistan and Iraq, or those that trigger an emotive response from the Western pub-lic, such as the 2004 Asian tsunami disaster. People suffering in situa-tions that have a low political and media profile get less help than others. The pattern of humanitarian aid is more closely related to donors' interest than to the needs of the affected communities.

This is not to say that humanitarianism has suddenly become "politicized." It has always been affected by major political trends, and from time to time politics converges more closely with humani-tarianism or even takes it over. Similarly humanitarianism sometimes takes the form of a reaction to narrow political interests. For example, Oxfam[1] is one of several aid agencies that have highly political origins. During World War II, the British government refused to allow relief supplies into occupied Greece, despite a famine that is thought to have claimed 250,000 lives, mainly children. Citizens around the United Kingdom set up committees to protest against this policy, lobby Parliament, and send supplies through the blockade, defying the authorities. The Oxford Committee for Famine Relief was promi-nent among them. After the war it broadened its scope and renamed itself as Oxfam, and subsequently as Oxfam GB (OGB), to distin-guish it from other national Oxfams that had been established in various countries (later joined by other northern NGOs under the umbrella of Oxfam International). In contrast, at about the same time, the Cooperative for American Remittances to Europe (CARE) was founded with the aim of helping the US government deliver surplus US Army food parcels across post-war Europe (Stoddard 2003:27). It later changed its name to the more neutral Cooperative for Assistance and Relief Everywhere, Inc. Western nongovernment aid agencies have always been close to politics, either supporting political initia-tives or reacting against them.

The current trend is toward greater assertiveness by the Western powers and less consensus about their legitimacy. During the Cold War period, the superpowers provided arms to various regimes but did not intervene directly (except in their own "backyard"), for fear of coming into confrontation with their prime enemy. For instance, the

United States was extensively involved in the wars of Central America throughout the 1980s, but refrained from intervention farther afield, notably in Africa. Now there is little to stop the United States from doing as it likes, usually with the support of other major aid-giving countries. These geopolitical shifts and tensions send shock waves through the humanitarian profession.

Much depends on whether the person receiving assistance accepts the political baggage that comes with it. If individuals feel that their suffering is being exploited in order to make a political point, they may feel angry—especially if they do not agree with the point being made. This tension may be particularly acute in cases of conflict and war. People in need of assistance may have very different perceptions of political issues than do the givers of aid. Their perceptions may not be the same as those of local organizations or their national government. There can be serious implications. They may refuse to cooperate with aid agencies or withhold information that might be important for security. All this creates, at the very least, an uncomfortable feeling for the aid giver, and uncertainty about whether and how to be transparent about the sources of funding. There is also a fear of becoming a tool of Western politics.

Hence the "politicization" of aid is an important topic of debate. Aid workers do not necessarily want to be detached from politics, but they want to know if they are being manipulated by interests that they do not support, and they want to know the risks that arise from the political agendas that surround them. All these factors affect their relationship with the person in need of assistance.

There are, however, positive aspects to Western assertiveness and its closer linkage with humanitarianism. Aid has come closer to the center of public and political attention, giving the agencies greater profile, more resources, and more influence. But the same dynamic also leads to greater expectations: is it not reasonable to expect that with such advantages the aid agencies should be able to address the root causes of problems?

The continuing killings in the Darfur region of Sudan have demonstrated that the "new world order" will not solve every problem and may indeed create new ones. Cold War politics continues to block humanitarian responses—not through the single US–Russian confrontation of the past, but in the form of a complex web of trade-offs played out in the UN Security Council. The United States actively considered military intervention in Darfur, but China stood in the way because of its oil interests.

British ministers wanted to apply pressure on the Sudanese leaders through the International Criminal Court (ICC), but the United States did not want to give the court legitimacy. No one can be sure if the reasons given in public for a political stance are the real reasons. Speculation abounds. Aid workers live amid constantly shifting perceptions of themselves, the West, and the nature of humanitarianism.

To add to all this, the "global war on terror" (GWOT) now dominates the political landscape. NATO's intervention in Kosovo was described by the British Prime Minister as a "humanitarian war"; the aim was to bring an end to unacceptable and unnecessary human suffering. Political factors were certainly involved, but humanitarianism was also a leading motive—although, as the Prime Minister observed at the time, it made a difference that the issues were played out within Europe, rather than in some distant part of the globe. But after September 11, 2001, Western security has come to dominate all other agendas, moving aid and humanitarianism even farther toward the core of politics. The threat has been linked variously to Islamic peoples, unstable states, and poverty. In the eyes of politicians, humanitarianism has now become a means to another end (that of Western security), rather than an end in itself.

Outwardly aid agencies have been extremely successful over the past decade. Budgets have increased dramatically, and the agencies have been welcomed into policy discussions at the highest levels. They have been both embarrassed and gratified to find themselves regarded as part of the political establishment and assumed to be allies in the GWOT.

Greater resources have allowed more time for research, reflection, training, and improvement in systems. On the ground there is a sense of greater professionalism and more confidence in knowing what needs to be done, at least in terms of techniques and standards. But aid workers also have a number of serious concerns, especially concerning their relationships with local partners and people. Issues of accountability remain unresolved and uncertain. As Western politics draws humanitarianism closer to itself, the distance from people in need seems to increase. Tensions play out within the aid agencies between different levels of decision making.

Current trends mean that although they have more resources, humanitarians are less in control of their work than they were in the past. This situation points aid agencies toward a more ambitious or maximalist view. We should aim higher. We should not only address immediate needs but also tackle the causes of vulnerability and insecurity, even though these are likely to be political in character.

NEEDS VERSUS RESOURCES

The fact that makes me most uncomfortable today is that, despite many individual successes, the system as a whole is not functioning effectively in terms of its basic purpose. The most fundamental principle of humanitarianism—stated in both the Red Cross Code (IFRC 1994) and the Sphere Charter (The Sphere Project 2004)—is that the response must be based on needs, not on any other factor such as political interests, cultural affinity, or availability of resources. This is known as the "humanitarian imperative." But, looking around the world, we can see at a glance that agencies' responses are not based solely on an assessment of needs. They strongly reflect political and cultural factors. The war in the Democratic Republic of the Congo (DRC) is thought to have caused as many as four million deaths in the last few years (WHO 2005), but it barely features in the global portfolio of many of the largest agencies, whereas Iraq, which scarcely qualifies as a humanitarian disaster at all, consumes far greater attention.

The Asian tsunami of December 26, 2004, evoked a massive public response and has since totally dominated the budgets and activities of many aid agencies; but in comparison with other ongoing challenges to humanitarian agencies, such as conditions in Sudan and the Congo, the needs of the tsunami survivors are not exceptional. The most senior and experienced staff, and the advocacy experts, tend to focus on high-profile areas rather than those where the need is greatest. Field staff are drawn from other programs to deal with the challenge of spending huge sums of aid donations in high-profile areas within a reasonable period of time. The opportunity cost of the tsunami disaster has been considerable.

Although each aid worker may gain satisfaction from doing a good job in her or his own location and from scrupulously following the "humanitarian imperative," the system as a whole is not in compliance. Global responses bear little relationship to global needs. It would be hard to prove that this situation never happened in the past, but a series of papers produced by aid agencies suggests that there is a trend toward greater discrepancy (Christian Aid 2004; Cosgrave 2004; Oxfam GB 2003). Although the point has been registered, the agencies have not emphasized it in their publications and comments on the issue. This is surprising because the failure of the entire humanitarian system to follow its most fundamental principle is surely a matter of considerable importance.

Perhaps the agencies lack confidence that they can change the way in which their funding works. They rely on the Western public for donations, and they feel that they cannot influence the emotive way in which people respond to one disaster and ignore another. Similarly political preferences are likely to follow national interests, especially security. But the agencies' silence suggests a lack of resolve to challenge either the institutional donors or the public. At worst it gives rise to a suspicion that they simply want to maximize resources, regardless of whether those resources can be used in a principled manner. For example, aid agencies in the United Kingdom could challenge the British government for not allocating aid according to need, as required by the Public Service Agreement of the Department for International Development (DFID). Certainly this would amount to "rocking the boat" and might lead to worsening relations with a major provider of resources. But, if the boat is far off course, raised voices may be the only way of attracting the attention of the captain.

After a certain point, a few agencies decided to stop accepting public funds for the tsunami disaster. Some advised their donors and supporters to give to other more needy causes. But, without concerted action by the agencies, donors simply switched their gifts to another organization that was considered more accommodating. Without concerted action, individual agencies could not succeed in raising the issue in a sensible and thought-provoking way. In the end, competition seemed to be the overriding factor. No doubt competition has its value in spurring the agencies to greater efforts, but there should be a limit to competition when the final result is such serious distortion of humanitarian principles.

In order to raise the profile of this issue, it would be useful to have a system for monitoring the allocation of resources in relation to needs. The mechanism most widely used at present is the United Nation's Consolidated Appeals Process, whereby the percentage of an appeal that is being met by donors is used as an indication of whether needs are being met. However, the system itself is deeply flawed (Darcy and Hoffman 2003) and is based not on an assessment of needs but on almost random bids by UN agencies and others. This practice provides only the crudest possible indicator of the relationship between global needs and responses. Such is the importance of the issue that aid agencies should devote much more energy to devising a method for establishing a reliable measure of needs and responses on a global basis—a simple map of the humanitarian system in operation. This method could become a tool in managing the global humanitarian system in a more effective and strategic way.

NEUTRALITY

There is a widespread expectation that aid agencies will not take sides in conflict. This principle was effective during the Cold War in allowing aid agencies to operate freely in conflict situations despite the confrontation of the superpowers. For example, agencies working in Ethiopia under the regime of Haile Mengistu were not to be accused of being pro-Russian, nor were those who worked in the rebel areas to be accused of being pro-American. Nevertheless it would be wrong to suppose that certain prejudices and loyalties did not exert an influence. Agencies working through the mujahideen in Afghanistan were well aware that they were participating in a US strategy to make the Russians leave. Many of them saw this as an unfortunate side issue. They argued that they were responding to need and would have been willing to help people on the Russian side if opportunity arose. There were also, however, a few aid workers, and some agencies, that saw it as a legitimate purpose to drive out the Russians.

In much of Central America there was no room for neutrality, even during the Cold War. As Martha Thompson describes the situation in relation to El Salvador:

> There was no middle ground. Debate and dissent were erased, as was the concept of neutrality. If an institution defined neutrality as independence from the government, it became suspect. When civilians stayed in a war-zone, even if they did not take up arms, they were regarded as guerrillas. In counter-insurgency, where the state must control everything, "non-government" means "anti-government."
>
> (Thompson 1996:327)

The GWOT has affected aid workers deeply and resulted in a wider confusion between humanitarian and political objectives. There was little pretense of impartiality or neutrality when aid agencies followed the Western forces that defeated the Taliban in Afghanistan. Humanitarian actors were placed firmly under military control through provincial mechanisms, and the overall aid strategy was derived from politico-military perspectives. Similarly in Iraq, aid agencies were coordinated through a system run by the Western military. It was practically impossible to operate without collaborating with the armed forces. US leaders made it clear in both cases that they regarded aid agencies as their allies—with special responsibility for "hearts and minds."

This follows a long-term trend toward "coherence" between Western political, military, and aid strategies. In the United Kingdom, the government's grip on aid has tightened. The maverick former Secretary of State for International Development, Clare Short, did not survive the war on Iraq. Considerable government attention has been given to weak or "failed" states deemed to be potential sources of terrorism. The solution is thought to be a combination of military, political, and aid inputs. Accordingly DFID's resources have been pooled with those of the Ministry of Defence (MoD) and the Foreign and Commonwealth Office in order to facilitate "joined-up government." DFID has to follow the lead of general government policy, rather than taking a distinctively humanitarian or developmental perspective.

By implication, agencies that accept DFID funding may find that, especially in sensitive conflict situations, the decision about their grant has been filtered by political and military strategists other than aid managers. By taking such funds, they are in effect accepting political direction. Does this matter? The Western public has expressed no negative feeling about this phenomenon; indeed some may welcome the news that their charities are being more "patriotic." The volume of humanitarian aid continues to increase, and agencies benefit from a synergy between political interest and aid programs. It creates profile for their work. The system may not suit the aid worker on the ground, but it is successful in generating resources for itself.

In the wider perspective, neutrality is only one form of humanitarianism, and perhaps a peculiarly British one. The common model in the United States is the Wilsonian agency, following the view of Woodrow Wilson, the US president at the end of World War I. Such agencies are basically an extension of the state into charitable activity. They readily accept a responsibility to reflect the interests of their own country, acknowledging that they depend primarily on their fellow citizens for donations. Reflecting the views of donors is therefore seen as a form of accountability. By contrast, the tendency in the United Kingdom has been to try to base decisions on moral principle, to change opinions, and to challenge the state. This school of thought is reflected in the Dunantist type of agency that abides by Red Cross principles, including that of neutrality.

Recent critiques of humanitarianism have mainly come from a Dunantist perspective. Michael Ignatieff (1998) and David Rieff (2003) have advocated a return to humanitarian detachment. But most aid workers seem to find this impracticable. In the words of one senior Oxfam GB policymaker, the Dunantist position has been blown out of the water."[2] In practice there has been a shift, at least by the bigger agencies, toward more Wilsonian stances. This has tended to leave the more Dunantist agencies such as Médecins Sans Frontières in "niche" positions, often behaving differently from the majority.

All this seems to suggest that humanitarianism is not an absolute principle, but instead a cultural phenomenon that may be closely linked to Western values, perceptions, and politics. Observers around the world may always have seen it in such a light, but now aid workers are beginning to see themselves not as maverick idealists but as part of a Western cultural system. That may be difficult to accept, but, as Southern NGOs become more assertive, there will be no escape.

One opportunity that this trend creates is the chance to consider other forms of humanitarian response. Why do people in non-Western countries not create agencies like CARE and Oxfam? Are they doing something else? Once we start to recognize that our own Western form of humanitarianism is not the only one, we begin to look more carefully at phenomena such as *zakat,* the Islamic requirement to give a significant proportion of income and assets to others in order to create a more equitable society. We may notice that human suffering is prevented in the "failed state" of Somalia because thousands of Somalis who have left their home country send funds back through social structures that have evolved to perform the function of banks. Their actions achieve humanitarian results, even if they bear little resemblance to classic models.

Humanitarianism is not, as we may have believed, the new religion that needed to be promoted around the world, but rather one of many religions, each with its own positive and negative factors. This reflection should make Western agencies more wary of proselytizing and more responsive to their local societies and counterparts.

Neutrality is culturally and historically determined. During the Cold War there was a degree of scepticism about government positions and a sense that "ordinary people" could stand up for peace and humanity despite political animosities. The GWOT has accorded to governments a greater legitimacy for their international behavior, especially when they justify their actions on grounds of national security. The public are less inclined to support neutrality if they think that it might reduce their own protection. There is a suspicion that terrorists may evolve from precisely the kinds of anarchic and poverty-stricken environments in which the aid agencies operate. Hence there is less willingness to let them do what they think is best. If aid agencies have to be accountable to donors as well as to beneficiaries, as required by the Red Cross Code, they cannot be neutral.

If the abandonment of neutrality leads to a closer engagement with other cultures and perspectives, it may be to the good. If it means simply following the Western consensus, there will be times when humanitarianism will not be true to itself, most notably in making the response proportionate to the needs. My concern is that agencies may be a little too concerned about their own size and will tend to avoid tackling difficult issues because they fear that they might lose public support and hence slide down the rankings. This is not a good enough reason for compromises on the principle of neutrality.

In practice, perception is just as important as principle. If agencies diverge too far from the neutrality principle, they will become targets of those who want to make a target of the West. The individual agency has no escape from this problem. The people who attack or block a road may not know the difference between one agency and another, or the difference between private agencies and the United Nations. It is common in Russia and the former Soviet republics, for example, for every agency to be called the Red Cross. Potential enemies judge the system, rather than the agency. This may be another reason that it is time for agencies to do the same.

Today's humanitarianism is essentially pragmatic. It succeeds through a diversity of approaches, rather than through having a single form that suits all situations. If CARE is unable to work in one place, maybe Oxfam can. And if Oxfam is blocked, maybe Médecins Sans Frontières or a local organization can still deliver assistance. The big agencies may need to accept that they cannot be everywhere and that they must take greater responsibility for the success of the system as a whole, rather than for the success of their own agency only: in other words, they need to demonstrate more altruism and less selfishness.

If the political environment has caused a shift in the humanitarian system, how does this come across to people "on the ground?" This is not simply a matter of political connections and loss of neutrality. Other changes have happened in the past decade, arising from pressures within the system itself.

STANDARDS AND CODES

The increase in humanitarian budgets has led to an expansion and pro-liferation of relief agencies. This reflects a shift in the focus of Western attention from development to security. From the late 1980s, Oxfam began to realize that competition between agencies could lead to lower standards. The organization was particularly concerned about the way in which some agencies were drawing attention to themselves, rather than to issues and problems. Although a low profile had often been nec-essary during the Cold War, publicity now became the way to achieve success, through fundraising and media attention. At the same time, journalists came under increasing pressures to deliver reports based on less research and lower travel costs. They became more reliant on the aid agencies, and the agencies became more willing to become the focus of the story.

We began to consider what really set "good" practice apart from "bad." The issues were clearly wider than the media and the competi-tion for profile. What constituted quality? With decades of experience accumulated by the older agencies, it seemed time to try to codify what they had learned and use it to influence the new agencies that were con-stantly forming. This process led to the Red Cross Code of Conduct, published in 1994.[3] The Code took what is now described as a develop-mentalist position: saving lives was taken for granted as the immediate need, but it was not seen as the sole objective of emergency relief. Local capacity was to be supported, and future vulnerabilities should be reduced. There should be consultation with local people, of course, but the real mark of quality was that those affected by a crisis should be involved in decisionmaking. The Code also specified the meaning of impartiality—that there should be no discrimination on grounds of race, sex, age, caste, and so on. The Code pushed agencies to go further than they would otherwise go toward a "maximalist" position.

The Code became a popular "badge" for aid agencies. Because there were no compliance criteria, anyone could sign up to it. So anyone and everyone did, including security companies.[4] The big mistake was not to set up any mechanism for monitoring compliance, for interpreting the

Code, and for making it widely known among decisionmakers and practitioners. As a result it had little practical impact and was almost immediately overtaken by one of the defining events of twentieth-century humanitarianism: the 1994 genocide in Rwanda. The process that led to the formulation of the Code was later restarted, but it was strongly influenced by the specifics of the Rwanda experience.

The genocide exposed many weaknesses in the humanitarian system. It was a shock to everyone, insiders as well as outsiders. The media had taken little interest in this small and uneventful francophone country in central Africa. Aid agencies were present but had shown little awareness of the tensions building up in the region and had no clue that such a dire event was being planned. Many of their activities over the preceding years probably made things worse, by strengthening an oppressive leadership (Uvin 1998). Even after the genocide began, agencies did little to bring it to the attention of the world until it was too late.[5] Because of geopolitical factors, notably US unwillingness to mount another military operation in Africa after the Somalia debacle, the Western powers ignored the killing, and the United Nations proved incompetent even in passing on messages and warnings (Melvern 2000).

To add to this appalling catalogue of failure, the response of the aid agencies was not only too late but also chaotic and competitive. Hundreds of organizations poured into the camps in eastern Zaïre. Small organizations with no significant experience "took charge" of relief camps and were given mandates by the United Nations that they could not fulfill. People died unnecessarily because of the incompetence of the relief operation. Aid workers suffered the psychological strain of ministering to the killers. In some cases they had not been warned that this would be the case: they believed that they were going to help the innocent survivors. In the refugee camps they could not help noticing that aid was finding its way into the hands of the leaders among the killers, or *génocidaires,* and enabling them to regroup and carry out further attacks. The aid workers pondered on "man's inhumanity to man." Some decided that they lacked the motivation for further humanitarian work.

Faced with such an unparalleled crisis, the agencies came together to produce a joint evaluation (Borton et al. 1996). This report documented the failures in detail and included the suggestion of minimum standards in humanitarian action. The recommendation was vigorously taken up as a way of ensuring that some good would emerge from all the failures. The outcome was the Sphere Charter (The Sphere Project 2004), reasserting the "humanitarian imperative," and the Sphere Standards, intended to ensure that agencies could be held accountable against specified levels of good practice. Sphere was intended also to ensure that donors should provide adequate resources for humanitarian operations.

Sphere has undoubtedly had a profound influence on humanitarian agencies, but its impact has fallen short of its loftiest aims. Donors have never committed themselves to ensuring that Sphere Standards will be met, and they have been able to shrug off responsibility for failure by blaming each other. The emphasis on relief responses and technical standards has tended to reinforce a minimalist approach focused on saving lives, rather than tackling the causes of problems and dealing with them in a sustainable way.

Aid workers often express appreciation to Sphere for helping them to know where they stand. Although Sphere has had a positive effect on the morale of Western aid workers, it has had unintended negative effects on local organizations. The desire to exclude undesirable Western agencies has led to exclusion of local ones that may lack the resources to respond at the level prescribed by Sphere but do have other valuable qualities. A further problem is that, although Sphere Standards are readily applicable if people are displaced into camps, they are far less easily applied in other situations. After the 2001 Gujarat earthquake, for example, many agencies decided that Sphere Standards should not be applied (Disasters Emergency Committee 2001).

But perhaps the greatest impact of Sphere, derived from the Rwanda experience, has been a tendency to separate humanitarian relief from development. It has thus generated a "back to basics," or minimalist, school of thought that has tended to undermine developmentalist positions as set out in the Red Cross Code. Sphere tends to limit the response to saving lives, emphasizing basic professional processes, such as assessment, monitoring, and evaluation. It strongly asserts the rights of individuals but weakens the claim of local organizations that, under Red Cross principles, might claim support for capacity building and a role in the long-term reduction of vulnerability.

One reason for this is that Sphere was to some extent a reaction to the failure of development workers to predict or address the Rwanda genocide. This came on top of a series of cases in which development staff had resisted pressure to switch over to humanitarian responses (Vaux 2002, especially chapters on Ethiopia and Sudan). Because of internal departmental divisions in the aid agencies, the issue often revolved around the willingness of existing program staff to hand over decisionmaking power and resources. Sphere tended to equalize the status of the humanitarian and development branches within the agencies, leaving senior managers to make the strategic decisions. This in turn has arguably made the agencies more susceptible to public and political pressures in their home constituencies.

The back to basics approach ran counter to an increasing awareness among aid workers that even the simplest forms of relief were subject to manipulation and political influence, especially in situations of conflict. David Keen, for example, had demonstrated that humanitarian aid to Sudan was blocked by the deliberate strategies of merchants who wanted to profit from higher food prices and distress sales of animals (Keen 1994). He showed that this was a widespread phenomenon that could be characterized as "the benefits of famine" (Keen 1994:2). Through the 1990s a series of studies showed how aid was habitually manipulated by those involved in conflict (Le Billon 2000).

These efforts led to the awkward conclusion that there was no form of aid that was simply "saving lives." There were always hidden side effects, including the possibility that aid was fueling or prolonging war. Faced also with the awareness that Western powers were often deeply involved in the military and political aspects of conflict, the agencies began to wonder if they could sustain a policy of simply counting the people who needed help and providing the necessary inputs under Sphere Standards. Added to this, the aid agencies' own public policy departments were drawing attention to Western economic factors such as oil interests and trade restrictions that might also count as factors causing conflict and other humanitarian disasters.

It was clear that the Western powers could achieve almost anything if they had the will to do so. This led some aid workers in dire situations to question whether their activities were simply designed to make the situation bearable so that the international community was not forced into taking more drastic action. They had noted that the slaughter in the Balkans was ended only after the Srebrenica massacre. Against such a backdrop, it seemed unethical to continue with a focus on delivering a certain volume of water and food that contained a certain number of calories.

The desire to understand and integrate an understanding of conflict into aid strategy remains one of the most contentious areas of humanitarian policy. Minimalists argue that it is impossible to reach a full understanding and so it may be better not to try. Maximalists argue that agencies have a responsibility to ensure that relief aid does not increase the likelihood of conflict. Underlying this debate is a fundamental ambiguity inherent in the notion of saving lives. Does it mean providing the necessary bodily inputs, or does it mean protection against security threats? The awkward reality is that providing relief aid, as in the refugee camps after the Rwanda genocide, can create new threats to human life.

My own view is influenced by the experience of meeting people in conflict zones who say that security protection is much more important to them than anything else. They are ready to suffer lack of food and even starvation rather than face violence against themselves and their families. One of the starkest lessons for me was in the 1980s, when Ethiopian peasants continued to support a war to overthrow a hated regime, even though they knew that the result would be famine. I have been haunted by calls from many refugees to stop the war.

Of course, I could not stop the war, but I feel an obligation to do as much as I can in that direction. That is why advocacy about the causes of and solutions to war has always been important. But it is not enough. Today's protracted conflicts arise from profound crises of governance, economic factors, and social relations. They are not ended simply by peace talks but depend upon the transformation of all these factors. Half the wars that were thought to have ended in the past decade have since resumed (World Bank 2004). Humanitarian aid should play a role not only in saving lives today but also in saving lives tomorrow—and this means contributing to a just society. Issues such as participation, consultation, gender equity, and respect for minorities are not just "quality" aspects of a humanitarian response. They may be its essence, if they contribute to peace.

The support of Western powers has given aid agencies greater power, and with that comes greater responsibility. A minimalist position may be safe, but is it an adequate response to the challenges of Darfur or Congo? Would it be acceptable in Colombia to heal the wounded and ignore the geopolitical battle raging among drug producers and traffickers, US interests, national politics, and local elites? Civil society organizations in Colombia have repeatedly made it clear that it is not acceptable.

For the past three years I have been engaged with others in developing methods of conflict analysis that can be used to direct aid-agency strategies.[6] Aid agencies have been mainly influenced by the work of peacebuilding organizations. Various "do-no-harm" principles, checklists, and guides are widely available (see, for instance, Africa Peace

Forum et al. 2004). These suggest a range of "good-practice" standards
for working in conflict situations. One limitation of this approach is that
it does not alter the agency's overall strategy. It does not say whether it
should focus on advocacy or direct response, or whether livelihood
needs should be addressed as well as physical needs. Nor does it give a
road map for reducing conflict.

Second, the "do-no-harm" approach does not address the specifics
of each conflict. The approach is based on general principles and lessons learned—but the critical issue in understanding conflict is to
understand that particular case. It is the political economy of war that
really matters, and this varies considerably. There is a need for a method
that begins without preconceptions, maps out the issues relating to conflict, and then helps aid agencies to decide between the strategic options
available.

There is now a degree of consensus about such strategic methodolo-
gies. The approach pioneered by Jonathan Goodhand for the Department
for International Development has been adapted for use by the United
Nations Development Programme[7] and is very similar to the method
used by the World Bank.[8] Until quite recently the approach to analyzing
conflict was to send in a team of experts, but their reports were found to
have little impact on decisionmaking. This led to demands for more participatory methods, basing the analysis on the outcome of workshops
for aid-agency staff, key stakeholders, and a range of other informants
and commentators. The result may not be a polished report, but the participants are likely to be strongly committed to it, and at the very least
different perceptions will have been shared in a way that may encourage team building. In addition to formal inputs to strategy, this approach
also brings benefits in terms of each individual's ability to make decisions that are based on a wider understanding of the relationship
between the agency's program and the conflict.

A further refinement, pioneered with Tearfund in Darfur (see also
Riak 2000), includes a wider stakeholder analysis before the workshop, especially a consultation with some of the affected people.
Using Participatory Rapid Appraisal (PRA) methods, Tearfund examined the capacities and vulnerabilities of the affected people and integrated the findings of this research into the workshop process. The
result was a strategy in which aid and conflict were no longer separated: positive and negative interactions, as well as perceptions, were
understood. The workshop also provided impetus to Tearfund's international advocacy and suggested new channels for peacebuilding. A

single set of workshops is unlikely to change the overall course of events in Sudan; but, applied on a wider scale among aid agencies, it could arguably make a considerable difference. It is a way to resolve the age-old problem of coordination.

Agencies including Tearfund and ActionAid are now beginning to wonder whether the same sort of analysis should also be applied to so-called natural disasters (which generally involve "man-made" factors: security, political, economic, and social). Although richer people only very occasionally suffer the immediate effects of natural disasters, poor people have to live in dangerous places and take further risks in order to survive. Although richer people have sources of support such as insurance, poorer people are prone to real disaster. Their lives are fundamentally insecure even in normal times, just as they are in times of conflict. In many poorer countries, conflict is a regular threat, along with rain failure and flood. The distinction between the two types of threat does not hold, especially in relation to the poorest and most vulnerable people. This points the way toward "Human Security Analysis," in which security is taken to include all kinds of threats to life and livelihood.

The reaction to the Rwanda disaster has now run its course. Humanitarian actors now have less to fear from development colleagues. For more than a decade, resources have flowed in their direction to the point where they can well afford to go beyond the minimum of saving lives. They may need to embrace elements of developmentalism. Uneasy about the political pressures applied on them by Western governments and local elites, aid workers now need some kind of protection from manipulation and mistake. This seems most likely to come from deeper understanding and deeper engagement.

NATIONAL AND INTERNATIONAL NGOs

The tsunami disaster of 2004 indicates that national NGOs have not followed the trend toward minimalism. Most are rooted in particular situations or dedicated to particular long-term issues concerned with improving society. Disasters are incidents along the way, rather than the sole focus of attention. Western assertiveness and the global war on terror have put pressure on the principles of these agencies, and they have passed this pressure on to national NGOs with the added factor of Sphere Standards.

Over many years the aid agencies have created and supported cadres of national NGOs, many of which might now be regarded as taking developmentalist positions. But this is not simply a matter of ideological fads. Inevitably local people play a far greater role in shaping national NGOs than they do in influencing Western aid agencies.

Western aid agencies such as CARE and World Vision are now transnationals that include large national NGOs, although the flow of resources leaves the underlying power relationship basically unchanged. The Red Cross movement has worked through its own national societies for a very long time, but until recently the International Federation of Red Cross and Red Crescent Societies (or IFRC, which acts as a secretariat to national societies) was able to take a fatherly control of the overall process.[9] But in its response to the tsunami in Sri Lanka and India, the Federation has found itself severely constrained by the policies and limitations imposed by national Red Cross and Red Crescent Societies, which have demanded respect for their sovereignty to the extent of excluding international responses.

The loss of any semblance of neutrality has had particularly strong effects in Asia, in areas where there are large Muslim populations and some chafing under Western hegemony. India aspires to be a member of the UN Security Council. Malaysia has been openly critical of the West. The invasions of Afghanistan and Iraq, and perceived partiality toward Israel, have sent political shock waves across the continent.

After the tsunami disaster, NGOs in India and Sri Lanka openly criticized Western agencies for not knowing enough about the situations in which they work. In India local NGOs express concern that international agencies have intensified inequalities. In Sri Lanka there is a fear that Western aid could increase pressures that might lead to a renewal of fighting. As this criticism mounts, there is a temptation for aid agencies to retreat into a focus on systems and "good practice," including Sphere Standards. Others, such as ActionAid, have pursued a path of decentralization. In its tsunami response Oxfam International (OI) was caught in a difficult position, without a national OI counterpart in India, and faced with highly assertive national NGOs. It chose to channel much of its resources directly to local NGOs and community-based organizations, bypassing more prominent organizations.

In general, aid agencies have reached an accommodation with their donor public and governments, but this involves some loss of principle in relation both to neutrality and the "humanitarian imperative" and has left them open to the suspicion that they are acting as tools, willing or unwilling, of Western interests. For the more assertive national NGOs this is now a sensitive and important issue. They feel that they have a right to question Western agencies and, because those agencies are compromised, seek a more equal balance of power.

In much of Latin America the issue has long been settled through the concept of solidarity: the role of the Western NGO is to support, not to decide. This was partly a reaction to the perceived illegitimacy of US political interests in the region during the Cold War. Now a parallel process can be seen in the Middle East and parts of Asia. Western NGOs today are under pressure to establish a solidarity relationship. But this goes against both the Wilsonian pressure to align with Western governments and the Sphere-based pressure to pursue standards set in the West. There is room for compromise: some national NGOs may become more sympathetic to an agenda of "global security" and give greater recognition to Sphere, but in much of Asia the issue is in the balance.

One danger is that the process will lead to the emergence of elite national NGOs, empowered by their control over Western resources. It is not yet clear whether smaller NGOs will be able to exert further downward pressure and make the whole system more democratic. If they did, it is likely that the prevailing policies and principles might need to be revised. The perceptions of people in need are likely to be different than those of people who have never experienced poverty or disaster. Different cultural attitudes would emerge and shape a new and genuinely global humanitarianism.

As an indication of what might happen, consider the Self-Employed Women's Association (SEWA) in India, a union of more than half a million working women. Because decisions are democratic, the leaders' perspectives have shifted toward a sharper focus on livelihoods in humanitarian disasters. The members of SEWA argue that relief inputs are of little value and often continue far too long when people want to take back charge of their own lives. They contrast the helplessness generated by dependence on relief supplies with the sense of confidence that they gain from pursuing their own livelihoods and supporting their families. SEWA has accordingly lobbied the government to establish stand-by arrangements to support livelihoods within days after a disaster.

Such trends are far less noticeable in sub-Saharan Africa, where most NGOs lack the assertiveness of their Latin American and Asian counterparts. The humanitarian response in Darfur is dominated by white faces, cohorts of foreign "experts" with little experience of Sudan and operational styles of response.[10] The more senior positions are held by the 800 international agency staff, not by the 5,000 local staff.

I wonder whether this lack of assertiveness on the African side reflects a similar lack of assertiveness in the political dimension, with exaggerated respect for "the big man," whatever his faults? It is easy to envisage that the indigenous people of Brazil, India, or Indonesia will one day manage their own humanitarian responses, with or without national societies funded by Western counterparts. In China this is already the case. But it is not so easy to see such a future in many African countries, where NGOs remain fragmented and submissive, regimes change but corruption and conflict continue, and bad governance keeps people in permanent destitution, with or without democracy. The rest of the world shows some progress toward the Millennium Development Goals. Africa does not, except in a few specific cases.

CONCLUSIONS

Western aid workers today have less control of their actions than formerly, because they are under increasing pressure from assertive Western governments, especially after the declaration of the "War on Terror." The Western public is generally supportive of this state of affairs. Aid agencies can make general calls for action and for political will, but they have been reluctant to press for the humanitarian agenda to take precedence over the security agenda. As a result the allocation of resources for humanitarian needs is highly biased toward areas that pose security-related concerns for the West. The minimalist approach of focusing simply on saving lives makes this easy. Agencies accept the focus given to them by Western powers and then ask in relation to specific cases how lives can be saved. The agencies, the public, and Western governments collude in a distortion of humanitarian ideals. Aid workers in the field face increasing skepticism from local organizations and local staff, and in some cases pose greater security risks.

Information becomes distorted to suit the system. The media, governments, and agencies focus on the places where they already operate and on issues they have already been addressing. It becomes ever more difficult to shift attention to areas where needs are greater but where there is less funding and less media attention, despite perhaps greater hardship. So far the aid agencies have avoided taking responsibility for the overall impact of humanitarianism, preferring to focus on specific cases. A process of monitoring and publicizing the relationship between humanitarian needs and responses would be a good start.

Aid agencies should also move on from the minimalist perspectives of the post-Rwanda period. They have the capacity and resources to be far more ambitious and to accept greater responsibility. In the case of conflict they should ensure that every action has the most beneficial outcomes, and in other disasters, such as the Asian tsunami, they should ensure that they not only meet immediate needs but also reduce vulnerability for the future. In simple terms, it may be time to bring the Red Cross Code more in balance with the Sphere approach.

But a renewal of the humanitarian principle will require more than this. It will require a more collective approach among the agencies and greater willingness to challenge public opinion and the self-interest of Western donors. They may need to rely more heavily on their local partners and their partners' perspectives. This implies decentralization and much greater democracy in the long chain of relationships between giver and receiver. There is evidence of such trends. Agencies are more transnational than they were, and local partners more assertive. But there is still a very long way to go.

NOTES

[1] Unless indicated, "Oxfam" is used to designate any of the national affiliates of Oxfam International, while "Oxfam GB" is referred to as "OGB."

[2] Paul Smith-Lomas, then OGB Humanitarian Director, personal interview 2004.

[3] Available at www.ifrc.org/publicat/conduct/code.asp (retrieved October 6, 2005).

[4] Armor Group, for example, became a signatory to the Code.

[5] With a few honorable exceptions, OGB among them (Mackintosh 1997).

[6] Notably Jonathan Goodhand at the School of Oriental and African Studies (SOAS) at the University of London.

[7] Conflict-related Development Analysis. More information can be found via UNDP's Bureau for Crisis Prevention and Recovery at www.undp.org/bcpr/ (retrieved October 6, 2005).

[8] Conflict Analysis Framework. More information can be found via the World Bank's Conflict Prevention and Reconstruction Unit at http://lnweb18. worldbank.org/ESSD/sdvext.nsf/67ByDocName/ConflictAnalysis (retrieved October 6, 2005).

[9] These remarks are based largely on personal observation during visits to India and Sri Lanka in May 2005.

[10] My own observation from visiting in October 2004. See also Herson 2005.

REFERENCES

Africa Peace Forum, CECORE, CHA, FEWER, International Alert and Saferworld (2004) "Conflict-Sensitive Approaches to Development, Humanitarian Assistance and Peacebuilding," resource pack available free at www.conflict sensitivity.org/ (retrieved October 6, 2006).

Borton, John, Emery Brusset and Alistair Hallam (1996) *Humanitarian Aid and Its Effects Study III: The International Response to Conflict and Genocide: Lessons from the Rwanda Experience,* Copenhagen: Steering Committee of the Joint Evaluation of Emergency Assistance to Rwanda.

Christian Aid (2004) *The Politics of Poverty: Aid in the New Cold War,* London: Christian Aid.

Cosgrave, John (2004) *The Impact of the War on Terror on Aid Flows,* London: ActionAid.

Darcy, James and Charles-Antoine Hoffman (2003) *According to Need? Needs Assessment and Decision-making in the Humanitarian Sector,* Humanitarian Policy Group Report 15, London: ODI.

Disasters Emergency Committee (DEC) (2001) *Independent Evaluation of the Response to the Gujarat Earthquake,* London: Disasters Emergency Committee.

Herson, Maurice (2005) "Real-time Evaluations in Darfur: Some Suggestions for Learning," *Humanitarian Exchange* 30(June):16–19.

Ignatieff, Michael (1998) *The Warrior's Honor: Ethnic War and the Modern Conscience,* New York: Metropolitan Books.

International Federation of Red Cross and Red Crescent Societies (IFRC) (1994) *Code of Conduct for The International Red Cross and Red Crescent Movement and NGOs in Disaster Relief,* Geneva: IFRC.

Keen, David (1994) *The Benefits of Famine,* Princeton: Princeton University Press.

Le Billon, Philippe (2000) *The Political Economy of War: An Annotated Bibliography,* Humanitarian Policy Group Report 1, London: ODI.

Mackintosh, Anne (1997) "Rwanda: Beyond 'Ethnic Conflict'," *Development in Practice* 7(4): 464–474.

Melvern, Linda (2000) *A People Betrayed: The Role of the West in Rwanda's Genocide,* London: Zed Books.

Oxfam GB (2003) *Beyond the Headlines–An Agenda for Action to Protect Civilians in Neglected Conflicts,* Oxford: Oxfam GB.

Riak, Abikök (2000) "Local Capacities for Peace Project: The Sudan Experience," *Development in Practice* 10(3&4): 501–505.

Rieff, David (2003) *A Bed for the Night: Humanitarianism in Crisis,* New York: Vintage.

Stoddard, Abby (2003) *Humanitarian NGOs: Challenges and Trends,* Humanitarian Policy Group Report 14, London: ODI.

The Sphere Project (2004) *The Sphere Handbook English: Humanitarian Charter and Minimum Standards in Disaster Response* (2nd revised edition, with CD-ROM), Geneva: Sphere Project.

Thompson, Martha (1996) "Empowerment and Survival: Humanitarian Work in Civil Conflict, Part I," *Development in Practice* 6(4): 324–333.

Uvin, Peter (1998) *Aiding Violence: The Development Enterprise in Rwanda,* West Hartford, CT: Kumarian Press.

Vaux, Tony (2002) *The Selfish Altruist: Relief Work in Famine and War,* London: Earthscan.

World Bank (2004) *Breaking the Conflict Trap,* Washington, DC: World Bank.

World Health Organization (2005) "Democratic Republic of the Congo: Response, Health Status, WHO's Activities," report presented at Health Action in Crisis Forum, WHO, Geneva, July 1.

First published in *Development in Practice* 16(3&4): 240–254 in 2006.

PART 1

The Politics of Violence: Humanitarian Responses

Two

The Politics of Emergency and the Demise of the Developing State: Problems for Humanitarian Advocacy

Vanessa Pupavac

CHAPTER SUMMARY

This chapter discusses humanitarian advocacy in the contemporary world within the wider crisis of political vision. Humanitarian advocacy over the past fifteen years, by drawing attention to how crises have been precipitated by state policies, has sought international intervention to protect people. It has consequently become associated with challenging the national sovereignty of the developing state. The author contends that the weak state is the problem and suggests that the existing paradigm of humanitarian advocacy helps to legitimize the erosion of equality among sovereign states and the reassertion of international inequalities.

THE RISE OF HUMANITARIAN ADVOCACY

Médecins Sans Frontières (MSF) pioneered contemporary humanitarian advocacy under the motto "Care for and Testify," thus challenging the reserve of traditional humanitarianism. The award of the 1999 Nobel Peace Prize to MSF was a mark of international recognition of the contribution played by humanitarian advocacy. Since the end of the Cold War, humanitarian organizations have not simply become more involved in lobbying for more official aid and campaigning to increase private donations (in appeals of the Band Aid type), but have sought to intervene directly in international politics. MSF made prominent appeals in the Western media for military intervention in Bosnia, and a willingness to support the concept of military action is now widely evident in the humanitarian sector. Representatives of Save the Children–UK (SCF) were among those lobbying Western governments to intervene militarily in Kosovo. SCF's work has always been underpinned by advocacy on child rights, but this form of advocacy was new.

More recently Oxfam GB (OGB), which from the 1960s defined itself as a development organization, lobbied for the right of humanitarian intervention to be widened and for a change to the principle of noninterference enshrined in the UN Charter, albeit as a last resort (Oxfam GB 2005). In the same vein, OGB appealed for "robust action" in the crisis in the Darfur region of Sudan (Oxfam GB 2004). Indeed OGB now ascribes equal importance to advocacy, to development work, and to emergency relief work. This is just one example of how development NGOs have increased their advocacy and campaigning on human rights, a trend reinforced by their adoption of the rights-based approach to development. Many NGOs have also become more closely involved in campaigns on issues such as debt relief or the reform of international trade rules that might previously have been left to specialist organizations such as People and Planet (formerly Third World First).

In addition to their own advocacy work, many British NGOs also run joint campaigns under banners such as Make Poverty History (MPH). For instance, MSF is involved in a campaign to make cheap generic drugs available to developing countries. Moreover a growing number of NGOs are focused primarily on advocacy rather than on delivering aid, while human rights organizations such as Amnesty International have expanded their remit to include advocacy on international humanitarian law and cooperation with humanitarian organizations. Other human rights organizations, such as the Aegis Trust and Genocide Watch, are dedicated mainly to advocacy and do not conduct individual casework. The trend corresponds to general patterns of public engagement in the West. In the United Kingdom, for instance, organizations such as the National Society for the Prevention of Cruelty to Children (NSPCC) have moved away from direct involvement in child welfare and protection in favor of advocacy work on child rights.

Humanitarian advocacy was embraced as part of a fresh approach when the crises immediately following the collapse of the Berlin Wall cast doubt on traditional humanitarianism. It promised to reinvigorate a demoralized humanitarian sector and forge new partnerships with populations in the South. Recent humanitarianism has been preoccupied with the unintended consequences of humanitarian assistance, but humanitarian advocacy has serious ramifications too. This chapter discusses the problems of humanitarian advocacy in an unequal world, drawing upon examples from British NGOs. These NGOs' conscious identification with progressive politics makes their advocacy work interesting because it has frequently attracted staff or volunteers who aspire to move beyond emergency work and promote social change. The chapter begins by considering the wider crisis of purpose in international politics at the end of the Cold War, which helped to raise the profile of humanitarian advocacy. Since the early 1990s, humanitarian advocacy, drawing attention to ways in which humanitarian crises have been precipitated by state policies, has sought international intervention to protect people. Consequently, it has become associated with challenging the sovereignty of the developing state. However, this chapter will argue that the weak state, rather than the strong sovereign state, is the problem that lies behind today's humanitarian crises.

In challenging the authority of the developing state, humanitarian advocacy has complemented international politics and economics. It has complemented international political developments that challenge the equality of sovereign states. It has also complemented economic policies that hollow out the developing state and abandon national development, thereby undermining the position of developing countries within the international system. At the same time, humanitarian advocacy for military intervention has encouraged the politicization and militarization of humanitarian aid, which makes it harder for NGOs to resist precisely the same trends in the "global war on terror" (GWOT).

This chapter suggests that the existing paradigm of humanitarian advocacy legitimizes the reassertion of an unequal international order, while too many of the high-profile NGO campaigns risk oversimplifying the causes and degrading the meaning of political engagement at precisely the time when they seek to be key players in efforts to revitalize such engagement.

INTERNATIONAL POLITICS OF THE EMERGENCY

Humanitarianism acquired new significance in post–Cold War international relations. Aid agencies are already nostalgically looking back at the 1990s as (if not a golden age for humanitarianism) an interregnum when "the tide was definitely moving in the right direction" (Christian Aid 2004:2):

> Here was a chance for a brave new world. One in which rich countries would lift emerging nations out of poverty and help them to stand on their own, equal partners on a new, more equal and more prosperous stage.
>
> (Ibid.:10)

The GWOT is portrayed as canceling gains made by humanitarianism and ushering in a New Cold War, which subordinates humanitarian principles to security concerns (Christian Aid 2004; Cosgrave 2004). Yet there is more continuity in international politics than aid agencies may care to acknowledge, perhaps because they confuse their own presence in government policymaking with progressive international politics. Arguably the high profile of humanitarianism in the 1990s was due less to a flourishing humanism than to the way in which humanitarian advocacy complements the contemporary politics of emergency (Furedi 2002; Laidi 1998). The ending of the ideological divisions of the Cold War without major international conflict suggested new possibilities for a peaceful world order and boosted somewhat idealistic accounts of international relations, certainly in Europe, if not in the United States. Yet its end also revealed profound problems in domestic and international politics. Initial euphoria at the West's "triumph over communism" quickly gave way to pessimism about the future. Premature declarations of "the end of history" soon rang hollow and came to suggest the abandonment, not the realization, of grand historical projects. Indeed security analysts were soon referring nostalgically to the Cold War period.

It is important to recognise that the demise of the ideological divisions of the Cold War also eroded political meaning and the legitimacy of public institutions in the West. Rivalry for influence in the developing world had fostered rival political visions of national development. A modernist project was galvanized in the West by international pressure to produce an alternative to counter the Soviet model of progress, something that also helped to give a sense of purpose to Western societies. Consequently the loss of the political framework of the Cold War was experienced as disorientating rather than liberating. Progressive politics has fragmented in the West, and the emerging discourse exhibits disenchantment with mass politics and universal visions. Western politicians struggle to identify sources of meaning and common values around which their societies can cohere. In this search for an elusive meaning, the relativist age finds the Holocaust or similar contemporary catastrophes to be almost the only remaining moral absolutes against which it can define itself. Western societies increasingly seem to come together only in tragedy, whether the sentimental mourning for Princess Diana in the United Kingdom or the public outrage in Belgium against the murderer and pedophile Marc Dutroux. This problem is repeated at a local level, where city councils in the United Kingdom, such as that of Nottingham, seek to reconnect to the public by recreating a civic ethos based on outrage against violent killings. The lowest-common-denominator definition of the good citizen as "not a violent killer" or "not a pedophile" reveals the exhaustion of progressive politics and illustrates how civic life is being reorganized around insecurity, rather than a positive vision of the future.

Political disorientation has intensified feelings of vulnerability and of being at risk. This fuels the urgent sense that "something must be done," but the responses themselves lack the coherence that would derive from a larger vision (Furedi 2002). The demise of grand historical projects has truncated political vision and encouraged short-term policymaking. Politics increasingly resembles crisis management, as politicians lurch erratically from one issue to another, seeking to project a sense of purpose through action—or the politics of emergency (Laidi 1998).

Against this backdrop, recent humanitarian emergencies have resonated in the Western imagination, in part because they are symptoms of the failure not only of past political projects but also of contemporary politics that finds it difficult to do more than manage the present (Laidi 1998). A disenchanted polity has an opportunity to feel engaged and vicariously vent its existential anxieties in the struggle for survival represented by the humanitarian emergency. Moreover the politicization of such emergencies turns them into modern morality plays for Western audiences. Catharsis is experienced through somebody else's emergency (Ugresic 1998). Victims and villains are identified and new moral certainties are found in the absolutes of life and death.

At the same time, however, those populations that are cast as villains have found their plight ignored in international humanitarian circles as well as by international politics, a fact that compromises the principle of universal concern for those in need, irrespective of their beliefs or politics (Fox 2001; Vaux 2002). The nostalgia for the 1990s ignores how its politicized humanitarian advocacy has the potential to jeopardize humanitarian work to alleviate suffering.

If humanitarian advocacy in the 1990s focused on complex political emergencies, the new millennium has witnessed efforts to raise the profile of poverty and development as issues that promise to move beyond the politics of emergency and address the long-term problems of people in developing countries. NGO campaign work is seen as addressing the vacuum in Western politics and engaging young people who remain uninspired by traditional party politics. In this vein one OGB initiative is aptly named "Inspired Action," and its 2006 campaign is titled "I'm In."

I now turn to two core themes of contemporary NGO advocacy—sustainable development and human security—before returning to the nature of humanitarian advocacy as political engagement. This analysis suggests that there are deeper problems with NGO advocacy, which fails to take us beyond the politics of emergency, with adverse consequences for developing states and their populations.

THE ANTIMODERNIZATION PHILOSOPHY OF DEVELOPMENT ADVOCACY

An important aspect of today's truncated political vision is that it offers low horizons to the developing world, which in turn can only increase the likelihood of more humanitarian emergencies. NGO development advocacy has enjoyed a radical reputation with the general public and has not been as internally contentious as humanitarian advocacy for military intervention. However, its horizons are also low: the normative goals remain ambitious but are increasingly detached from material transformation. Developing countries have long found themselves caught between the contradictions of the market and international development policies. Here I want to highlight influences that have shaped NGO development philosophy and its antimodernization stance before considering some of the implications of the divorce between material conditions and normative goals in development advocacy.

The need for long-term development aid over short-term emergency assistance has been a perennial theme of NGO advocacy, but

NGO development philosophy has been wary of imposing Western development models on non-Western societies. It has largely defined itself as being opposed to a Western modernization model of national development and industrialization because this is seen to be destructive of the environment, alienating, and harmful to the interests of communities. The "sustainable development" approach champions strategies that respect local cultures, address the needs of individuals or communities, and emphasize rural rather than urban development. NGO development thinking is encapsulated in the much quoted maxim: Give a man a fish and you feed him for a day. Teach a man to fish and you feed him for life. The proverb has been repeatedly invoked since its first use in the 1960 UN Campaign Against Hunger.

Historical Antecedents of Opposition to Industrialization

The anti-industrialization position of NGO thinking has long antecedents in romantic hostility toward industrialization, expressed by writers and artists such as William Blake and William Morris. In the context of international development, it may be traced back to Western anthropological perspectives, which in turn informed colonial administrations. Leading twentieth-century anthropologists were partly inspired by doubts about their own societies, notably the alienating consequences of modernity and a desire to find alternative ways of life that would support their progressive reform agenda at home by demonstrating the possibility of different ways of organizing society. Anthropological thinking therefore considered it important to preserve cultural pluralism because it was thought that traditional communities could provide insights for modern society. Western anthropologists often expressed alarm at how contact with modernity was destabilizing the societies that they studied. Hence they had serious reservations about the perceived aspiration of international development policy to transform the world on the lines of the advanced industrialized societies. Concerns about modernity's destabilizing impact on traditional societies were taken up by colonial administrators and shaped colonial thinking on development as it tried to deter nationalist movements (Duffield 2005).

NGO development advocacy continues to understand itself as posing a radical challenge to a modernization orthodoxy that requires countries in the South to follow a Western path of national development. Yet this self-image is set against a straw-man model of modernization that has long since lost favor with Western governments. Indeed the growth of Western development NGOs and their increasing prominence in international development has been founded on Western scepticism about industrialization in the South, articulated in both official and radical circles. Western governments arguably embraced a modernization agenda for developing countries purely as part of their strategy to contain the influence of the Soviet Union: they remained wary about the industrialization of these countries, fearing that it might challenge their own status or have a destabilizing effect and promote political radicalism, with broader consequences for international peace and security (Pupavac 2005).

Alarm about modernization among Western policymakers was captured in E.F. Schumacher's book *Small Is Beautiful* (1973), which became the bible of the "sustainable development" approach adopted by NGOs. Its publication during the 1970s oil crisis, which suggested that developing countries might challenge Western access to cheap raw materials, secured a large audience for Schumacher's arguments. Schumacher argued that modernization policies were damaging communities and livelihoods while promoting greed and frustration, and therefore ran counter to international peace and security. Development strategies should reject the goals of industrialization and universal prosperity and concentrate on small-scale production and meeting basic needs, maintaining traditional communities and livelihoods by disseminating low-tech solutions. This retrenched international development agenda and its rejection of policies such as nationalization also complemented the shift in the West from Keynesian to neoliberal economic policy, with the state playing a smaller role as employer and welfare provider. Western governments accordingly began to channel more of their development aid through NGOs, rather than bilaterally, thus helping to sponsor the spectacular growth of the NGO development sector since the 1980s. Following the end of the Cold War, the development of countries in the South to the level of industrialized nations is simply not an aspiration of the West, although developing countries are nevertheless subject to extensive externally imposed reforms.

Radical Opposition to Modernization

Official concern about modernization strategies was complemented by the counterculture critique of mass society that influenced radical politics in the 1960s and 1970s. If Western policymakers were fearful that urbanization might promote political radicalism, radical politics has the opposite concern. In trying to understand why the masses did not embrace radical politics, critics suggested that modern consumerism anesthetised people and created conformists (Marcuse 1964). Political radicalism could emerge only from those outside the processes of the modern industrial state; therefore radicals should oppose the idea of developing countries becoming modern industrial states like their own. Radicals were also becoming disenchanted with the communist model and the Soviet Union's suppression of dissent in Eastern Europe. State sovereignty was associated not with national independence struggles but with violence, whether through the superpowers' military interventions or their support for military regimes in the developing world. The counterculture critique idealized an authentic life of peasant farmers and independent artisans producing traditional crafts, perceived as still existing in parts of the South but being crushed by development.

This vision was further supported by the rise of environmentalism within Western thought, expressed in books such as Rachel Carson's influential *Silent Spring* (1962), which condemned industrialization as destroying the planet's resources. Its holistic vision wanted to minimize humanity's imprint on the planet and return to a simpler way of life, balancing human needs against those of the environment. Environmentalist perspectives were absorbed into the antimodernization critique as it became codified into the concept of sustainable development. Small-scale nonwaged production is viewed as being less destructive of the environment and also less exploitative than large-scale production, by spreading ownership of the means of production (Sen 1975). These ideas inform NGO advocacy, which does not envisage people in developing countries adopting Western consumerist lifestyles, but retaining more "authentic'" simpler ways of life within a modified market economy.

In short, both official policy and NGO advocacy on sustainable development reject the idea that countries in the South should achieve Western levels of economic development, while at the same time retaining normative goals—even though these countries are marginalized within a global market economy. This policy convergence does not imply that NGO development advocacy is irrelevant. Rather, it helps to legitimize the rejection of the goal of transforming the material conditions of developing countries by giving this rejection a radical gloss. Campaigns such as "Make Poverty History" appear ambitious in their demands to end poverty, but closer examination reveals that they do not aspire to prosperity for all, but effectively redefine poverty eradication in terms of managing survival through better self-reliance. "Making Poor Poverty Management History" may be a less snappy slogan, but a better description of the approach.

SOME CONTRADICTIONS OF DEVELOPMENT ADVOCACY

Sustainable development advocacy complements the erosion of the welfare-state model and makes a virtue of people having to create their own employment opportunities to support themselves in the face of structural adjustment reforms that reduce both state welfare and public employment. NGOs talk in terms of promoting "sustainable livelihoods" and the position of the "poor in markets"; they argue that "[c]orruption and the abuse of power prevent the benefits of free trade, privatisation and political change reaching the poorest" (Oxfam GB 2003:18). The theme of empowering people with the skills and confidence to start up their own microenterprises chimes with the ideology of neoliberal economics. As Mark Duffield observes, "Sustainable development shifts the responsibility for self-reproduction from states to people reconfigured as social entrepreneurs operating at the level of the household and communities" (Duffield 2005:152).

In this vein, the Africa Commission aims to "empower poor people to shape their own lives, including by investing in their health and education . . ." and emphasizes the need "to foster small enterprises" (Commission for Africa 2005, Chapter 7:2). Similarly Christian Aid's Web site (www.christian-aid.org.uk) declares that it "believes in strengthening people to find their own solutions to the problems they face," and OGB speaks of people coming together across the world "[t]o end poverty for themselves, for others, for each other" (Oxfam GB 2003–2004). Under the banner of neither patronizing nor imposing upon them, NGOs are effectively telling people living in poverty how better to fend for themselves.

At its best, giving priority to meeting basic needs—such as UNICEF's GOBI program for infants—has had significant success in improving survival rates, despite the worsening economic situation in many developing countries (Black 1996). Impressive though such programs might be as lifelines for populations in precarious circumstances, they cannot be described as development or poverty eradication. Overall, the sustainable development model leaves most of the world's population relying on household production, their lives dominated by the forces of nature, and highly exposed to risk and insecurity without the safety nets that citizens of post-industrial states expect.

To be sure, proponents of sustainable development have not wanted to abandon efforts to promote social improvement, even if the basic needs approach seeks to lower people's material expectations. However, the relationship between social progress and material advancement is being broken, and normative change is increasingly what is meant by development. Consider the Millennium Development Goals (MDGs) project, which describes itself as "an expanded vision of development" (www.un.org/millenniumgoals/). It does not aspire to create universal prosperity, but expects states to achieve its normative agenda by 2015—including universal primary education and gender equality—without having advanced materially. Rather its vision makes changing culture and individual behavior the primary means of social advancement by "vigorously [promoting] human development as the key to sustaining social and economic progress." In effect pre-industrial societies are expected to adopt post-industrial norms, although they are still based on enhanced traditional household production and must forgo the material comforts and welfare enjoyed in the West. Typically, for example, spending on basic community health care meets with approval, but spending on high-tech hospitals is viewed as an inefficient use of resources.

Crucially the sustainable development model does not address the limited capacity of the developing state, which without a developed economy and infrastructure can hardly become a progressive redistributive state that guarantees its citizens' welfare. Insofar as the problem of the weak state is belatedly being recognized by official donors and NGOs, the problem is moralized in terms of corruption or bad governance. This ignores the material conditions underlying the weak, illiberal state and social or economic inequalities. NGOs' reluctance to address contradictions in their development models relates to their antipathy toward their own modern industrial societies, associating these with violence and injustice, together with their romantic perceptions of non-Western populations' self-reliance, nonmaterialist expectations, and restraint. Such beliefs contrast with earlier progressive politics that, while often heavily critical of Western modernization models, nevertheless saw social progress as contingent upon material advancement. However, the demise of the drive to national development is not returning countries to a simple holistic life in harmony with nature, but has brutal and competitive effects. The reality of a society organized around small-scale family producers or pastoralists and strong communal or kinship ties is likely to be able to support only a precarious state with a weak relationship to the population and characterized by a nepotistic public sphere.

At the same time NGO advocacy for sustainable development makes inequality between developing and developed countries an indefinite condition, because abandoning the technological advancement of developing countries essentially means abandoning the advancement of equality. For example, advocacy for fair trade assumes unequal means of production between developed and developing countries, with the latter engaged in low-tech or medium-tech microenterprises, as opposed to large-scale automated production; it also assumes their trading in international markets through a paternalistic relationship with ethical Western companies or NGOs, not independently. Moreover, like microcredit conditionality, the proposed conditions for fair trade presume the right to dictate extrafinancial terms, based on the Western advocates' vision of the ethical life. So although NGOs are wary of developing countries following Western paths of economic development, they are in effect intervening in developing societies to change social and political norms.

Advocacy for sustainable development originally evaded the political consequences of effectively making inequality an indefinite feature of the international system, but since the 1990s human security advocates have plainly been abandoning the principle of sovereign equality. Ironically, the anti-development critique, despite its avowed antipathy toward modern industrial societies, now endorses in the human security model the idea of those very states having greater powers to use against developing countries. The assumptions of human security advocacy belie the idea current in NGO circles that the 1990s offered developing countries the chance to become "equal partners on a new, more equal and more prosperous stage" (Christian Aid 2004:10).

HUMAN SECURITY ADVOCACY AND INTERNATIONAL EQUALITY

If the sustainable development model complemented the anti-state policies of neoliberal economics, the human security model that evolved in the 1990s assumed the inability of developing states to protect their populations, and the necessity of reordering international relations in order to deal with this reality. The 1945 UN Charter established a collective, self-policing, international system, underpinned by the principles of national sovereignty and sovereign equality between states. Each state is presumed to represent the interests of its own people and to have the capacity to guarantee its own security. Interference in the internal affairs of other states is outlawed in the Charter. Thus the viability of the international security system has been dependent on developing the newly independent states. These looked forward to securing their capacity in the heady early days of international development, but incapacity has become an indefinite condition for many states in the face of the demise of international development, weakening the possibility of their being equal subjects in international terms, or moral agents able to secure the welfare of their own population in domestic terms. Furthermore the collective self-policing security model is made untenable.

The concept of human development as distinct from national development has captured the imagination of the demoralized international development community. The associated concept of human security concerns the enforcement of human development norms and harnessing the higher priority (and resources) that Western policymakers give to security (King and Murray 2001; Mack 2004). Against the assumptions on which the Charter is based, the concept of human security highlights the fact that states may fail to protect the interests of their population, and that too often the state may violate individuals' security. Despite their wide appeal in development circles, the concepts have been criticized for being attractive in terms of rhetoric, but of limited practical application for populations (ibid.).

Predictably, human development rankings categorize many developing countries as widely failing their populations; conversely the advanced industrial countries are depicted as generally securing their populations' welfare. Yet the Human Development Index (HDI) was inspired by the desire to demonstrate that social progress is possible without material advancement. A broad correlation between per capita income and HDI ranking is hotly contested in the literature, and cases countering this linkage are emphasized, although the commonly cited examples of China and Cuba might point to rather different conclusions than those usually drawn! Developing countries find themselves caught between the contradictions of an antimaterialist development outlook and idealized accounts of international relations. Importantly for low-ranking developing countries, there has been a tendency to interpret their position in the HDI as a moral rather than a material ranking.

Human security scales are implicitly used to distinguish unethical states, which violate their population's security, and responsible states, which provide human security. Strategies to protect human security by force entrust the international community (of responsible states) to intervene on behalf of vulnerable populations in those states that are perceived to violate human security. Thus human security advocacy essentially challenges the legitimacy of developing countries and pro- motes that of Western powers to intervene around the world, undermin- ing the principle of equality among sovereign states.

Contrary to the provisions of the UN Charter, intervention is posi- tively endorsed in the human security model. NGOs that are challenging the right to national sovereignty and the principle of noninterference are essentially arguing for a change to the UN Charter in favor of interna- tional rights to enforce human security. The prohibition against such action was based on fears of its potential abuse by powerful states. Tellingly discussions about human security advocacy have neglected the potential conflict of interest between intervening states and the popula- tions of developing states, or indeed between Western NGOs and the pop- ulations of developing countries. This neglect is striking, given that the concept of human security draws attention to the conflict of interests between a state and its population. NGOs talk of international relations in terms of belonging to an intimate global community, as if we are living in one big inclusive extended village, where people enjoy an equal voice and mutual ties of accountability, where wealth does not matter, and individ- uals in the South can just pop along to their neighbors in the North at times of need. In this vein OGB extols "interconnectedness" as follows:

> Oxfam is a worldwide network. A community that's crossing conti-
> nents. Linking villages, towns, countries. Connecting individuals who
> live thousands of miles apart. And from Bangalore to Bolton, from
> Tokyo to Tajikistan, this community is changing lives. People across
> the world are coming together with a shared goal.

(Oxfam 2003–2004)

NGOs are assuming a direct disinterested relationship that bypasses the developing state and allows them to claim to be voicing the interests of people in developing countries in place of their delegitimized govern- ments. In this unequal relationship, NGOs are political gatekeepers, determining which voices in the developing world they will represent, and how their problems are represented and addressed, often along with their implied role as economic gatekeepers in fair trade or debt relief.

The possibility that NGOs might be drawn to viewpoints that reflect their own thinking is overlooked, as is the unequal distribution of power in such relationships.

"Humanitarian war" was a concept that humanitarian organizations themselves helped to legitimize in their demands for military enforcement in the Balkans during the 1990s. Official policymakers now take for granted that intervention, including military enforcement, is acceptable to aid organizations; and they talk about mechanisms for more efficient coordination between Western governments and NGOs in global governance. The possibility that intervening states and humanitarian organizations may have conflicting objectives is disregarded. The level of acceptability is such that Western governments have frequently found themselves criticized by aid organizations for not intervening *enough* in crises around the world, even following the controversial military invasion and occupation of Iraq. The collapse of humanitarian space in Iraq caused serious disquiet because humanitarians were identified with the Western military forces as legitimate targets; but it has not prevented various organizations from demanding more robust intervention elsewhere since then, including interventions that would bypass the UN Security Council (Oxfam GB 2004).

Western governments can happily live with criticism that calls for them to have a greater role in world affairs. The recasting of human insecurity in developing countries in moralized terms has provided something against which Western states can define themselves, and the endorsement of humanitarian enforcement has given them a flexible foreign policy tool. When the alleged presence of weapons of mass destruction proved to be shaky grounds for the invasion of Iraq, the British government played the humanitarian card. Western politicians frequently observe that they cannot intervene everywhere, but the idea that they should be intervening has boosted their weakened sense of purpose and helped them to manage their crisis of domestic legitimacy. They have at least been able to take a moral stand and point to violations of human security in the developing world, even if they have found it difficult to identify common values at home.

MORAL PROJECTION

The problem of human security in developing countries is real. However, the call to erode equality among states and expand Western governance of developing countries is an alarming and antidemocratic approach that reverses the political progress made in the international system during the twentieth century and resurrects the idea of liberal imperialism. The human security model proposes only third-class social justice for populations in developing countries. The experience of Bosnia can be considered as perhaps the best and most comprehensive case of governance beyond borders. Yet after a decade of international administration, unemployment in Bosnia still exceeds 40 percent, and the public welfare system is being reduced, not expanded. The population is expected to create its own employment through microenterprise and to provide its own welfare through private insurance. In fact, post-conflict economic recovery in Bosnia under international administration has been far weaker than its recovery after the World War II. International administrators seem happier elaborating social policies that are susceptible to moralizing or bureaucratic target setting (such as quotas), rather than designing policies that can generate real improvements in the political, social, and economic prospects of the population.

Within international humanitarian work, the growing preference for moral advocacy over material aid is increasingly clear. Live Aid's mission in 1985 was to send aid direct to Ethiopia; Live 8's mission in 2005 was about promoting an awareness of poverty among a Western audience. Consider the two UN ad hoc criminal tribunals for the former Yugoslavia and Rwanda: at their height, these (especially that in the former Yugoslavia) swallowed up 20 percent of the UN's funds, the main beneficiaries of which have been human rights advocates and other professionals (like me!), rather than the victims of the violations. This preference is being repeated in relation to other crises, encapsulated for me at a meeting about the crisis in Darfur in 1994. The UN humanitarian coordinator, Mukesh Kapila, was highly animated in his address, urging the international community to prosecute war crimes, but he devoted rather less time to the refugees' pressing needs for humanitarian aid. His conscious or unconscious priorities may seem a trivial matter, but they illustrate how humanitarian advocacy is becoming distorted. The perverse consequences of this bias can be seen in the United Nations' warning that refugee rations might be cut to levels below caloric requirements—in the same month that it announced that the International Criminal Court was taking up the case of violations of human rights in Darfur. The discrepancy in resources suggests that the international community is keener to take a moral stand on Darfur than to provide proper nourishment to the very refugees whose suffering it is invoking.

The degree of international commitment and sustained efforts to provide security and create a viable state in Bosnia are probably the exception rather than the rule. More striking is the rather arbitrary, superficial, and short-term character of foreign interventions, which do not seem to be based on a rational analysis of security risks or clear plans of what to do once they have taken place. The interventions create much sound and fury ("shock and awe"), but their purpose remains vague. Policy is made on the hoof. Similarly the literature on advocacy for humanitarian intervention is now dominated by the right to intervene militarily, but it has had relatively little to say about what happens next. In the words of Zaki Laidi, there is a desire to project moral and military authority in the absence of a clear political project (Laidi 1998). Consequently today's interventions are not evolving into the same formal or embedded relationships between ruler and ruled that prevailed during previous eras of liberal imperialism. Phrases such as "empire-lite" (Ignatieff 2003) or the more damning "hyperactive attention deficit disorder" (Ferguson 2004) are being applied. NGO advocacy and informal interventions are proving to be useful media for today's ad hoc global engagements.

MUSCULAR HUMANITARIANISM?

The relegitimization of international inequality between states, and the informal political role being delegated to NGOs in governance beyond borders, create serious problems for humanitarian advocacy. It is too easy for aid agencies to become cheerleaders for Western posturing over the state of the developing world. Despite the extensive soul-searching in the 1990s, the humanitarian sector as a whole still underestimates the ramifications of this reordering for humanitarian work. Interestingly, considering that MSF pioneered today's politicized humanitarian advocacy, one of the strongest recent warnings on the dangers of humanitarianism becoming dangerously entangled with Western military missions comes from the research director of the MSF Foundation (Weissman 2005). Fabrice Weissman's report pointedly observes that humanitarians' endorsement of the concept of humanitarian war has compromised the meaning of humanitarianism. He argues that humanitarian organizations must therefore bear some responsibility for becoming targets and being unable to work in places such as Iraq or Afghanistan. In the light of NGOs calling for intervention in Darfur, Weissman asks: "After the

Iraqi and Afghan populations, will the Sudanese people on the wrong side of the front line become the newest victims, abandoned by humanitarian organisations forced to evacuate the country after their symbol has been militarised?" (Weissman 2005).

If MSF has burned its fingers by being too closely associated with Western foreign adventures, other humanitarian organizations are less wary. Those NGOs that are becoming more prominently involved in international politics through lobbying for reform of the UN Charter and intervention in individual crises are taking some risks. Least wary in advocating military interventions in the name of humanitarianism are probably the newer human rights organizations: because these are not themselves engaged in relief work, they do not have to face the consequences of their stance on the ground. If they worry about too close an identification of contemporary military humanitarianism with past imperialism, they try to square this with the idea of ground troops coming from non-Western countries. But such niceties actually echo past colonial strategies of "getting savages to fight barbarians" (Duffield 2005).

Generally, insofar as awareness of a changed climate is expressed, this is too easily put down to the global war on terror, as if humanitarian advocacy could continue as usual if only Western security priorities did not divert aid from humanitarian concerns. The humanitarian organizations have been slow to acknowledge the fact that their own political advocacy has facilitated this reordering, despite the compelling research produced by individual NGO staff members on the political, social, and ethical problems created by "humanitarian enforcement." Indeed, this reordering would be formalized by the changes to the UN Charter for which some NGOs are lobbying. And NGOs have been inconsistent in criticizing the failure to secure a prior UN Security Council resolution authorizing military intervention in Iraq, while they were previously and subsequently willing to dispense with this same requirement in demanding military intervention in Kosovo or Darfur in the name of humanitarianism. Clearly the practical consequences for specific missions, such as the collapse of humanitarian space in Iraq, have registered more with aid agencies than have the broad ethical dilemmas raised by the concept of humanitarian enforcement. Moreover the huge response to the 2004 Asian tsunami has helped to reinforce complacency that humanitarianism will be all right after all, and to reduce the impact of some perceptive reflections on its future. The growing emphasis in official circles as well as among NGOs on "the right to intervene" has yet to confront the fact that, even with unrestricted intervention and the willing compliance of developing countries, the normative development agenda is unrealizable without complementary material advancement.

ADVOCACY'S NARCISSISM?

I wish to make one final general observation on the growth of humanitarian advocacy. Tony Vaux provocatively titled his book *The Selfish Altruist* (Vaux 2002). Perhaps today we should speak of the "narcissistic altruist." The contemporary preference for advocacy is not unrelated to the narcissistic cult of publicity. There exists a long-established philosophical notion that for charitable acts to be truly virtuous and not an expression of vanity, they should be secret. These ancient strictures may be harsh and impracticable (how would an aid agency raise funds for its programs?), but they are worth highlighting because today's desire to be seen doing something in high-profile emergencies is distorting aid priorities and undermining the principle of universalism. There is an obvious temptation to undertake advocacy rather than offering material aid when relief assistance has been criticized for damaging economies and feeding killers. Advocacy directly raises an organization's profile in a manner that the ordinary provision of aid does not. Advocacy can allow one to claim the moral high ground—without the stresses and responsibilities of implementing assistance programs on the ground. Nor is it necessary to deal with potential contradictions between policy and practice. In other words, advocacy can in some cases represent a disingenuous flight from responsibility for social problems, rather than deeper engagement with them.

In addition, the distinction between doing good and being seen doing good is getting lost in high-profile contemporary campaigning, which seems too often focused on appearances. Its style flatters individuals into believing that they are changing the world through superficial gestures, without needing to sacrifice time or money. "It only needs to take you a matter of minutes every month, but it will help us to literally change the world," states the MPH Web site in promoting its white-wristband initiative (www.makepovertyhistory.org). It goes on:

> By wearing one you are part of a unique worldwide effort in 2005 to end extreme poverty—you're saying that it's time to stop the deaths of more than 200,000 people every single week from preventable diseases.

The wristband campaigns of the "noughties" (displacing the badges of the 1980s and the ribbons of the 1990s) epitomize the trivial fashion statement masquerading as commitment. Throughout history, items of clothing have been used to symbolize allegiance to a particular political, religious, or moral cause. However, today's symbolic gesture has become the action itself, emptied of any meaning. Wristband wearers are being asked to project a moral position, but without having to commit themselves to anything beyond the gesture. Tellingly the MPH Web site states:

> Wearing the White Band in 2005 is about sending a message that you want poverty to be stopped. You can wear it any way you like. . . . The really important thing is that you just wear it.

The phrase "[y]ou can wear it any way you like" is the language of fashion magazines and appeals to a consumer culture, rather than countering it. Revealingly, the stress is on *you,* on *your* wearing and showing the wristband, and *you* demanding that something must be done: *"The important thing is that you show your support and say enough is enough."*

This approach runs the risk of rendering such campaigns vacuous. A student involved in the MPH campaign at the University of Nottingham alerted me to the potential frustrations:

> I thought the whole white wristband idea for MPH was a really good idea [. . .] to make charity cool, but in fact, since doing some campaigning on campus for the trade justice part of the MPH campaign, I'm left very much undecided [. . .]. On the stall we had people coming up asking to buy the white bands saying "Oh, I've been looking for these everywhere," but actually they knew nothing about the campaign, what it stood for, or what we were doing. A lot couldn't even take the time to tick a box to vote for trade justice, let alone ask or be told what it was all about. [. . .] Charity wristbands are the new cool, and yet no one knows or cares anything about what the charities stand for or who they help.[1]

So the campaign's endorsement of minimalist gestures masquerading as participation risks demoralizing those who want serious engagement with the issues and want to engage others meaningfully.

This lowest-common-denominator type of politics is somewhat at odds with the impression that NGOs have created a vibrant mass movement in support of their activities. Rather, they appear to be trying to will into existence a mass movement by projecting the image that it exists. This simulation trivializes the idea of political struggle and invokes a false universal community and a faux political movement. Talking up the symbolic gesture of buying and wearing a wristband as a form of political engagement both patronizes individuals and also flatters the organizations involved into believing that they are leading a political movement, while at the same time trivializing the causes that they have embraced. Stopping poverty is treated as merely an act of will, embodying the consumer expectations of instant gratification whereby desire is equated with realization. Popular campaigns, rather like Western politics more generally, may be good at projecting themselves, but it is often at the expense of substance. Analysis is kept to the minimum, as are the expectations of people's capacity to be politically engaged, in what amounts to an expression of disenchantment with the possibilities of political action. Rather than engaging people through analysis, the focus is on sensationalist accounts. The approach implies a dim view of people and does nothing to arrest the erosion of progressive politics. The superficial nature of people's engagement suggests that rather than being genuinely involved in grassroots advocacy, some NGOs are now much more comfortable with lobbying in official circles.

CONCLUDING REMARKS

In this chapter I have criticized the nature of much existing humanitarian advocacy as tending to reinforce international inequalities rather than overturning them, by casting conditions in the developing world as moral rather than political and material issues, with dubious results for those in whose name the advocacy is conducted.

Insecurity is an inevitable condition for most people in developing countries because a weak state without a developed economy and infrastructure will lack the capacity to guarantee their welfare and rights, whatever its political hue and whatever the level of international supervision. Humanitarianism is ultimately concerned with affirming a universal humanity and recognizing the humanity of every individual. International inequalities make humanitarian relief necessary, but inherently difficult to get right, and also inadequate when most of the world's population is governed by necessity. Humanitarian aid is an important symbolic act of empathy in an unequal world. It can also alleviate suffering. But it remains at best a gift that can be given or withheld.

Premature declarations of membership in a global community cloud the reality of unequal relations and the significance of sharply divergent material conditions of existence. And such declarations are belied by the minimalist engagement with the Western domestic public established by NGO advocacy, while humanitarian advocacy offers the temptation to project a sense of moral purpose against conditions in developing countries—without the responsibility of potentially getting it wrong.

NOTE

[1] Frances Wakefield, e-mail correspondence, June 29, 2005.

REFERENCES

Black, Maggie (1996) *Children First: The Story of UNICEF, Past and Present,* Oxford: Oxford University Press.
Carson, Rachel (1962) *Silent Spring,* Harmondsworth: Penguin.
Christian Aid (2004) *The Politics of Poverty: Aid in the New Cold War,* London: Christian Aid.
Commission for Africa (2005) *Our Common Interest,* available at www. commissionforafrica.org/ (retrieved September 30, 2005).
Cosgrave, John (2004) *The Impact of the War on Terror on Aid Flows,* London: ActionAid.
Duffield, Mark (2005) "Getting Savages to Fight Barbarians: Development, Security and the Colonial Present," *Conflict, Security and Development* 5(2):141–159.
Ferguson, Niall (2004) *Colossus: The Price of America's Empire,* London: Allen Lane.
Fox, Fiona (2001) "New Humanitarianism: Does It Provide a Moral Banner for the 21st Century?," *Disasters* 25(4):275–289.
Furedi, Frank (2002) *Culture of Fear: Risk-taking and the Morality of Low Expectation,* London: Continuum.
Ignatieff, Michael (2003) *Empire-Lite: Nation-Building in Bosnia, Kosovo, and Afghanistan,* London: Vintage.
King, Gary and Murray Craig (2001) "Rethinking Human Security," *Political Science Quarterly* 116(4):585–610.
Laïdi, Zaki (1998) *A World without Meaning: The Crisis of Meaning in International Politics,* London and New York: Routledge.
Mack, Andrew (2004) "The Concept of Human Security," in Michael Brzoska and Peter J. Croll (eds.) *Promoting Security: But How and For Whom?,* Bonn: Bonn Center for Conversion (BICC).

Marcuse, Herbert (1964) *One Dimensional Man: Studies in the Ideology of Advanced Industrial Society,* London: Routledge & Kegan Paul.

Oxfam GB (2003) "Oxfam GB Strategic Plan 2003–2006," Oxford: Oxfam GB.

Oxfam GB (2003–2004) "Annual Review," available at www.oxfam.org.uk/about_us/annual_review/downloads/Oxfam_review_2003-4.pdf (retrieved September 30, 2005).

Oxfam GB (2004) "EU Must Act to Stop Violence in Darfur," press release, November 22.

Oxfam GB (2005) "Oxfam Challenges Governments—Back Annan's Vision, Save Lives," press release, March 21.

Pupavac, Vanessa (2005) "Human Security and the Rise of Global Therapeutic Governance," *Conflict, Security and Development* 5(2):161–181.

Schumacher, E.F. (1973) *Small Is Beautiful: A Study of Economics as if People Mattered,* London: Blond & Briggs.

Sen, Amartya (1975) *Employment, Technology and Development,* Oxford: Clarendon Press.

Ugresic, Dubravka (1998) *The Culture of Lies,* London: Phoenix House.

Vaux, Tony (2002) *The Selfish Altruist: Dilemmas of Relief Work in Famine and War,* London: Earthscan.

Weissman, Fabrice (2005) *Military Humanitarianism: A Deadly Confusion,* Paris: MSF.

First published in *Development in Practice* 16(3&4):255–269 in 2006.

THREE

Post-war Aid: Patterns and Purposes

ASTRI SUHRKE AND JULIA BUCKMASTER

CHAPTER SUMMARY

A recent report by the World Bank reiterates the widely held view that donor agencies commit large amounts of funding in the immediate post-conflict phase, only for the funding to taper off to more "normal" levels once the crisis is over. The World Bank criticizes this phenomenon, referred to as "frontloading," and claims that it damages the prospects of economic growth, which in turn undermines the peace. This chapter argues that the Bank's analysis is flawed because it does not distinguish between commitments and disbursements, or take sufficient account of other factors influencing aid patterns over time and in different settings. Moreover, the link between official aid and post-war economic performance is of only marginal significance. Any critique of aid policies must be based on detailed analysis of what is delivered rather than what is promised, and of the impact of donors' assistance on the ground.

(World Bank 2004)

THE PATTERNS OF POST-WAR AID

Conventional wisdom within aid circles holds that assistance strategies in post-conflict situations are driven by the "CNN effect." Donors supposedly rush in with aid when peace is declared—but rather than staying for the long haul, they rapidly scale back their giving when the situation is no longer newsworthy. The result is a distinct and dysfunctional frontloading of aid. This belief seems widely accepted as a sad fact of life by aid practitioners and also by recipients, and has been given further currency by a major study prepared for and promoted by the World Bank, which supports the thesis with elaborate statistical analysis (World Bank 2004). But is the thesis correct? More careful examination of aid in post-conflict situations currently being undertaken with support from the Norwegian Research Council shows a far more complex picture.[1] Frontloading occurs only in certain kinds of post-conflict situations, not in others. Similarly, only some types of aid are frontloaded; others are not. Changes in the volume of aid can be better explained by discrete political events than by the supposed CNN effect. Overall, we find nuances in aid patterns that suggest deliberate and varying strategic rationales. Post-war aid, in other words, must be understood as politically strategic behavior in pursuit of what is commonly called "peace building." The patterns of aid and their rationale form the subject of this chapter.

Our point of departure is the World Bank report noted above, which was prepared by Paul Collier and associates (World Bank 2004).[2] Addressing the aftermath of civil wars and similar types of violent conflict, the report concludes that donors frontload aid by rushing in extra money during the first couple of years after peace is announced, but that this aid soon tapers off to much lower levels. Collier and associates argue that this is sub-optimal behavior, and recommend instead that donors gradually increase aid to peak in the middle of the first post-conflict decade before tapering off to "normal" levels. They argue that this aid strategy will maximize economic growth in the post-war period—and growth, they claim, is important to sustain the peace.

The notion that economic growth sustains peace in the immediate post-war period will be discussed further below. Let us first look at actual donor behaviour. We took the data set that was used for the World Bank study and looked at aid volumes for the first post-conflict decade, but we also made a several distinctions that the study did not consider. First, we distinguished between types of aid, and between commitments and disbursements.[3] Second, we used annual figures rather than four-year averages. (In the figures in this chapter, each year after the war ended is coded as year 1, 2, 3, etc.). And third, we took into account changes in the evolution of the international aid regime by separating conflicts that ended in the 1990s ("new conflicts") from the earlier ones ("old conflicts"). Recognizing these distinctions, which are elementary from the perspective of practitioners, yields a far more nuanced and varied picture.

PATTERNS OF AID

In looking at patterns of aid, we distinguished between development aid and humanitarian relief aid, which the World Bank study does not.[4] Not surprisingly, we got different results. As shown in Figure 3.1, based on a sample of seventeen post-conflict countries, only relief aid is front-loaded, whereas other types of aid are gradually phased in and peak in the third year following the peace settlement (after which, admittedly, the aid then tapers off). Using four-year averages and lumping all aid together (as the World Bank study does) would produce an overall front-loading pattern. This would be a misleading interpretation, however, because it conceals the separate role of and rationale for humanitarian aid in the immediate post-conflict period. The primary purpose of such aid is not—and arguably should not be—to promote economic growth. Viewed in this light, frontloading humanitarian aid is eminently rational and appropriate donor behavior.

Second, we took account of the fact that the international aid regime has changed dramatically in recent years, especially since the

Figure 3.1 Development and Relief Aid.

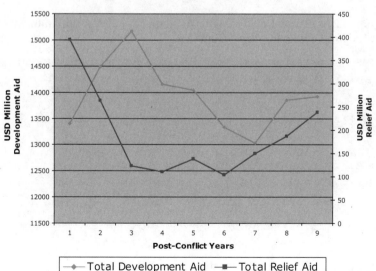

end of the Cold War. With respect to aid for humanitarian assistance and post-war reconstruction, a comprehensive, multilateral aid regime has evolved to address post-conflict situations. This change has entailed a progressive standardization of international responses to post-war situations with increasingly agreed-upon formulas for the nature and sequencing of aid, improved coordination, and clearer division of labour among aid agencies. It was during this period (specifically, the early 1990s) that the term "post-conflict" became standard among international financial institutions (IFIs) and aid agencies. When analyzing aid patterns it therefore makes sense to distinguish between the "new" post-conflict situations from the 1990s and those that occurred before, rather than combining conflicts spanning more than three decades into one group, as the World Bank report does. After sorting the cases (with "new" conflicts being those that ended after 1990, and "old" conflicts being those that ended before) we found that the aid responses indeed differed. Post-war aid after old conflicts was phased in much more gradually than after the new conflicts with respect to both relief aid and development assistance. Although the sample was small,[5] the trend is suggestive: the development of a comprehensive, multilateral aid regime in response to post-conflict situations has entailed a greater emphasis on moving aid in quickly in the early post-war years.

Another issue ignored by the World Bank study is the distinction between commitments and disbursements. The tendency for aid distribution to lag behind promises has been noted in some post-conflict

Figure 3.2 Official Development Assistance (ODA): Commitments and Disbursements in "New" Conflicts.

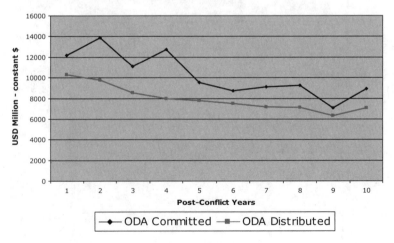

situations (e.g., in post-Taliban Afghanistan), and has been a standard source of claims, counter-claims, and tension in recipient-donor relations. The reality is more nuanced. Looking at aid to fifteen conflicts that ended after 1990 (Figure 3.2), we do see a discrepancy between commitments and disbursements in terms of ODA totals, but mainly during the first phase of peace. By the middle of the post-war decade, commitments tend to come down to a more "realistic" level—in other words, closer to the actual disbursements. Figure 3.2 also helps to explain why it is widely assumed that aid is rushed in during the early years of peace but then declines sharply. The commitment curve follows the dynamic of frontloading: big promises are made in the early post-war years but then show a marked decline—and big promises attract attention. Actual disbursements, by contrast, tend to be steadier. Although less visible in terms of international profile, disbursement is what actually counts in terms of impact on the ground.

COUNTRY CASES

Turning to individual country cases, we use total ODA figures (i.e., relief and development), and only include new conflicts that ended in the 1990s and were followed by increasingly standardized post-conflict aid strategies. The results show significant differences in the level and timing of aid, which in turn suggest different strategic rationales. These appear more clearly when country cases are considered in pairs.

Bosnia and Cambodia

The Bosnian post-war phase opened with the Dayton peace agreement, signed in December 1995. As Figure 3.3 shows, except for one year, there is little difference between aid commitments and aid disbursement. The remarkable aspect of the aid picture is that the very high volume of aid in the first four years is followed by a dramatic decline. While the curve does not suggest sharp frontloading of aid—the build-up during the first three years after Dayton is quite steady—the mild frontloading is accentuated by the subsequent sharp reduction. A CNN effect is hardly sufficient to explain this dramatic change, as the World Bank report claims. On closer examination, the abrupt decline can be better explained by reference to distinct political events.

Figure 3.3 Official Development Assistance (ODA) to Bosnia and Cambodia.

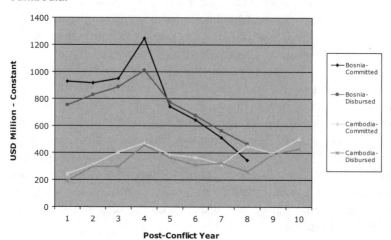

First, donors were becoming increasingly aware of the dysfunctional aspects of large aid transfers in the environment that prevailed in post-war Bosnia. Major reports published in mid-1999 revealed how aid had generated systematic new corruption and helped sustain the power of wartime and pre-war elites in ways that failed to further the Dayton agenda of democratic development and economic recovery. The recognition was gaining ground that institutional developments had to precede liberalization to ensure that aid would be used effectively. Media reports of spectacular waste (for instance, schools being repainted four times) underscored the point. Between 1999 and 2000 these concerns came to a head, partly because the initial commitments had been made within a four-year framework. At the same time, the NATO intervention in Kosovo (1999) led to major new demands for aid and reinforced donors' determination to reassess their initial capital-intensive approach to post-war reconstruction and peacebuilding in Bosnia. The formal reassessment was announced in the Brussels Declaration of the Peace Implementation Council in May 2000, in which a change of aid strategy was outlined entailing lower commitments and a greater emphasis on institution building.

The high level of aid to Bosnia during the first four years is remarkable. It represented about three times the amount disbursed to Cambodia in the equivalent post-conflict phase—yet Cambodia has more than twice the population of Bosnia and had suffered arguably far more destruction, and a few years earlier the international community had been equally instrumental in bringing the conflict in Cambodia to an end. Why this extraordinarily large amount of aid to Bosnia? This degree of engagement not only reflected the significance of Bosnia to the major donors and the intensity of the war's political and social impact on Europe and the United States, but NATO's military intervention and the US orchestration of the peace agreement had also given the major donors a strong sense of ownership of the peace process. It was to a great extent "their" peace. The Dayton Accord and the government it left in place in Sarajevo represented a victory for the declared interests of the United States and Europe in Bosnia, and the donors had strong political incentives to secure their investment and demonstrate their commitment. Massive aid transfers served this purpose. Moreover, important clauses of the peace agreement could only be implemented with external financing. This was particularly true regarding the return of refugees and internally displaced persons (IDPs), which was an integral part of the Dayton Accord and its underlying principle of restoring a multicultural Bosnia. Donors also cited strong economic reasons for immediate and large aid transfers. Both the World Bank and the EU argued that repairing the severely damaged infrastructure could help jump-start the Bosnian economy (World Bank 1996).

In Cambodia, by contrast, the peace agreement concluded in Paris in October 1991 contained a remarkable clause on post-war assistance. The Declaration on the Rehabilitation and Reconstruction of Cambodia appended to the peace agreement specified that such aid must be phased in slowly: "The implementation of an international aid effort would have to be phased in over a period that realistically acknowledges both political and technical imperatives" (para. 5). The most critical imperative in this respect was political. The Paris agreement left in power the Vietnamese-installed and supported government of Hun Sen. None of the major donors supported the Hun Sen government, and the United States vehemently opposed it for reasons related to its own defeat in Vietnam. Only Moscow was a friend of Hun Sen. The peace agreement was orchestrated by the large powers, but this was not the donors' peace in the same way the Dayton Accord would be. All the major powers and donors hoped that the elections scheduled for 1993 would bring a different government to power. The donors consequently had little incentive to rush in aid before the outcome of the elections was known. (The UN operation—UNTAC—had a comprehensive mandate but was financed separately.) The 1993 elections produced an uneasy compromise and a coalition that included a still-powerful Hun Sen. By the end of the decade, Hun Sen was still prime minister but had become more palatable to the donors (particularly in comparison with other Khmer political figures), and aid came to fluctuate at a slightly higher level than in the first post-war phase.

El Salvador and Nicaragua

A striking aspect of the post-war aid pattern in El Salvador is the huge initial gap between commitments and disbursement. Not long after the final peace agreement was concluded in 1992, promises of aid totalled more than US$ 1,200 million, although only around US$ 400 million was disbursed, and even less the next year (as shown in Figure 3.4). By then, commitments also fell drastically, and both curves stay around the US$ 270 million mark for most of the rest of the post-war decade. The most common criticism of the post-war aid policy in El Salvador was that disbursements were sorely inadequate in the first phase—in other words, that aid was not sufficiently frontloaded. The peace agreement had an ambitious agenda for socioeconomic reform (which was one quid pro quo for the FMLN to lay down arms), as well as standard provisions for post-war demobilization and the return of refugees and IDPs. All required significant financing, but the Salvadoran government's ability

Figure 3.4   Official Development Assistance (ODA) to El Salvador and Nicaragua.

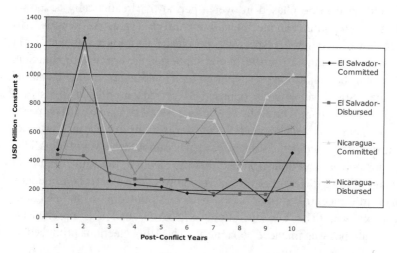

to provide this was undercut by its agreement with the international financial institutions to impose macroeconomic reforms to promote stability and also undertake economic structural adjustment to aid post-war recovery (de Soto and del Castillo 1994). International aid, had it been forthcoming in the quantities promised, would have given the government greater freedom to finance the peace agreement as well as observing the IMF strictures on macroeconomic stability.

It remains somewhat of a puzzle why aid was first promised in huge quantities and subsequently fizzled out. One explanation is that the donors (both in Europe and the United States) were prepared to finance the envisaged land reform, which was explicitly recognized in the peace agreement as a condition for the FMLN to demobilize and hence to secure the peace. Slow implementation of the reform schedule during the first year of peace indeed threatened to jeopardize the cease-fire. A new schedule was negotiated, but it encountered serious political and bureaucratic difficulties (del Castillo 1997). As the land reform came almost to a halt, the projected need for aid declined accordingly. Somewhat later the emphasis shifted toward general economic recovery through a national policy that emphasized sectoral restructuring and private sector-driven growth. In this policy framework, development assistance was assigned only a limited role.

Within the UN system, a major lesson from the case of El Salvador was clearly registered, namely the need to coordinate the economic and political aspects of a peace agreement in the negotiating phase. This lesson was pointedly referred to a few years later when the UN Secretariat assisted the peace talks in Guatemala. As a result, the World Bank and the IMF were brought into the peace negotitions rather than negotiating separately with the government as they had done in El Salvador. The general profile of post-war aid to Guatemala is nevertheless quite similar to that of El Salvador. In both cases the annual level is around US$ 250 million, although Guatemala's population is almost twice that of El Salvador. Aid disbursements are steady, in fact almost identical year by year for an entire six-year period following the 1996 peace agreement. The Guatemalan agreement had an even more ambitious agenda for socioeconomic change than its Salvadoran equivalent. But there was no frontloading of aid, as assumed and criticized by the World Bank report, or as advocated by other observers as being necessary to finance a peace agreement.

In the case of Nicaragua, the overall level of assistance is higher than for both El Salvador and Guatemala, probably reflecting a US strategic interest in building up a client regime. This would also account for the timing of aid. First, and again contrary to the World Bank study, the evidence shows no clear frontloading in terms of disbursements, but instead shows peaks and troughs. The first and most marked peak occurred in 1991, the year after the elections that signalled the end of the war. Surprisingly, the elections were won by the pro-US anti-Sandinista faction, with Violeta Chamorro becoming president. For the United States and its supporters this signified the transition to a democratic system and a favorable election outcome. To consolidate this trend, aid for "governance" increased sharply, accounting for part of the peak (US\$ 350 million). Subsequently, however, the anti-Sandinista coalition became deeply split, leading to what one observer calls "five years of raw confrontations over every issue" (Spence 2004:12). This seems to have produced some disillusionment among donors, which led in turn to unpredictable aid levels.

Mozambique and Rwanda

In both these countries, aid patterns (shown in Figure 3.5) conform more closely to the profile identified as a general tendency in the World Bank study. But the frontloading in both cases rests on a compelling and specific rationale.

Figure 3.5   Official Development Assistance (ODA) to Mozambique and Rwanda.

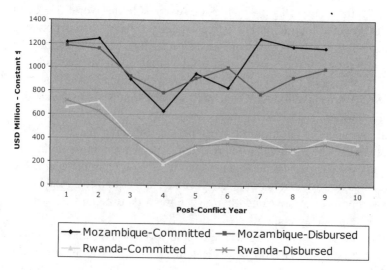

In post-genocide Rwanda, massive aid in the second half of 1994 and through 1995 expresses the deep sense of guilt felt in the international community because of its failure to stop or stem the genocide, and then by the relief needs of the enormous refugee movements that followed in its wake. The abrupt decline in 1996 and 1997 marks the fall from donor grace of the new government of Rwanda as its troops invaded neighboring Zaïre (now the Democratic Republic of Congo) and were credibly accused of committing massacres among the refugee populations linked to the *génocidaires*. In subsequent years, aid seems to find a steady "normal" level, reflecting conflicting views among the donors. Some cited a continued obligation to help the victims of the genocide, represented by the new government of Rwanda, while others claimed that the regime's authoritarian tendencies undermined the effectiveness of aid (Uvin 2001). The government's resistance to external conditionality, and a tendency to lay down its own conditions for accepting aid, further cools relations with donors.

In Mozambique the strategic rationale for frontloading aid was to finance the 1992 peace agreement. This had a tight schedule of demobilization and for the return of refugees, both of which were to precede and make meaningful the elections scheduled for 1994 (Hume 1994). Both these items were costly, and the elections themselves more so as the entire infrastructure for registration and voting had to be established. The elections were, however, an essential element of the peace strategy by helping to move the conflict between Frelimo and Renamo from the military to the political arena. Once the two-year program for implementing the peace agreement had been completed, the extraordinary expenditures could cease. Aid subsequently reverted to general development assistance and stabilized at between US$ 800 and US$ 1,000 million a year. By any criterion, this is a very high level of aid, which reflects both Mozambique's continued deep poverty (in 1995 the country ranked as the poorest in the world according to World Bank indicators) and the existence of faithful donors that have consistently supported the Mozambican government from the time of independence and throughout the war.

CONCLUSIONS

As the above analysis has shown, donors do not simply rush in with aid in the aftermath of war and then rapidly scale back. Post-war aid rather follows varied patterns that reflect distinct strategic rationales. Frontloading aid, which the World Bank report finds to be a general trend, is in fact only one of several patterns, and is most clearly reflected in commitments; donors tend to rush in with great promises to support a peace agreement but stay a much steadier course when it comes to actual disbursements. When donors move in with large funding in the immediate post-war years, they do so in response to strategic interests rather than simply reacting to the newsworthiness of peace. The three most important rationales our study found for frontloading aid are as follows:

- Humanitarian (e.g., relief aid provided in the aftermath of war)
- To implement a peace agreement (which typically carries an agenda with a price tag and a schedule)
- To support a client regime or favored peace agreement

Regarding the last point, it seems that peace settlements that are orchestrated by donors (as in the case of Bosnia), or that lead to donor-favored regimes (such as Nicaragua), tend to attract major initial funding. Peace agreements that leave in place regimes that are *not* favored by donors start off with much more modest funding (as in the case of Cambodia). But even favored peace agreements or regimes can quickly lose funding once the immediate post-war phase with its initial implementation schedules and sense of emergency is over (typically three to four years). Reassessment leading to sharply reduced funding may be based on criteria relating to its effectiveness (as in Bosnia), human rights considerations (as in Rwanda), or the general role of aid in the policy for economic recovery (as in El Salvador).

In all the cases studied here, peace prevailed for at least a decade. Why then, does it matter whether or not aid is frontloaded? No one has claimed that the timing and magnitude of aid are decisive in making or breaking a peace. Rather, the argument in the World Bank report is that frontloading post-war aid has a negative *effect* on peace. The argument is twofold: first, that rapid economic growth in the post-war decade serves to sustain the peace; and second, that to maximize economic growth, aid should be phased in slowly to peak in the middle of the first post-war decade, at which point it should be doubled before tapering back to "normal" levels. Both claims are uncertain.

The conclusion about the positive impact of economic growth on post-war peace rests on one statistical analysis undertaken earlier, also by Collier and associates (Collier and Hoeffler 2000). This study examines the probable occurrence of civil wars, and does not take into account specific aspects of post-war situations, such as the legacy of previous violence and integration of ex-belligerents. Moreover, it found that economic growth was only one of numerous factors that increased the likelihood of rebellion. Other factors include low population density and a highly mountainous terrain. A related World Bank study showed that in fragile war-and-peace situations, truly spectacular growth rates would be necessary to bring down the statistical probability of war even a few notches.[6] The impact of post-war aid on economic growth is in itself highly uncertain. A statistical retest found that the effect was 120 percent *less* than that estimated by the initial study used for the World Bank report (Suhrke, Villanger, and Woodward 2004).

These findings have significant policy implications. If the relationship among aid, growth, and peace in post-war situations is indeed uncertain or only marginally important, it frees policymakers to give more weight to other objectives in formulating policy. As we have shown here, this is what policymakers in fact tend to be doing, and, arguably, in some cases this is what they ought to be doing as well (i.e., providing immediate humanitarian relief and financing the implementation of a peace agreement). To assess the legitimacy of such strategic rationales and to formulate a policy critique therefore requires at a minimum the identification of actual aid patterns of the kind we have made here.

NOTES

[1] The research project, titled "Aid in post-conflict situations," is conducted at the Christian Michelsen Institute in Bergen, Norway.

[2] Paul Collier, Professor of Economics at the University of Oxford, was research director at the World Bank at the time of the report's preparation. The conclusions in the Bank study regarding post-conflict aid draw heavily on Collier and Hoeffler (2004).

[3] We used the aid figures in the OECD/DAC database, International Development Statistics, available at www.oecd.org/dataoecd/50/17/5037721.htm. Values are in US$ at 2002 rates. To analyze the conflicts, we used a slightly revised version of the country sample used by Collier and Hoeffler for their 2004 study (with corrections for coding errors, and adding data for Cambodia and Bosnia), which in turn was drawn from the widely used dataset on civil wars, Correlates of War (University of Michigan). For further discussion of the coding issue, see Suhrke, Villanger and Woodward (2004).

[4] The OECD data are disaggregated by sector. For "Relief Aid," we used Emergency assistance + Relief food aid + Non-food emergency and distress relief. The last item also includes a certain amount of aid to refugees in donor countries, as there is no separate category for this item. For "Development Aid" we used total Official Development Assistance (all sectors except those included in Relief Aid).

[5] To avoid very small subsamples, we used an earlier and larger version of the Collier-Hoeffler selection, which yielded eleven old and fifteen new conflicts.

[6] Using Zaïre (pre-DRC) as a model, the study found that an increase in economic growth from 2 percent to 8 percent would reduce the risk of civil war from 70 percent to 64 percent (Collier and Hoeffler 2002).

REFERENCES

Collier, Paul and Anke Hoeffler (2000) *Greed and Grievance in Civil War,* Working Paper Series No. 18, Oxford: Centre for the Study of African Economies, University of Oxford.

Collier, Paul and Anke Hoeffler (2002) *Aid, Policy, and Peace: Reducing the Risks of Civil Conflict,* Working Paper Series 2002/01, Oxford: Centre for the Study of African Economies, University of Oxford (later published in *Defence and Peace Economics* 13(6): 435–450).

Collier, Paul and Anke Hoeffler (2004) "Aid, Policy, and Growth in Post-conflict Societies," *European Economic Review,* 48: 1125–1145.

del Castillo, Graciana (1997) "The Arms-for-Land Deal in El Salvador," in M.W. Doyle et al. (eds.) *Keeping the Peace: Multidimensional UN Operations in Cambodia and El Salvador,* Cambridge: Cambridge University Press.

Hume, Cameron (1994) *Ending Mozambique's War,* Washington, DC: United States Institute of Peace.

de Soto, Alvaro and Graciana del Castillo (1994) "Obstacles to Peacebuilding," *Foreign Policy,* 94 (Spring): 69–74.

Spence, Jack (2004) *War and Peace in Central America: Comparing Transition toward Democracy and Social Equality in Guatemala, El Salvador and Nicaragua,* Cambridge, MA: Hemisphere Initiatives.

Suhrke, Astri, Espen Villanger and Susan Woodward (2004) "Economic Aid to Post-Conflict Countries," paper presented at UN/Wider conference, Helsinki, June 4–5.

Uvin, Peter (2001) "Difficult Choices in the New Post-conflict Agenda: The International Community in Rwanda after the Genocide," *Third World Quarterly* 22(2): 177–189.

World Bank (1996) *Bosnia and Herzegovina—Toward Economic Recovery,* Report No. 15668, June 30, Washington, DC: World Bank.

World Bank (2004) *Breaking the Conflict Trap,* Washington, DC: World Bank.

First published in *Development in Practice* 15(6): 737–746 in 2005.

FOUR

Humanitarianism and Politics: The Dangers of Contrived Separation

VOLKER SCHIMMEL

CHAPTER SUMMARY

Humanitarianism and politics are more often than not considered to be separate from each other, despite the increasing complexity of contemporary conflict. This chapter highlights the specifics of the flight of one renegade soldier and some 300 of his men from the Democratic Republic of the Congo (DRC) to Rwanda, at a time when the international community was plotting the road map for an ideal solution that all parties could have approved. The chapter explores what caused the relevant parties to forfeit such a solution and recommends ways to improve operational coordination and complementarity among international actors.

INTRODUCTION

The relationship that has evolved between humanitarian and political action and actors in responding to human needs in contemporary conflicts is characterized by fundamental ambiguities, both moral and operational. This chapter argues that although humanitarian and political actors are, in the words of Sadako Ogata, the former UN High Commissioner for Refugees, "uncomfortable bedfellows" (Ogata 1998), the biggest problem lies in policies that artificially separate the two. Instead of such separation, constructive and coordinated engagement is needed in order to achieve positive humanitarian and developmental outcomes.

Traditionally humanitarianism and politics have been perceived as polar opposites. From its inception, humanitarianism has always insisted on its nonpartisan—and thus nonpolitical—nature. One of the oldest humanitarian organizations, the International Committee of the Red Cross (ICRC), invokes the notion of *espace humanitaire* [humanitarian space] and emphasizes the importance of maintaining neutrality and independence as opposed to taking sides in a conflict, i.e., being political. The United Nations in general, and its specialized agencies in particular, were from the very outset defined as being humanitarian, which again meant nonpolitical. For many years now, scholars and practitioners alike have considered the limitations of conceiving of humanitarian action as being free of politics; the classic dichotomy of "good humanitarianism" versus "bad politics" has broken down. A first landmark event was the Biafra conflict in the 1960s, but the nadir of the late twentieth century was the humanitarian support given to perpetrators of the 1994 genocide in Rwanda.

Since that point, there have been attempts to come to terms with the interconnected nature of politics and humanitarianism. Today it is generally at least acknowledged that there probably is some sort of interaction, even if it is in the form of complementarity. Thus Ogata's statement has often been qualified by pointing out that the bedfellows' discomfort stems from the fact that humanitarianism and politics are so closely intertwined.

A prominent example of the links between humanitarianism and politics is the way in which refugees can be manipulated. This chapter will address this issue by considering whether, when, and how irregular (rebel) forces can return to civilian life and, crucially, the kind of operational interaction between political and humanitarian actors that such a process requires.

The chapter does not seek to address the conceptual question of whether it is better to be political or humanitarian, nor does it pursue simplistic legal arguments citing conventions and protocols. Rather, it deals with operational realities and consequences resulting from clinging to obsolete definitions of conflict that lead to an artificial perpetuation of the humanitarian–political divide. The challenge is not to define which is the better form of action (i.e., humanitarianism *or* political engagement), but to determine how humanitarian and political actors can most effectively cooperate and interact. The chapter seeks to show how a refusal to interact operationally can have negative political and humanitarian consequences, with reference to the case of Colonel Jules

Mutebutsi and the role of the international community and the government of Rwanda (GoR) in the aftermath of the various crises in North Kivu and South Kivu in the Democratic Republic of the Congo (DRC, known until 1997 as Zaïre) between 2003 and 2005.

There are three interrelated issues underlying this argument. The first is that Rwanda has both economic and security interests in the DRC, some of which are based on bringing to justice the perpetrators of the 1994 genocide. The second point is that Rwanda still uses the genocide to justify its foreign policy objectives, something which donor governments find difficult to counter. Third is the image-conscious way in which the GoR projects its foreign policy, claiming that it generally wants to "do the right thing." At the same time, the transition to democracy and the rule of law in the DRC has legitimacy and will succeed only if impunity is challenged and the rule of law is respected. Hence, the example of Colonel Mutebutsi is a small but essential step toward this goal.

A BRIEF HISTORY OF RWANDA'S LINKS
WITH THE KIVUS

The dynamics of this case study can be understood only by reference to the DRC's recent history and the role played by its Rwandaphone population (or *Banyarwanda* people). There is a historic link between the Kivus and Banyarwanda. For centuries Rwandans have migrated westward, whether for economic reasons or under duress and flight from persecution, either because of displacement by colonial powers or because of territorial expansion under various kings (Mamdani 2001:234–263). One of the first group to migrate were Tutsi settlers in South Kivu, who labeled themselves *Banyamulenge* in order to distinguish themselves from Rwandaphone populations that followed much later. Importantly the Banyamulenge population was never fully integrated, either in Zaïre under Mobutu or in the DRC under Laurent Kabila or later under Kabila's son Joseph. Many had migrated in the nineteenth century and settled in the Kivus but were not granted citizenship at independence. In a move to win over the increasingly influential Banyamulenge, Mobutu granted them citizenship in 1972, only to revoke it nine years later, when he exploited the unpopularity of the Banyamulenge community to marginalize them further. Little has changed since then, and discussions about the new citizenship bill have confirmed the marginalized status of the Banyamulenge (Nzongola-Ntalaja 2004:6–8).

Furthermore, in the aftermath of the 1994 genocide, millions of Rwandan Hutus fled westward over the border. Although they were swift to integrate, because Hutus had migrated to Zaïre throughout the twentieth century, this displacement was destabilizing for the entire region. Banyamulenge self-defense militias sprang up, and the GoR, led by the Rwandan Patriotic Front (RPF), invaded its neighbor. This culminated in the toppling of Mobutu by Laurent Desiré Kabila, whose rebels had significant Rwandan and Banyamulenge backing. Soon, however, alliances shifted, and Kabila decided to use Hutu rebels rather than the RPF and their Banyamulenge allies to strengthen his position.

After a clash with his backers, Kabila became embroiled in another conflict in 1998, which subsequently drew six foreign countries into what some have labeled Africa's Great War. The conflict lasted five years, causing some three million deaths and creating seemingly insurmountable humanitarian challenges. It was brought to an end by the 1999 Lusaka Ceasefire Accords and subsequent agreements, and—in relation to Rwanda—by the 2002 Pretoria Peace Agreement. The Inter-Congolese Dialogue was concluded with the April 2003 Sun City Agreement, which drew up the parameters for the transition to democracy and the rule of law, most notably the *espace presidentielle* [presidential space] whereby President Joseph Kabila is flanked by four vice-presidents, each belonging to a different group previously involved in the conflict. One of these parties is the *Rassemblement Congolais pour la Démocratie Goma* (RCD-G), which has its power base in the Kivus in eastern DRC. Since its founding, it has had very close ties with the GoR.

This process of establishing *le Congo aux Congolais* [Congo for the Congolese], the slogan of former Prime Minister Patrice Lumumba, conflicts with Rwanda's strategic economic and political interests in the Kivus, both because the Kivus are endowed with valuable natural resources and because the area is a hideout for perpetrators of the genocide. In the past, the region was a strategic buffer against attacks on Rwandan territory carried out by successors to *Interahamwe* rebels (Braeckman 2003:241), and there is a clear cultural connection because many Rwandaphone Congolese live in eastern DRC. Various justifications have been given for Rwanda's influence or presence in the Kivus, but the Rwandan elite exercised de facto control over North and South Kivu from 1998 to 2002. The Pretoria Peace Agreement brought an end to the presence of foreign troops on Congolese territory, after which Rwanda's influence became much more indirect. Indeed, the RCD-G became an important means by which Rwanda could influence Congolese politics. Alphonse Furuma, one of the RPF's founding members, called Rwanda the "invisible hand" that pays and supports proxies in the DRC (Braeckman 2003:243).

Since 1994 the GoR has pursued the *génocidaires* in eastern Congo. Initially this campaign responded to real concerns about security and was motivated by the desire to bring to justice those who had committed crimes against humanity. Hence, there was widespread understanding of Rwanda's position and its actions in Zaire at the time. However, the security-based justification for Rwandan involvement in Congolese politics became ever more contentious. Since Rwandan and Rwanda-backed forces reached Kinshasa in 1996, claims that they were unable to deal with the threat of genocidal fighters seem superfluous and not credible.

Over the years Rwanda had extracted millions of dollars in the form of natural resources from the DRC, and economic interests became the driving force behind Rwanda's behavior toward its neighbor. The most concrete evidence of this is the report by the UN Panel of Experts on the Illegal Exploitation of Natural Resources (UN 2002) and the Panel of Experts on the Arms Embargo (UN 2003). Security concerns regarding Hutu extremists and their base in the Kivus were superseded by the concern to maintain profits and economic security, especially for the Rwandan elite and their networks. These in turn are now linked with international criminal networks that can operate only in a partially failed state such as the eastern DRC.

If indeed the profit motive is inextricably linked to the overt or covert Rwandan security presence in the Kivus, then Rwanda and its proxies must be viewed as potential spoilers in the Congolese transition, in that there is more money to be gained from the status quo of a failed state than from a successful transition. The elite groups who run these spoiler operations have been aptly referred to as "entrepreneurs of insecurity" (Reyntjens 2004:207).

The importance of this entrepreneurship underpins the basic premise of this chapter, which is that Rwanda has a strategic interest in the DRC that manifests itself in opposition to the Congolese transition process. Because Rwanda is always eager to be seen as "doing the right thing" internationally, it did not object to the Pretoria Peace Agreement, which would lead to the complete removal (repatriation) of armed foreign

elements from Congolese soil. Its image-conscious way of doing politics is brilliantly described elsewhere (Pottier 2002:130–178).

Rwandan interests in the Kivus and the GoR's wish to do the right
thing came into play during the rise of Colonel Jules Mutebutsi and
should have been exploited in attempts to solve the ensuing problems
posed by Mutebutsi and his fellow combatants. In order to understand
the specifics of their case, we need to look more closely at the events in
eastern DRC leading up to Colonel Mutebutsi's flight in 2004.

COLONEL MUTEBUTSI AND
THE BUKAVU CRISES IN 2004

Colonel Jules Mutebutsi is from the Banyamulenge community in the
Minembwe plateau. After military training in Burundi, he joined the
Alliance of Democratic Forces for the Liberation of Congo (AFDL)
in its early years. His career with the RCD-G started in Kalemie and
subsequently led him to Baraka and his first brigade command in
Uvira. Within the spectrum of RCD-G politicians, he is opposed to the
Ruberwa wing that has engaged in the DRC transition process, which in
turn brings him closer to the GoR position (*Le Soft* 2004).

The withdrawal of Rwandan forces from DRC under the Pretoria
Agreement made the empowerment of Congolese proxies a strategic
necessity if the GoR was to maintain influence over the course of the
transitional process—a nation-building exercise that is supposed to end
with the first elections held since Congolese independence in 1960.

In December 2003 an important step in the Congolese transition
was to unify the various armed factions under a central army command
of Armed Forces of the Democratic Republic of the Congo (FADRC).
The refusal of several officers to adhere to this unified command created
the friction that eventually erupted into renewed clashes in the Kivus in
February and May 2004. Behind the February crisis was the planned
reorganization of the army and the creation of new military regions (the
eighth region includes South Kivu, and the tenth includes North Kivu).
Military commanders were named in January 2004 according to their
affiliations. At that point the GoR felt that it had ceded control over
South Kivu to Kinshasa-friendly forces, because General Nabyolwa of the
People's Party for Reconstruction and Democracy (PPRD) became com-
mander of the tenth military region, and only his second-in-command,
Colonel Mutebutsi, came from the ranks of the RCD-G.

In February 2004 Nabyolwa accused several RCD-G members of arms trafficking, as several weapons caches were found—notably that of a former RCD officer, Major Kasongo. Following Kasongo's arrest, Mutebutsi mounted attacks, and fighting broke out in Bukavu. Rwanda immediately closed the border in order to dissociate itself from the problem. Calm was restored, and Nabyolwa was replaced by General Mbudja Mabe. This left Mutebutsi effectively in charge of the security situation, and Mabe curtailed Mutebutsi's excessive freedom of movement, including movement to and from Rwanda, only toward the end of May that year. Eventually men loyal to Mutebutsi clashed with soldiers of the tenth military region, when the latter wanted to stop their free movement to the Rwandan border. This prompted the May/June crisis in Bukavu, during which another renegade general—Laurent Nkunda, based in Goma—became involved. Again Rwanda closed its borders with DRC, but by that time some 3,000 refugees (mostly Banyamulenge) had already fled to Cyangugu.

Although fighting in Bukavu ebbed after about ten days, the wider region remained tense, and clashes continued in Kamanyola (in June), around Minova and Kalehe (July/August), around Goma (September/October), and in Kanyabayonga (December). On each occasion the GoR followed events closely, with growing indications that it would not remain inactive if the unrest continued. The clearest example of this was President Kagame's threat to redeploy the Rwandan army in DRC, issued the very week after the Dar es Salaam Declaration on the consolidation of Security, Stability and Development in the Great Lakes region (November 20, 2004). Although the UN Peacekeeping Mission in DRC (MONUC) never confirmed an alleged Rwandan presence in DRC immediately following this open threat, many observers in Goma were in no doubt that there was an initial deployment.[1]

Taking into account Rwandan strategic interests and the ways in which the GoR can maintain a direct or indirect presence in the DRC, the transition can work only if there is at least the perception that the DRC's future is in the hands of the Congolese and not those of foreign governments. Critically, after the atrocities and crimes committed in Bukavu by Colonel Mutebutsi and his men, the only way to avoid betraying this principle was to combat his impunity. This would have required putting Mutebutsi and his supporters on trial. Ironically, the GoR, which had always lamented rampant impunity in the DRC in relation to the Hutu rebels, provided refuge for Mutebutsi and, in so doing, precluded a concerted multilateral effort to bring him and his men to justice.

This episode adds a second dimension to the basic premise of this chapter, which is the GoR's ability to sign up to international agreements and to express continued support for them while covertly sabotaging their execution. This is captured by Collette Braeckmann, who accuses President Kagame of playing a regional version of the board game Stratego, an abstract game of military strategy. She sees symptoms of a split personality in the behavior of the GoR, which takes tea to discuss development with donors and visitors while waging war next door (Braeckman 2003:211). The international community in Rwanda must take some blame for too readily accepting official declarations without ensuring that they were followed through, particularly if they were politically contentious. Here a coordinated response (cross-border as well as within Rwanda) could have offered a legitimate and face-saving solution to both governments as well as to the international community.

LACK OF CROSS-BORDER COORDINATION

When serious fighting erupted in and around Bukavu in late May 2004, the consequences, both humanitarian and political, were felt immediately on the Rwandan side. Refugees, mostly Banyamulenge, came across. They settled close to the border, contributing to the tensions of the already politically charged situation. In its broadcast of May 27, 2004, Radio Rwanda lost no time in claiming that Banyamulenge in Bukavu had been subjected to genocide. This was later disproved by an investigation led by the MONUC human rights division in June 2004, which showed that there had been 143 civilian casualties, 31 rapes, and 147 homes pillaged. But the broadcast claims suggested the direction in which the GoR was moving. Although Kigali was not affected at all, there was mounting pressure on the international community to endorse the GoR's position concerning the claim of genocide.[2]

It was in this context that Colonel Jules Mutebutsi first transited through Rwanda and finally sought refuge there. After FADRC troops under General Mabe had quelled the Mutebutsi-led rebellion, he was allowed into Rwanda via an official entry point in early June.[3] Shortly afterward Mutebutsi was found fighting in DRC again near Kamanyola. This area is often claimed as a Banyamulenge area of origin, and the subsequent vicitimization of the Tutsi population was used to legitimize Kigali-friendly forces in DRC. On June 21, Mutebutsi officially fled to Rwanda, claiming persecution and asking for refugee status.

The GoR swiftly accorded him and his followers refugee status without any formal screening, let alone any officially verified demobilization. This was contrary to various international conventions to which Rwanda is a signatory, but although it was challenged from the outset by UNHCR, in all official documentation as well as on national radio and television, the GoR referred to Colonel Mutebutsi and his approximately 300 co-fighters as "refugees." The slightest criticism or qualification voiced by the international community was met with strongly worded references to its having given support to perpetrators of the genocide in 1994.[4]

The GoR brought the group to Ntendezi, roughly 25 kilometers from the border with Bukavu. Authorities claimed that the group had been fully disarmed and demobilized, and that all the fighters were cantoned (confined to military quarters). The confiscated arms were never seen or presented, however, and because the site did not even have a proper perimeter, the term "cantonment" was hardly accurate. Having already accorded refugee status to Mutebutsi and his group, the GoR then made various appeals to international NGOs, UN agencies, and the ICRC mission in Rwanda for assistance. The United Nations quickly dispatched an assessment mission in order to recommend the next steps. Although MONUC was present during that mission, the peacekeepers were unable to take the lead or even to push for certain actions by the UN Country Team (UNCT), which had agreed to a concerted effort in view of the heavy political pressure.

Ultimately MONUC was too preoccupied with the aftermath of the Bukavu crisis, which it had mismanaged. Moreover, MONUC was more concerned with pursuing Brigadier General Nkunda, who on an ad hoc basis had been an ally of Mutebutsi in May and June 2004, but had since moved north toward Kalehe and Goma. MONUC's position is understandable to some extent because the peacekeeping mandate covers the DRC, and Nkunda was still on DRC territory. But it impeded an effective reaction on the Rwandan side, considering that MONUC is best placed to act as an international interlocutor between Rwanda and the DRC. Indeed, this function was part of the rationale for opening a MONUC liaison office in Kigali. The problems and failures with regard to MONUC's response, including decisionmaking procedures and internal coordination, are summarized in a March 2005 report by the UN Department of Peacekeeping Operations (DPKO) Best Practices Section (see also BERCI International 2005).

MONUC should have been in a position to direct the assessment mission and to provide all the necessary background information regarding Colonel Mutebutsi's role, which largely eluded the international community in Rwanda. This did not happen, and the MONUC presence in the DRC learned only after the event that such a mission was being undertaken. In the opinion of many of those involved in the DRC (including MONUC), Colonel Mutebutsi did not deserve any special attention, let alone assistance, from the international community. However, this was a political decision that did not take into account what the group was entitled to in terms of a transition to civilian life and eventual determination of their refugee status (although there was a strong likelihood that such status would be refused). Nor did the decision take into consideration how these humanitarian entitlements might have been woven into a comprehensive political solution to further the DRC transition process.

This, of course, was accompanied by the legitimate fear that the GoR was trying to legitimize a group of irregulars who had committed serious abuses of human rights. A report by Human Rights Watch, issued immediately after the events, cites the following abuses by soldiers who were under the control of Mutebutsi and Nkunda:

> In Bukavu, soldiers raped a mother and her three-year-old daughter on June 3 in the center of town. The mother was gang-raped by six soldiers in front of her husband and other children, while her young daughter was raped by another soldier. After the rape, the soldiers looted the house, taking most of the family's possessions. One local organization documented twelve cases of rape committed between June 2 and 4, including three girls of [age] three . . . and five girls in their teens. In one case, on June 3 soldiers entered a home where four teenaged girls were hiding. The soldiers demanded money, asked their ethnicity, and questioned them on the whereabouts of pro-government soldiers. Each of the girls was then raped more than once. In another case, twelve women and girls had taken refuge together in the same home for safety. On the evening of June 4, six soldiers entered the house. They said to the women: "we're going to show you that these girls are women like you." They then raped two three-year-old girls and did not rape the others.
>
> (Human Rights Watch 2004:3–4)

Mutebutsi himself was suspected of involvement in this raping and looting. International agencies on the Rwandan side were fairly oblivious of these facts and allegations; they treated Mutebutsi and his men like another group of second-tier troublemakers. It is not, therefore, surprising that the United Nations sent an assessment mission to find out more about the situation, which established further that it would be acceptable to offer humanitarian assistance to this group. This came as a shock to their counterparts in the DRC, particularly MONUC in Bukavu.[5]

In the end, the assessment mission that made recommendations to the humanitarian coordinator did not include any information or concerns from MONUC in the DRC. Subsequently, on June 29, 2004, the UNCT offered the prospect of humanitarian assistance (not to be confused with assistance for refugees), based on the fulfilment of four criteria:

- Verifiable renunciation of their status as combatants
- Verifiable cantonment
- A full list of names and rank
- Establishment of their legal status in the DRC

This cross-border policy mismatch within the international community overall and the United Nations in particular caused some friction and a series of exchanges at all levels between officials in the DRC and in Rwanda. However, the UNCT took a sensible line that avoided alienating the GoR while still providing the space for a comprehensive solution—even if it was forfeited soon afterward.

This opportunity to reach a solution was missed because of a lack of coordination among the relevant actors in Rwanda, a direct consequence of insisting on the artificial separation between humanitarianism and politics. Although cross-border coordination was a sufficient condition for a proper resolution of the Mutebutsi problem, straddling the humanitarian–political divide within Rwanda and coordination among actors in Kigali was the necessary condition. This was the area in which the contrived separation between the two would manifest itself most openly as a problem.

LACK OF COORDINATION IN RWANDA

Within Rwanda, the operational logic for the international community has been that of development, particularly since the end of the transition in 2003. Humanitarian issues or conflict-related questions have been sidelined. At the same time, the political space has narrowed, and high-level political criticism rarely goes unpunished. Following incidents in which expatriates have been expelled for being too critical of the government, the independence of the international community in Kigali has been compromised. Given how easy and comfortable life can be in Kigali, there is a deep reluctance to get into conflict with the government over big political issues, especially if they are not even related to domestic matters, as was the case with Mutebutsi.

Furthermore the legacy of 1994 is a factor at every turn. Quite rightly, the GoR never ceases to remind the international community of its share of guilt, a stance that yields strong commitments, financial and otherwise, in support of its position. Some observers have referred to this as "genocide credit" (Pottier 2002:130–151). Similarly, the GoR feels free to denounce critical statements and unpopular decisions by the international community.

Soon after Colonel Mutebutsi arrived in Rwanda in June 2004, Foreign Minister Muligande went on record with BBC World Service–Africa to declare that the international community was ready to assist *géno-cidaires* in 1994, but not refugees (i.e., Mutebutsi) in 2004.[6] It was in this context that Mutebutsi had fled and that international NGOs and UN agencies were asked to intervene. However, ICRC, NGOs, and UN agencies receded into passivity instead of making sure that consultations took place among the agencies. The standard justification was that "humanitarian agencies do not engage with military elements."[7] In the minds of international decision makers in Kigali, this was an either/or matter. This is the crux of the entire episode, in which international humanitarian decision makers deemed an issue too difficult and politically charged for them to get involved, even though a solution was at hand. In order to avoid involvement, all of them, without exception, "played the humanitarian card," leaving politics—and thus Colonel Mutebutsi—to others. The situation turned into a never-ending game of passing the buck.

The obvious first step would have been to advocate Mutebutsi's extradition within a matter of hours, which could have been done only by members of the *Comité International d'Appui Technique* (CIAT) [International Technical Support Committee] in DRC and MONUC. This option was not considered until months later, and despite the issue of an international arrest warrant by the Kinshasa government more than a year after Mutebutsi had fled, no extradition arrangement had been discussed at the time of writing. This speaks volumes about the

Congolese transition in its own right, but it certainly did not mean the end of all options; nor should it have meant that the international community in Rwanda became passive.

Every international actor in Kigali had an excuse for doing the wrong thing. Some UN agencies cited the need to deal with civilians rather than with soldiers, and on the same grounds several international NGOs refused to get involved. The ICRC argued that it was not mandated to deal with this group because they had left the territory in which they had been embroiled in a conflict. Other more development-oriented UN agencies wanted simply to provide one-time assistance and quickly forget about the issue altogether. The World Bank–sponsored multinational demobilization program (MDRP) could intervene only if asked to do so by the governments of both Rwanda and the DRC—a somewhat unlikely prospect. In short, all the relevant agencies interpreted their own mandates as narrowly as they could, without seeing—let alone understanding—the mandates of others. This failure to understand each other's mandates and activities was a major impediment to attempts to address the increasingly protracted crisis.

Following the four conditions set out in the UNCT position, the GoR decided to relocate Colonel Mutebutsi and his men in order to provide a more verifiable and credible form of cantonment. They were transferred to Coko camp in Gikongoro province on August 24 and 25, 2004. Interestingly the GoR immediately declared its willingness to comply also with the remaining three conditions.

However, because of the lack of a coherent position and the GoR's ability to put pressure on individual actors rather than on the UNCT, a growing number of UN agencies came to regard one-time assistance as the easy way out of their dilemmas. Once again, the justification for providing such assistance was based on a neat separation between humanitarian issues and politics. This also meant that no priority was given to establishing comprehensive dealings with Mutebutsi and his men after the granting of humanitarian assistance (i.e., demobilization and refugee-status determination). The group's disarmament and cantonment were accepted quickly by the UNCT in order to consider them civilians. This process should have been seriously challenged on three grounds. First, there are major doubts about the effectiveness of the cantonment, as several soldiers disappeared in August 2004 and the number of persons cantoned fell from 350 to 315. In a meeting with representatives of the international community in the same month, a government representative claimed that perfect cantonment is not possible, and that it would be normal for some fighters to escape "much like prisoners do." That said, according to the local authorities any cantoned combatant was supposed to leave only for medical treatment at a neighboring hospital (Mthembu-Salter 2005:15&38). However, Colonel Mutebutsi was sighted in Kigali as well as in Gisenyi/Goma,[8] and throughout 2005 the number of combatants cantoned at Coko fluctuated between 100 and 250, according to various assessment missions by MONUC, military attachés, and diplomats. To top it all, Mutebutsi's deputy, Eric Rurihombere, was apprehended along with forty-six others near Uvira in the DRC in September 2005. He was the second on the list of cantoned soldiers.

Moreover, to date no valid renunciation of their status as combatants has been forthcoming. In other words, there is no clear evidence that the demobilization is intended to last. Diplomats in Kigali referred to it as "part-time demobilization." In an interview conducted by the author in June 2004, Colonel Mutebutsi said that he and his men were not ready to lay down their arms because their home country might require their "services."

Finally, this was not a humanitarian situation or crisis that called for an intervention in the first place. A situation in which just over 300 persons are in need of food and nonfood items is nothing that a government with the control and access of the GoR could not handle. Yet the issue was pursued by high-ranking Rwandan politicians, who seldom care much about refugee issues. This political engagement made it seem like an effort to legitimize the group by having a UNHCR flag waving above the camp. No other option was ever discussed or accepted for discussion.

The GoR's push for assistance was not, therefore, matched by an adequate political assessment on the part of the international community. Instead the promise of humanitarian assistance was seen as an easy way out—the line of least resistance. Added to this, MONUC's self-marginalization in Rwanda impeded the search for a proper solution to the crisis. The peacekeepers were in the unfortunate position of being "UNAMIR's successors," criticized for having failed the Rwandan people in 1994—nothing unusual in Kigali. MONUC's position made it equally difficult for others to associate themselves with the peacekeepers, thus isolating the obvious engine to drive a coordinated and proactive response. The UN agencies in particular were afraid that their association with MONUC would make them immediately suspect and susceptible to the same stigma, so—rather than seeking meaningful cooperation—the easy path of dissociation was chosen.[9] This reinforced the logic and rhetoric of insisting on humanitarian roles, which enabled UN agencies to put some distance between themselves and the more political MONUC. Hence, as the situation progressed, MONUC stopped engaging; and the UNCT failed to involve it, largely because the Rwanda mission is not viewed as a full-fledged member of UNCT because of its status as a liaison office.

Compliance with all conditions set by the UNCT, however, remained elusive. Eventually in late October 2004 the Rwandan Ministry of Foreign Affairs (MINAFFET) summoned all the UNCT members in order to reassess the situation, given that pressure on individual agencies at lower levels had not yielded results. The GoR made it clear that it was not acceptable to withhold assistance to Mutebutsi and his men, given the efforts that had been made. The UNCT thus either had to stand firm on a principled and coordinated approach or yield to pressure. Given the complete lack of coordination among the various agencies or awareness of their different mandates, the UNCT agreed to giving one-time humanitarian assistance, in order to end what had already become a nuisance to various UN agencies.[10] This aid was justified exclusively on humanitarian grounds and was to be channeled through the Rwandan Red Cross in order to avoid high-profile visibility.

This decision singlehandedly rendered meaningless the conditions set out so promisingly in UNCT's initial position. There was significant government pressure on various actors and UN agencies during this time, and the lack of cross-border coordination, combined with inadequate information, made it difficult to continue to refuse to engage. More importantly, the lack of coordination within Rwanda made it impossible to exploit any complementarity among the agencies. The explicit unwillingness of humanitarian agencies to engage in issues related to peacekeeping, the manipulation of refugee situations, the DRC transition, and the refusal by political actors involved in it to take into consideration the humanitarian dimension of the problem meant that all parties had to stand their own ground in the face of exceptional pressure from the GoR.

Predictably the GoR requested toward mid-2005 that the group whom it considered to be refugees should receive the same kind of assistance as that accorded to other refugees in Rwanda. This time it was not about one-time humanitarian assistance but a long-term commitment. The GoR publicly repeated several times in 2004 and 2005 that Mutebutsi and his men were refugees, but that in line with international legal standards this fact would be established by a period of demobilization and refugee-status determination. UNHCR usually intervenes at the tail end of a process that necessarily involves other agencies, but that option was forfeited when the UNCT decided to go for disengagement through providing one-time humanitarian assistance without any coherent road map attached to it.

With better coordination among the UN agencies and within the international community (including international NGOs and ICRC) in Rwanda, a far better outcome could have been achieved. Assuming that a swift extradition was never an option, international actors should have cooperated in seeking to neutralize Colonel Mutebutsi and his men as spoilers of the DRC transition. This could have been achieved within the bounds of international legal norms and standards but would have required complementarity.

The international community, under the leadership of the UNCT, should have taken the GoR at its word in its willingness to neutralize Mutebutsi and set up a comprehensive and verifiable system of demobilization and cantonment. Clearly this would have required a road map that everybody would have had to sign on to, including the government of Rwanda. It was not in the latter's interest to be perceived as a renegade in international law, and indeed some RDF officers even considered Colonel Mutebutsi to be a nuisance that had to be dealt with. There was a possibility of cooperating meaningfully with the GoR on this issue. This is highlighted by the fact that Rwanda seeks to control (or be perceived as controlling) Mutebutsi. According to the independent newspaper *Newsline,* Mutebutsi was imprisoned in September 2005. Again this presented an opportunity to engage the GoR in a comprehensive solution, particularly because it followed a highly publicized agreement with the DRC and Uganda to deal with renegade elements and rebels jointly and swiftly.

A comprehensive agreement could have led to cantonment under ICRC monitoring or, if a narrow reading of the Red Cross mandate rendered this difficult, under MONUC or embassy- or attaché-led auspices. MONUC had the chance to become more proactive in Rwanda—an opportunity offered on a silver platter with the conclusion of the Joint Verification Mechanism in late September 2004. This enabled MONUC, as one of the monitoring partners, to "verify allegations of Rwandan logistical, technical and military support to any political and military entities in the Kivus." This could have covered the cantonment site for Mutebutsi. In the meantime, assistance could have been provided by a mandated NGO or by the German Technical Cooperation agency GTZ. This model was used in Burundi in cooperation with the European Union, where their respective mandates prevented other actors from providing assistance to combatants in cantonment sites. GTZ's more flexible status and mandate enable it to take an intermediary role. Given the state of German–Rwandan relations, this would also have been politically less contentious. Subsequent verification of demobilization could then have been carried out by MONUC, within a time frame determined by international precedents. The duration of demobilization before combatants can be considered civilians depends upon the degree of their involvement in combat and the suspected severity of any abuses of human rights committed by them. In the Mutebutsi case, this would have led to a maximum verification period of twelve months (da Costa 2004:38–51). This would verifiably have neutralized Colonel Mutebutsi and his men and, given the delay in their renunciation of combatant status, the verification period would have included the delayed election. Meanwhile it would have allowed UNHCR subsequently to consider them asylum seekers, which is in line with their claim. This in turn would have opened the door for proper refugee-status determination, which would have meant investigating crimes against humanity allegedly perpetrated by the entire group: if the allegations were proved, their claim to refugee status could have been disqualified, which would have delegitimized the group and anyone supporting them. This ultimate political outcome was what many humanitarian actors could not see, or chose not to see. Taking a long-term approach with a vision and a solution at its end would have meant traveling the humanitarian–political frontier, which is a complex process but one that is likely to yield more responsible results.

In essence this coordinated approach would have provided a legal and legitimate solution to the problem whereby none of the actors would have had to exceed its own mandate, thanks to workable complementarity. Neither the GoR nor Colonel Mutebutsi could have objected to such an approach without completely forfeiting their own legitimacy. In turn a proper investigation of their individual stories in Bukavu in 2004 would certainly have helped to combat impunity in the fragile DRC transition process.

CONSEQUENCES: PROSPECTS AND RISKS

Evidently, this coordination did not happen. Moreover, the GoR did not retract requests for assistance and has since resorted to a more confrontational strategy. Some observers therefore believe that Colonel

Mutebutsi and his men could eventually contribute to instability in the DRC once again.

Through state-owned media outlets, the GoR prepared the ground for justifying the combatants' departure due to "a lack of assistance provided by the international community" or through a program of "voluntary repatriation" organized by the government (*New Times* 2005; ORINFOR 2005). This is accompanied by rampant anti-transition rhetoric on the part of Mutebutsi himself. If it is indeed the case that Kigali does not yet have an interest in a smooth and successful conclusion of the DRC transition—this would be a convenient harmony of interests.

Eastern DRC will have to live with tensions for years to come, even after the elections. If the issue of Mutebutsi and his men is not addressed, it will become a permanent liability for post-transition DRC. It is not unusual in this area to hide out for a while and then strike at an opportune moment to jeopardize the political process. For instance, in August 2005 Mutebutsi's comrade Laurent Nkunda threatened to attack Kinshasa. Furthermore, the Kivus have been radicalized, and moderates have been silenced or killed, particularly in 2004. Some were deliberately targeted during the May/June crisis. This means that a small, localized conflict could easily recur, which could then be exaggerated as yet another genocide, providing yet another pretext for further military action. This could then spur the renegades to "protect" the Banyamulenge as a "humanitarian intervention," before monitors and observers could establish a clearer picture.

CONCLUSION

The traditional separation of politics and humanitarianism has been rendered increasingly irrelevant by the reality of complex emergencies. It can also undermine both the resolution of conflict and subsequent development. This is not to say that it is easy to straddle the divide, because doing so requires an awareness that often goes beyond individual mandates and operations and requires proactive coordination. A number of key issues emerge from this case study.

First, cooperation has to be enhanced and has to take place across the board, not solely within either the political or the humanitarian sphere. All parties must accept that there are some things that other agencies are better suited to address, and that it is important always to focus on the best way of combining mandates and resources. Although there have been examples of coordination, the case of Rwanda underlines the critical importance of including both sides. In any event, even a wider humanitarian group must take into consideration the political consequences of its actions and be proactive in engaging with them.

Such initiatives have to be aided and enhanced by a sound understanding of all mandates. Only if all the agencies and actors involved are aware of and understand what everyone else is allowed to do can there be comprehensive solutions. Equally such understanding will enable decision makers to engage in grey-area issues more readily as they arise, instead of losing time and missing opportunities. Had this been done in the case in question, a criminal could have been brought to justice for crimes against humanity, thereby contributing to a fragile transition process in the DRC. Crucially, this could have been achieved in perfect agreement with international laws, conventions, and precedents, and to the satisfaction of all actors, including the governments of Rwanda and the DRC as well as international humanitarian agencies. This opportunity was missed due to concerns about the grey area and resulting inaction. The nonpolitical nature of humanitarian actors was regularly invoked as a means of evading responsibility for the political consequences of their actions. This might be an acceptable position if it served to limit any exacerbation of conflict, but not as happened in the case described in this chapter, if it prevents a possible solution.

ACKNOWLEDGMENTS

The author thanks Greg Salter, Panos Moumtzis, and Leana Islam for their perceptive comments, without which this chapter would not have been written. The views presented in the chapter are those of the author, and are not to be attributed to the organizations to which he is or has been affiliated.

NOTES

[1] Interviews conducted in Goma. Statements made in these interviews about a Rwandan presence in late 2004 are coherent, but records differ as to whether the Rwandans withdrew or maintained a residual presence.

[2] Interviews with diplomats and senior UN staff in Kigali.

[3] Interviews conducted in Cyangugu.

[4] Foreign Minister Charles Muligande on BBC World Service–Africa, July 8, 2005.

[5] Interviews with MONUC officers.

[6] Foreign Minister Charles Muligande, interviewed by BBC World Service–Africa, July 8, 2005.

[7] Interviews with senior NGO, UN, and ICRC staff between July and December 2004.

[8] According to information gathered by the Forum on Early Warning and Early Emergency Response (FEWER).

[9] Interviews with senior UN staff in Kigali.

[10] Interviews with senior UN staff in Kigali.

REFERENCES

BERCI International (2005) "Peacekeeping Operations in the Democratic Republic of the Congo: The Perception of the Population," report commissioned by the Peacekeeping Best Practices Section (PBPS) of the Department of Peacekeeping Operations, available at www.un.org/Depts/dpko/ lessons/ (retrieved January 19, 2006).

Braeckman, Collette (2003) *Les Nouveaux Prédateurs,* Paris: Fayard.

da Costa, Rose (2004) "Maintaining the Civilian and Humanitarian Character of Asylum," *Legal and Protection Policy Series* (PPLA/2004/02), Geneva: UNHCR.

Human Rights Watch (2004) "D.R. Congo: War Crimes in Bukavu," HRW briefing paper, June, available at www.hrw.org (retrieved April 24, 2004).

Le Soft—édition internationale (2004) "Scission," N° 800 BIS, 28 August.

Mamdani, Mahmoud (2001) *When Victims Become Killers: Colonialism, Nativism and the Genocide in Rwanda,* Oxford: James Currey.

Mthembu-Salter, Gregory (2005) "The Wheel Turns Again: Militarisation and Rwanda's Congolese Refugees," unpublished paper, Geneva: Small Arms Survey.

New Times, The (February 9, 2005) "DRC Refugees Seek Repatriation," available at www.newtimes.co.rw (retrieved February 10, 2005).

Nzongola-Ntalaja, Georges (2004) "The Politics of Citizenship in the DRC," paper presented at the 2004 Annual International Conference on States, Borders and Nations, Centre of African Studies, University of Edinburgh, May 19–20.

Ogata, Sadoko (1998) "Keynote Address," Wolfsberg Humanitarian Forum, Wolfsberg, June 5.

ORINFOR (2005) "Exclusive interview avec le Colonel Jules Mutebutsi dans son camp de refuge à Coko," available at www.orinfor.org.rw (retrieved January 11, 2005).

Pottier, Johan (2002) *Re-Imagining Rwanda: Conflict, Survival and Disinformation in the Late Twentieth Century,* Cambridge: Cambridge University Press.

Reyntjens, Filip (2004) "Rwanda, Ten years on: From Genocide to Dictatorship," *African Affairs* 103:177–210.

Stedman, Stephen and Fred Tanner, (2003) "Refugee as Resources in War," in Stephen Stedman and Fred Tanner (eds.) *Refugee Manipulation: War, Politics, and the Abuse of Human Suffering,* Washington, DC: The Brookings Institution.

UN Panel of Experts on the Illegal Exploitation of Natural Resources (2002) Report to the UN Security Council (S/2002/1146), New York, October 16.

UN Panel of Experts on the Arms Embargo (2003) Report to the UN Security Council (S/2003/1027), New York, October 23.

First published in *Development in Practice* 16(3&4): 303–315 in 2006.

PART 2

Helping People Protect Themselves?

FIVE

Who *Really* Protects Civilians?

ANDREW BONWICK

CHAPTER SUMMARY

Current debate tends to suggest that the protection of civilians is something "done to" the passive recipients of international largesse. Whether in terms of macro-level interventions of the UN Security Council or micro-level attempts to reduce the negative side effects of relief action, those in need of protection are rarely seen as key players in their own futures. Although this type of external intervention can be valuable, it fails to take complete account of how people manage to survive the effects of conflicts. This concept of protection seriously underestimates the resourcefulness of people who have no choice, and results in missing opportunities to help communities as they are being forced to adapt to their new realities. Effective humanitarian action will thus not only focus on the actions of those with a responsibility to protect, but will also support and strengthen the rational decisions that people themselves take to try to ensure their own safety in conflict.

INTRODUCTION

[In Darfur] blatant breaches of the cease-fire agreements by all parties and the escalation of fighting, including rebel attacks and aerial bombardments by Government forces, have led to the evacuation of humanitarian staff. This has dramatically reduced our ability to deliver humanitarian assistance and protection for civilians.

(Egeland 2004)

These are the words of United Nations Under-Secretary-General for Humanitarian Affairs Jan Egeland, the United Nations' most senior humanitarian official. It would seem easy to conclude that "protection" is a commodity to be delivered to civilians alongside "'assistance": the basic goods and services required for subsistence, such as food, water, and medical care.

But is this comparison justifiable? This chapter examines the nature of protection and considers how people seek safety in the midst of armed conflict. It compares actions taken by external groups—from the UN Security Council to humanitarian agencies in the field—with the choices that people themselves make when they have few options. Finally it suggests ways in which humanitarian agencies can engage more effectively with people at risk in order to keep them safe or "protected."

UNDERSTANDING PROTECTION

So what does "protection mean"? Between 1996 and 2000, the International Committee of the Red Cross (ICRC) convened a series of workshops to encourage human rights groups and humanitarian organizations to address this question and search for common ground. A consensus definition was reached:

> The concept of protection encompasses . . . all activities aimed at ensuring full respect for the rights of the individual in accordance with the letter and the spirit of the relevant bodies of law, i.e., human rights law, international humanitarian law and refugee law.
>
> (Giossi Caverzasio 2001)

The workshops played an important role in promoting dialogue among diverse organizations. However, despite extensive use of the definition quoted above, its breadth has not helped agencies to find common ground, and as a result the coordination of humanitarian action at the field level has not improved. The rights-based definition covers everything from preventing the targeting of civilians by armed groups to preserving the right to marry and found a family. It thus allows almost all humanitarian activities to be reframed as "protection" without identifying issues of common concern across agencies—for

example, how to reduce levels of sexual violence against women in con-
flict-ridden areas, how to prevent people from being forced to return to
unsafe areas, how to prevent whole villages from being burned to the
ground—and thus does not catalyze coherent strategies to deal with
them.

Perhaps more important, it is not obvious that the language corresponds to a recognizable human reality. In 2004 Active Learning Network
for Accountability and Performance in Humanitarian Action (ALNAP)
published a pilot booklet of guidance on protection, which noted:

> Protection policy can often sound very state-centric. Thus it is essential
> to recognise that humanitarian protection is not merely a legal and
> programming conversation between agencies, states and armed groups
> that is over the heads of protected persons. On the contrary; wherever
> access and contact permits, humanitarian protection work is also about
> working directly with protected persons to identify and develop ways
> that they can protect themselves and realise their rights to assistance,
> repair, recovery, safety and redress.
>
> (Slim and Eguren 2004)

Protection is fundamentally about people. At its simplest, it is the challenge of helping people affected by conflict to stay safe—free from violence or fear, from coercion, and from the deliberate deprivation of
means of survival (Darcy and Hofmann 2003). A protection assessment
does not start with an abstract analysis of rights, but with the common-
sense question, "Who needs protection from what?"

This does not mean that international law and rights are not relevant. The law provides benchmarks for the way in which people can
legitimately expect to be treated. It can be used to locate responsibility
for the actions and inactions that threaten the safety of people caught up
in conflict. It can form part of a powerful argument to persuade individuals and governments to act. The law is a critical tool of protection,
but it is not its defining characteristic.

So if safety is the core concept underlying protection, how do
people stay safe? When humanitarian agencies consider the security
of their own staff, the aim is to manage risk. This can be done either
by reducing the level of threat, for example, through persuading military commanders to control their troops; or by reducing vulnerability
to the threat, for example, through avoiding danger by choosing not to
drive after dark. Exactly the same is true for protection, except that the

people whom we aim to keep safer are others—generally, although not exclusively, civilians.

REDUCING THE THREAT: PROTECTION AND THE UNITED NATIONS SECURITY COUNCIL

One of the key conclusions of the Joint Evaluation of Emergency Assistance to Rwanda (JEEAR), commissioned in the wake of the 1994 genocide, was that humanitarian action to pick up the pieces is no substitute for political action to prevent the violence in the first place.

The UN Security Council has increasingly taken an interest in the protection of civilians as a core part of its mandate. The importance of this step forward should not be underestimated. In the past the Council considered that the prohibition on intervening in matters that are essentially within the domestic jurisdiction of any state[1] debarred it from intervening in internal armed conflicts. During the Biafra conflict (1967–1970), the Security Council steadfastly refused even to discuss the plight of civilians, because it was felt that this would infringe upon Nigeria's sovereignty. Fortunately views have changed since then. In 1991 (Resolution 688) the Council demanded that Iraq act to halt the oppression of its minority populations, most notably the Kurds. In a series of resolutions on Somalia from 1992 on (Resolutions 733 ff), the Council decided that the magnitude of human suffering constituted a threat to international peace and security in its own right, and thus was a matter of legitimate concern.

By 2004 the question of Security Council jurisdiction over the situation in places such as Darfur simply no longer arose—it is now *assumed* that the protection of civilians is its concern. Indeed two resolutions (1265 and 1296) have been passed to affirm the protection of civilians—in the abstract.

The Security Council is being supported to develop its expertise in the area. In 2004 the UN Office for the Coordination of Humanitarian Affairs (OCHA) produced an updated Aide Memoire to guide the Council in its deliberations (UN-OCHA 2004). This encourages the Council to focus on issues from the security of internally displaced persons (IDPs) and access for humanitarian organizations through recommending measures to protect women from sexual violence. Its acceptance illustrates the significant progress that has been made at the policy level. Over the last five years, the language has shifted from the protection of humanitarian aid operations to the protection of civilians themselves. Peacekeeping operations—from Liberia to Haiti to the Democratic Republic of the Congo (DRC)—are now mandated to protect civilians in immediate danger, although the translation of this mandate into rules of engagement varies from force to force.

Despite this fact, even if there is sufficient agreement among Security Council members to reach a resolution, the types of measures available from such a distance are limited. Whether it is simply demanding action from states, using coercive measures ranging from sanctions to the threat of criminal prosecution, or even deploying UN troops on the ground, those who are expected to *deliver* this commodity of protection may be unwilling or unable to do so.

When the Security Council identifies governments that must take action, are these governments able to perform? Although the Sudanese government may be coerced into refraining from supporting the Janjaweed militia in Darfur, it is doubtful that it really has the power to rein them in, or indeed to bring long-running tribal conflicts in the area to an end. Similarly it is unrealistic to expect the nascent Afghan government to extend the rule of law far beyond the internationally protected haven of Kabul to areas where its poorly paid forces would need to challenge warlords' private armies.

When the Security Council deploys peacekeepers, its forces may have insufficient troops. The UN Secretary-General estimated that 35,000 troops would be required to enforce the safe havens in Bosnia. Only 7,000 were provided, with now infamous consequences at Srebrenica. Forces may also interpret their mandate narrowly or be unwilling to use the force necessary to carry out their operations effectively. Witness the time taken by the US forces in Somalia to accept that securing access for humanitarian aid necessitated the disarmament of militias—and their subsequent inability to carry out this larger task.

The protection agenda is not fundamentally incompatible with the Council's primary responsibility, which is to maintain international peace and security.[2] Indeed keeping civilians safe can be a steppingstone to peace, but this order of priority should not be forgotten. We have seen an example of this in the fear of compromising the North–South peace deal in Sudan by taking strong action on the abuses of civilians in Darfur (Greste 2004).

None of this is to say that the role of the Security Council is not necessary and important. The United Nations Mission in Sierra Leone

(UNAMSIL) played a vital role in stabilizing a country that was torn apart by a brutal civil war, and without the action of the Council the situation in Darfur risked being far worse. However, the inability of the United Nations to deliver protection on a consistent and widespread basis means that people caught up in conflict cannot rely on it as a guarantor of their safety.

REDUCING THE THREAT OR
REDUCING VULNERABILITY?

If protection offered by the Security Council is remote and inconsistent, at least it is relatively clear about its modus operandi: using a combination of persuasive and coercive interventions to encourage responsible authorities to take or to refrain from taking certain actions in order to keep civilians safe in conflict.

But what about protection for humanitarian agencies? In 2004 the Inter-Agency Internal Displacement Division sent out guidance to UN Humanitarian Coordinators (the most senior in-country UN humanitarian officials), defining protection at three levels: as an objective, as a set of activities, and as a legal responsibility (UN Internal Displacement Division 2004). In legal terms the following statements are rarely disputed:

> Primary responsibility for ensuring the protection of people affected by conflict rests with the national authorities, as prescribed by international human rights law. Additional legal responsibilities can be imposed under international humanitarian law on combatants in armed conflict (including non-state armed groups) and on occupying powers.
>
> Some agencies/offices, such as ICRC, UNHCR, UNICEF and OHCHR, are mandated with protection responsibilities for specific categories or groups of persons. These are considered "protection mandates."
>
> (UN Internal Displacement Division 2004)

Nonmandated agencies, including those of the UN and NGOs, have long worked alongside those with legal responsibility.

However, in terms of objectives, humanitarian agencies are far from agreeing about their role. Some limit their view of protection to ensuring that those whom they assist are not exposed to further harm by their assistance activities, whereas others believe that their role is to act as a witness: to monitor and denounce "violations" when they see them. The ICRC sees protection as all-encompassing, covering everything from persuading armed forces to respect the laws of war to ensuring that war-affected farmers have seeds to plant at the right time.

When it comes to activities, assumptions are made and not tested. In Darfur the first UN strategy for protecting civilians was built around "protection by presence": that is, it was assumed that the deeper the penetration of humanitarian staff or African Union observers into the field, the safer people would be (United Nations 2004). A major humanitarian organization is reported to have tested this assumption and concluded that the area under protection extended about 500 meters from their sites, and the protection lasted until around five o'clock in the evening.

Similarly, it does not seem credible that the detailed documentation of cases of sexual violence in the displaced people's camps in West Africa really reduces the likelihood of more women being raped, or that informing Colombian villagers of their "rights" genuinely increases their ability to exercise them when all the power is in the hands of the guerrillas, the paramilitaries, and the drug traffickers. Both activities have a role to play, yet neither is useful on its own.

It is perhaps these failed assumptions that provide the best pointer for the role of humanitarian agencies in protection. They are rarely, if ever, in a position to protect people from imminent harm. Although the Security Council *can* protect civilians but does not do so consistently enough to be relied upon, it is highly doubtful that humanitarian agencies can, to use Jan Egeland's words, *deliver* protection at all. This does not mean that such agencies cannot play a role in reducing the threats faced by civilians. Information, analysis, and political pressure coming from humanitarian agencies can spur action from those who are able to act effectively, whether they are as far away as New York and the Security Council, or as close to home as the national government or even the local police chief.

However, if humanitarian agencies are to realize their full potential for protection, they must understand how people *already* deal with the threats that they face. If, as in Darfur, women are most exposed to sexual violence when collecting firewood, then practical actions can be taken to reduce dependency on this activity for fuel or for income. Humanitarian agencies can support existing strategies, or help individuals and communities to develop new strategies to help them become just a little bit safer.

PEOPLE "PROTECTING" THEMSELVES

A rarely spoken truth about protection is that the main players in the protection of civilians in conflict are the civilians themselves. Rightly or wrongly, when civilians are most in need of protection, the humanitarian agencies are hardly ever present. The humanitarian presence in Chechnya is negligible. Agencies were absent from Western Upper Nile in Sudan when a massive offensive was burning people from their homes (Christian Aid 2002). As hundreds of thousands of people fled from their homes in Afghanistan in 2002, few agencies crossed the border from Pakistan.

This should not surprise us. On the one hand, the controlling authorities deny access to threatened populations. Their motive may be to maintain secrecy: a testimony, perhaps, to the power that aid agencies can have over authorities that want to be seen as responsible. Authorities may deny access because the authorities are unable to guarantee the security of the aid workers themselves; or because they doubt the motivation and impartiality of those demanding access. On the other hand, humanitarian agencies often *choose* not to be present, usually because they themselves deem it to be too dangerous, and they are not prepared to risk the lives of their staff.

Yet people survive. They are forced to make difficult choices between unpalatable options, basing their judgments on often inadequate information and analysis.

Their first line of defense may be to avoid the threat. At its most basic level, this means running away. Around 25 million people are internally displaced, and 17 million more are refugees beyond their own borders. However, flight is not the only option. People change their movements; they avoid taking particular routes or traveling at night. In northern Uganda, thousands of "night commuters" seek refuge in shelters in main towns every night because staying in their villages is too dangerous. Communities develop early-warning systems, networks of information to warn them of danger before it arrives. People hide their assets so as not to draw attention to themselves. In Colombia, many villagers, trapped between the army, the guerrilla forces, and the paramilitaries, feel that they will be safer if they do not associate with anyone, in particular with humanitarian agencies or human rights groups.

But people also submit to the threats. Taxes, official or unofficial, are paid. A colleague in Congo several years ago told of proudly using her humanitarian status to negotiate her way through a checkpoint on the outskirts of the city without paying—until begged by the driver to do so. The people from the checkpoint came to his house every night to demand the "tax" from him. There is a vast literature on gender-based violence that frequently talks of marriage with "the commander": a relationship that on the part of the woman is voluntary only in the narrowest sense, but is seen as "less bad" than any other option available. In Afghanistan joining the militias is often the only way of making a decent living and providing a modicum of safety for oneself and one's family. And in many, many places, people simply do what they are told to do by those who hold the power and the guns.

And finally, sometimes people will confront the threats that they face and fight back. Many of the tens of thousands of armed gangs that dominate the inner-city areas of Haiti originated as self-defense units for communities that felt threatened. They are now as much a part of the problem as they are a part of the solution.

So if this is the level at which people can really find protection, how can humanitarian agencies help? Minimally they should make sure that they are not undermining such protection strategies without offering a viable alternative. Despite the evident attraction of disarmament, taking away the guns that people use to defend their homes, without nullifying the threat, is likely to be counterproductive. Similarly it seems unethical to encourage communities to speak out in circumstances where staying invisible is how they stay safe.

Most agencies (although not every government) would not choose to arm people to defend themselves, nor would they encourage people to submit to the threats that they face. This leaves the option of helping communities to avoid the threats. The right assistance, provided in the right way, can play a vital role. Despite the threats that displaced people in Darfur continue to face, the assistance provided on a vast scale in the camps allows them to stay away from their home villages, where they would face still more danger. From the plight of internally displaced people in the southern Philippines to that of Burundian refugees in Tanzania, the world is littered with neglected crises that force people to return to dangerous areas because the official assistance has run out.

A second vital role performed by humanitarian agencies is to provide accurate, impartial information to people at risk, so that they can judge how to stay safer. It can be particularly important in contexts in which information is manipulated in order to maintain control. This can mean helping individuals and families to make their own informed decisions, independently of community "leaders." Ensuring that individual families could obtain impartial information about what was awaiting them was critical in helping Rwandan refugees to return home and restart their lives.

And finally, humanitarian agencies can give "voice" to those under threat, helping them to negotiate their own safety. This *may* mean raising their plight in the UN Security Council to call down help from on high, but it is just as relevant at the community level, where supporting the development of a civil society in a focused manner can challenge those who are abusing their power and neglecting their responsibility to protect civilians.

CONCLUSIONS

Protection can be a frustrating area of work for humanitarian agencies. Although negotiating the release of a group of prisoners may bring a more intimate sense of satisfaction than organizing a distribution to 200,000 people, the scale of achievement is often tiny, compared with the scale of the problems that civilians face. Furthermore, the time frames involved are often much longer. It took several years of lobbying by humanitarian organizations on the ground before the European Union deployed Operation Artemis to northeastern Congo, and even then only a modicum of security was provided to a relatively small number of people, in a relatively small area. However, even relatively small achievements should be valued when lives are saved. This is why the distant engagement of the Security Council remains important. It is why maintaining a presence in Darfur, even if it only deters attacks in a 500-meter radius and until five o'clock at night, remains important.

That said, rolling out standardized "protection activities," such as monitoring or denouncing violations or educating people about their rights, is analogous to some of the worst practices of the relief community twenty years ago.

Assistance has become more professional, a fact perhaps best illustrated by the Sphere Standards.[3] Donor agencies are demanding rigorous planning processes that use logical frameworks or similar tools to set objectives and check to see whether the activities carried out will meet those objectives. Equally important is the recognition that assistance will be at its most effective if it is designed in a participatory manner and builds upon the communities' existing or remaining capacities. One could say that the process is as important as the result, but in fact it is a good process that will deliver the best outcomes.

There are thus two keys to improving the protection of civilians. First, protection should be subject to the same rigors of program planning as are now expected of relief work. Objectives need to be clear— whether to reduce the level of the threats faced by civilians, or to reduce their exposure to them. And the activities chosen need to have a realistic chance of delivering against those objectives. Both denouncing violations and providing information about rights have a role to play, but their use needs to be limited to circumstances in which they will have an impact. Denouncing violations can be effective when those with the capacity to act decisively are likely to be shamed into action: for example, in response to the abuse of prisoners in Abu Ghraib prison in Iraq. Educating people about their rights can be effective if there is an interested authority with which to engage. However, in other circumstances a wider menu of response needs to be considered.

But perhaps it is more important to acknowledge that protection is not a commodity that can be delivered alongside food and water. Civilians themselves are central to their own safety. "Protection" is thus not a conversation conducted above the heads of those affected by conflict, but a process to support them in their daily lives. This understanding should be central to the protection work of humanitarian agencies.

NOTES

[1] Article 2(7), Charter of the United Nations.
[2] Article 24, Charter of the United Nations.
[3] For details on this interagency initiative, see www.sphereproject.org.

REFERENCES

Christian Aid (2002) *The Scorched Earth: Oil and War in Sudan,* London: Christian Aid.

Darcy, James and Charles-Antoine Hofmann (2003) *According to Need? Needs Assessment and Decision-making in the Humanitarian Sector,* London: ODI.

Egeland, Jan (2004) "Statement by Under-Secretary-General Jan Egeland at the Security Council Open Debate on the Protection of Civilians in Armed Conflict," paper presented to the UN Security Council, December 14; available at ochaonline.un.org/GetBin.asp?DocID=3579 (retrieved October 2, 2005).

Giossi Caverzasio, Sylvie (ed.) (2001) *Strengthening Protection in War—A Search for Professional Standards,* Geneva: ICRC.

Greste, P. (2004) "Analysis: Mixed Reaction to UN Summit," available at www.bbc.co.uk (retrieved October 2, 2005).

Slim, Hugo and L.E. Eguren (2004) *Humanitarian Protection—A Guidance Booklet,* London: ALNAP.

United Nations (1999) "Report of the Secretary-General Pursuant to General Assembly Resolution 53/35: The Fall of Srebrenica," UN Document A/54/549.

United Nations (2004) *Protection of Civilians—A Strategy for Darfur,* available at www.idpproject.org (retrieved October 2, 2005).

UN Internal Displacement Division (2004) "Implementing the Collaborative Response to Situations of Internal Displacement, Guidance for UN Humanitarian and/or Resident Coordinators and Country Teams," available at www.idpproject.org/IDP_documents/IDPPolicyPackage.pdf (retrieved October 2, 2005).

UN-OCHA (2004) "Aide Memoire for the Consideration of Issues Pertaining to the Protection of Civilians," New York: UN-OCHA, available through www.reliefweb.int.

First published in *Development in Practice* 16(3&4): 270–277 in 2006.

SIX

Colombian Peace Communities: The Role of NGOs in Supporting Resistance to Violence

GRETCHEN ALTHER

CHAPTER SUMMARY

Colombia's chronic war is one of the world's worst humanitarian crises. Amid armed actors, pervasive violence, and increasing militarization, many citizens experience hostility from all sides. This violence continues the historical marginalization of Afro-descendant, indigenous, and campesino communities and is intensified by the "global war on terror" (GWOT). Some peace communities are rejecting violence and seeking ways to survive within war—becoming protagonists in their own protection. This is risky: it draws accusations, threats, and attacks. Over time, the lack of sustainable livelihoods, weak internal cohesion, and antagonistic external dynamics test the determination of such communities. This chapter examines four peace communities and explores factors that generate and sustain grassroots protagonism. It ends by suggesting ways in which development organizations can enhance community-level protection and reinforce local peace processes in order to contribute to broader peacebuilding.

THE WAR IN COLOMBIA:
HIDDEN FACTORS OF VIOLENCE

The sensationalism of guerrilla warfare and drug trafficking obscures other aspects of Colombia's conflict, especially its roots in socioeconomic inequalities and the depth of its connections to US interests. The respective governments persistently use the drug trade, plus the more recent argument that this trade reinforces terrorism, to explain the conflict and argue for a militarized response. But Colombia's strategic geopolitical position should not be ignored, not least because Colombia (and the greater region) has oil—always a key consideration in US foreign policy. As the entry point to South America, and having both Pacific and Atlantic coasts, Colombia is also important to the neoliberal economic strategies generally associated with globalization. The control of land, natural resources, and economic structures is an important element in the conflict.

Insecurity in Colombia makes it difficult for the United States to advance its economic and political interests. In the effort to end this insecurity militarization becomes both a response to violence and a tool to advance a neoliberal development model.

Plan Colombia was created in 2000 under the Clinton administration with the goal of eliminating the production of illicit drugs, improving governance, and promoting peace. Much of Plan Colombia involves the aerial fumigation of illicit crops, which has proved harmful to rural populations and to the environment. In 2002 Plan Colombia was expanded to include counterinsurgency efforts (Global Security 2007; Human Rights Watch 2002). Between 2000 and 2005, US assistance to Colombia totaled US$ 4 billion, with 80 percent allocated to the security forces (Latin America Working Group Education Fund et al. 2005), making Colombia the top recipient of US assistance outside the Middle East.

Although Plan Colombia has failed to meet its stated objectives, as demonstrated by a growing regional drug trade, continuing impunity, and persistent conflict, aid levels remain constant, and militarized intervention continues to receive approval. As the GWOT has annexed the "war on drugs," an added threat to peace is the damage caused to existing democratic structures, human rights, and basic civil liberties in the process. Counterinsurgency strategies, which the GWOT tacitly condones, force individuals and organizations to choose sides, eliminating any "third way" to peace.

GRASSROOTS PATHS TO PEACE

Given Colombia's bleak situation, grassroots peace initiatives are significant. They illustrate other realities, offer models for opposing armed conflict, and propose a human-centered peace. Communities across Colombia are refusing to support violence by struggling to exercise their "right to peace" and creating mechanisms of self-protection. In opting for peaceful action, the "options" that these communities reject include taking up arms, remaining unarmed and accepting the unpredictable protection of an armed group, or remaining unarmed and accepting displacement. These initiatives demonstrate publicly that the country is not a "lost cause," and that other life-sustaining options exist. They also provide a basis upon which others can advocate for peaceful means of ending the war.

The grassroots peace movement in Colombia originated among traditionally marginalized sectors, including Afro-descendant, indigenous, and campesino communities. Along with the structural violence reflected in their poverty and poor health and education indicators, these communities are disproportionately affected by war. Afro-descendants and indigenous Colombians—who respectively comprise 25 percent and 4 percent of the national population—represent 50 percent of Colombia's estimated three million internally displaced people.

In an effort to confront the violence surrounding them, many marginalized communities have committed themselves to nonviolent resistance and popular participation. In many cases these are supported by national and international NGOs and religious groups. Members of these peace communities refuse to carry arms. Despite conscription their men refuse to serve in the armed forces. Most significantly peace communities refuse to support any armed actors (guerrillas, paramilitaries, or security forces), denying them food, supplies, refuge, transport, and information.

Resistance can be costly. Armed actors who are vying for territorial and socioeconomic control deny the validity of nonviolent "third options." Members of peace communities have been threatened, falsely accused, detained, blockaded, displaced, and assassinated. Without doubt, rejecting violence and claiming neutrality is more about surviving than it is about building peace. Nevertheless, these communities are examples of peaceful struggle over violence and retaliation. Their very survival obliges others to listen. Support for these grassroots movements not only defends people's lives, but also fertilizes the seeds of peace.

NONVIOLENT RESISTANCE AND GRASSROOTS PEACE INITIATIVES: A LITERATURE REVIEW

For centuries moral leaders have encouraged nonviolent struggle to counteract oppression and violence. Recent scholars have studied non-violent action and called for the development of nonviolent alternatives to armed conflict, particularly in "hard cases" in which people see little alternative to widespread oppression and killing, attempted genocide, mass displacement, destruction of indigenous communities, and social and economic injustice (Sharp 2003).

Noncooperation is the key to achieving change through nonviolent action, based on the theory that leaders derive power from the consent of their followers. When this consent is withdrawn and other forms of community organization are set up, this effectively reduces "the sources of power on which all rulers depend" (Sharp 2002:17). Scholars have reflected this theory in writings on communities of popular resistance in Guatemala, repopulated communities in El Salvador, communities in resistance in the Mexican state of Chiapas, and peace communities in Colombia. Seeing no other option, these communities defied violence and created their own ways of working for peace. For instance, in the 1980s, many indigenous Guatemalan communities refused to flee, even as the military razed their villages. In El Salvador displaced campesinos exercised their rights as civilians in conflict and returned to their homes. The example of local control in Chiapas is ushering in a new era of community mobilization. In Colombia, peace communities are proclaiming autonomy and turning their backs on violence.

The costs of noncooperation are high. During the 1980s the Guatemalan army eliminated more than 400 communities, most of them indigenous (Falla 1994). Leaders of El Salvador's repopulation movement were terrorized, and their communities were bombed. Similarly, defiant Colombian peace communities are targeted by armed groups of all persuasion, and hundreds of their members have been murdered. Their basic economic survival is also under threat.

Scholars and practitioners note that grassroots movements adopting nonviolent strategies can develop "protection capacities" that effectively withdraw the consent upon which control and oppression depend (Thompson and Eade 2004:7, reprinted in this volume), and challenge the domination of armed actors (Sanford 2003). Indeed, it "strongly appears that . . . nonviolent struggle can be used . . . to achieve and defend freedoms and to resist centralized repression" (Sanford 2003:16). There have been examples of nonviolent struggle in Argentina, Chile, India, Palestine, the Philippines, and South Africa.

John Paul Lederach, an expert in conflict resolution, proposes that the transformation of conflicts such as that in which Colombia is embroiled requires building peace through reconciliation, even at the grassroots level (Lederach 1998). He maintains that relationships are crucial: broken relationships generate conflict, whereas harmonious relationships generate peaceful solutions. Lederach's model suggests that peacebuilding must focus on several layers, from the grassroots to high political levels, each set of actors focusing on activities at their level of operation which interact to transform violence. Within this model NGOs can act as bridges between the grassroots and higher political levels (Lederach 1998).

Lederach has worked in Colombia with NGOs such as Catholic Relief Services (CRS) and the Mennonite Central Committee (MCC), and more recently with leaders of the Catholic Church. Several NGOs in Colombia consider themselves to be the bridges to peace that Lederach describes, although others question whether his theories are applicable. Theoretical models of multilevel strategies for peace and reconciliation may no longer feel relevant when people are tired of dialogue, when national organizations promoting peace and human rights are stifled and divided, and when civil society is weak and distrustful.

Other scholars point more directly to community-level resistance as the source of sustainable peace. Building peace from the grass roots rests on the idea that those who suffer most are those who best understand how to resist—and what that resistance means. In this view, a strong civil society ultimately redefines and rebuilds a society that is able to confront conflict positively (Hernández and Salazar 1999). Furthermore, the mere existence of grassroots peace initiatives implies the negation of war and creates spaces that can nurture peace (Sanford 2003:14).

Nevertheless, without adequate protection, communities that resist war face torture or a violent death, or violent displacement. In complex crises, NGOs often fail to deal with the need for sustainable protection, focusing instead on more immediate humanitarian measures (Paul 1999). Discussion is evolving about NGOs' duty and ability to provide and strengthen protection for civilian populations in situations of violent conflict. This discussion focuses mainly on situations in which international humanitarian agencies have a permanent presence and local people face physical danger. Less attention is paid to why and how communities can create their own protection mechanisms and how NGOs can and/or do support them to do this. In Colombia, where violence is widespread but not always detectable or immediate, protection takes on additional importance: it is about physical defense when armed actors are present, but also about creating longer-term mechanisms that both strengthen communities and help create spaces for peace. When a community is organized, it is better able to protect itself from sudden threat, and to start to develop its own protection capacities.

Many practical considerations influence communities' ability to protect themselves, and NGOs may therefore be involved in various ways, from supporting resistance to helping to develop a nonviolent strategy, and working to transform conflict. One factor that is often overlooked in theories of power based on mutual consent and the possibility of noncooperation is the community's ability to meet its basic needs, and how this affects its capacity to resist in the long term.

Diane Paul points out that when protection strategies are in place, those perpetrating violence will find ways to circumvent them (Paul 1999). This is especially true when armed actors are present in communities for any length of time and so can observe and infiltrate them, find out how they work, and identify key people. In addition, armed tactics may change. For instance, armed groups may start to undertake selective killings that fall under the threshold of massacre as defined by International Humanitarian Law (IHL). The mix of actors within a region may also change, which serves to complicate previously successful mechanisms of deterrence and protection. Protection strategies may need to be adapted accordingly (Paul 1999).

In most situations of (violent) conflict, people seek security by identifying with something personal and within their control. This is often related to identity or geography, and organized at the community level (Lederach 1998; Parcomún and Diakonía 2002). Such responses may be particularly true among communities who do not identify with the dominant culture. Three factors that support grassroots protagonism include the existence of a popular political project, an alternative vision for society, and increased external pressure on the government (Thompson and Eade 2004, reprinted in this volume).

Esperanza Delgado Hernández examines community-level experiences in Colombia from three angles: as experiences of peacebuilding; as options for self-protection and the assertion of legal rights, especially the right of civilians to immunity; and as an expression of noncooperation (Hernández and Salazar 1999). Hernández has since categorized grassroots movements into those attempting to deepen democracy, those resisting armed actors, and those opposing structural violence and prevailing economic models (Hernández 2004). Despite the many challenges, local and regional peace movements are becoming stronger and more numerous. Although they have emerged in areas in which violence continues or has even increased, these movements exemplify the desire of ordinary people to resist such violence (García 2004).

The literature is weak, however, in understanding the factors that induce and strengthen grassroots resistance and protagonism. It offers few concrete suggestions for how NGOs can support such protagonism in a situation like that of Colombia.

Furthermore, the nature of conflict in the post–Cold War era has shifted toward struggles within divided societies, often related to a government's inability to guarantee the basic needs of all citizens or to ensure broad social participation. Colombia's conflict is also fueled by the expanding small-arms industry, the narcotics trade, and other nonformal economic activities.

An environment that is largely hostile to peace and dialogue has obliged Colombian peace and human rights movements to temper their public protest and sometimes to hold back from voicing their own peace proposals. NGOs face the challenge of trying to support grassroots protagonism, despite the changing dynamics and the long-term and deepening nature of the conflict. This chapter addresses some of these issues and is largely based on the author's work with the American Friends Service Committee (AFSC) in Colombia from September 2003 to April 2004. (Interviews were undertaken during this period, unless otherwise stated.)

CREATING A THIRD WAY: COLOMBIAN PEACE COMMUNITIES

There are approximately fifty declared peace communities in Colombia, and possibly more. Some officially declare themselves peace communities, others do not—but all see neutrality as the only alternative in a war that forces people to choose sides and leaves little room for peaceful existence. The four peace communities examined below consciously use nonviolent tactics to oppose the war. Each represents at least one of many different forms of resistance, including proclaimed neutrality, participatory democracy, community organization, and self-protection.

Peace communities include Afro-descendant, indigenous, and campesino communities. Many have returned to their homes after being displaced. All struggle to resist, despite hunger, fear, and unjust economic and political systems. All Colombians who are living in poverty face some of the same challenges. But peace communities are unique because they have organized and asserted themselves as subjects in their own right. Their protagonism gives them strength and voice. Understanding and supporting these communities can protect lives, reduce the intensity of Colombia's armed conflict, and eventually be a source of broader, nonviolent change.

The Peace Community of San José

One of Colombia's oldest and best-known peace communities is that of San José de Apartadó, a municipality on the Caribbean coast. Campesinos first settled the area in the 1950s, many having been displaced by political violence. State presence was minimal, so people formed Communal Action Councils to petition for services.

Political and territorial struggles attracted the attention of insurgents, and San José became the scene of conflicts between the guerrillas, the army, and self-styled self-defense groups. A left-wing political party gained favor in the area during the 1980s, which engendered a violent right-wing reaction. The first assassinations at San José occurred in September 1996, when armed assailants killed four community leaders on the very day that the army had abandoned the area. Most of the population fled. The second killing occurred in February 1997, when a group of armed assailants captured, tortured, and killed a man and his son.

These experiences led the people of San José to ask the Catholic Church and national and international NGOs to help them develop ways to protect themselves. After a process of organization and dialogue, San José officially declared itself a peace community in March 1997. Today it comprises about 1,500 people in seventeen villages.

Five days after the declaration, a further three people were murdered, and the perpetrators ordered residents to flee. People had to decide whether to remain and resist, or to leave. Three thousand people left the villages of San José and fled to the municipal center. But rather than leave entirely, the people opted to reinforce community consensus about what being a peace community entailed, thus deepening their commitment.

Today the community uses a variety of protection strategies. They travel in groups. There is a security committee and a food committee. Members blow whistles to alert others to any armed incursion. Members do not travel where armed actors are present. There is permanent accompaniment by NGOs. They pray. They gather every morning and evening to review the day's events and ensure that all members are present. Members participate in community work. They agree that if one person stays behind, they all do. They practice transparency. They do not sell or consume alcohol.

Their commitment has not been easy. Since the catalytic events of 1996, armed groups have killed more than 100 community members, most recently in February 2005 (ABC Colombia 2005). The community is under constant observation and is the target of unwarranted detentions and searches. Pleas for official recognition as a nonviolent community go unheeded. A lack of economic resources and access to markets tests people's resolve. Nevertheless, San José views its commitment as the only dignified option for resisting armed conflict and forced displacement, and for protecting human rights. As one resident said: "For me, the Peace Community has been the only alternative to be able to survive in the middle of war, because without it, it would be very difficult to live here and I think it would be very difficult to survive" (quoted in Hernández and Salazar 1999:88).

An Afro-descended Community of Peace

In the mountains of southwest Colombia, edging the coastal plains, is the community of Congal.[1] The area was once dedicated to slave-holding plantations. Today, 90 percent of the population consists of Afro-descendants, and most depend on fishing, farming, or laboring. Like most rural people in Colombia, they face economic insecurity.

The construction of the Salvajina hydroelectric dam in 1985 flooded thousands of acres and displaced hundreds of people. In 1987 some Afro-descendants formed a peasant association to find a solution to their displacement. In 1992 the Colombian Institute of Agrarian Reform finally purchased the Congal farm for this community. The people formed a cooperative to manage the farm and implement sustainable family and community projects. Although they did not declare themselves a peace community, the families of Congal agreed not to participate in the conflict. Their commitment has required them to strengthen community organization, create security procedures, generate agricultural projects, participate in community work, and develop ties to the national and international community.

In July 2000 paramilitaries began to control travel and commerce in the region. They caused more than 200 disappearances and deaths in the area, including the Naya massacre in April 2001 that left an estimated 120 people dead and more than 4,000 people displaced (Amnesty International 2003). Although they are less frequent now, attacks, assassinations, and displacement continue.

Communities resist by acquiring their own lands (under "Law 70," Afro-descendants have the right to recover traditional lands and hold them collectively) and jointly defending what they create. The people of Congal believe that counteracting violence and displacement begins with reconstructing a rural community and developing practical, inclusive production alternatives. Congal's greatest tool is its unity. As community member Marta García explains:

> There are many armed actors here, and much fear. We've been killed and displaced. But we're united, and we've learned to use nonviolent methods to protect ourselves. When we see something strange, we advise the others and form a plan. If a stranger comes to my house, a neighbor comes for sugar or eggs—to see if everything's OK. But a united community is an obstacle for the armed actors. They are interested in power, but we subvert that. So they want to get rid of us any way they can. Unity is risky. But we think it's easier to take out one than 100. If we are united, it's harder for them.
>
> (Interview with the author)

There are many challenges for Congal and its neighboring communities. It is hard to meet basic needs. The lack of a peace structure at a national level means that communities often feel alone in their struggle. Armed groups are a risk to the community and an attraction for those who feel that they have no other economic option. The situation faced by young adults is the most critical. In the words of Marta García:

> Many young people go to the city for work. Some join gangs and get involved in crime. Others join armed groups that pay salaries. It's sad and dangerous. If my son joins the paramilitaries, we become enemies of the guerrilla. And if he joins the guerrilla, we become enemies of the paramilitaries and the army. It's best to remain neutral, but our youth need options.
>
> (Interview with the author)

Deepening Democracy: The Municipal Constituent Assembly of Mogotes

Mogotes is a municipality of 15,000 people in the eastern Andes. Inhabitants grow sugar cane, fruit, and sisal; raise cattle, goats, and pigs; and make fruit products, baskets, and molasses. Like many Colombian towns, Mogotes was barely within the periphery of the state. Politics was controlled by an elite that was prone to corruption.

This situation attracted the interest of guerrilla groups. Prior to local elections in October 1997, such groups used intimidation, kidnapping, and assassination to influence the results. On November 11, 1997, 150 guerrillas seized the town, killed three policemen and two public officials, and kidnapped the mayor on charges of corruption. The event divided Mogotes. Some pointed to corruption as the source of the problem. Others blamed the guerrillas. But with support from the Catholic Church, the local people were united in confronting what everyone agreed was an attack on their sovereignty. Thus began a process of community education, organization, and empowerment.

The people soon declared a Permanent Civil Assembly. In April 1998 they formed the Municipal Constituent Assembly (MCA) of the Sovereign Town of Mogotes. They successfully demanded the release of the mayor, whom they then forced to resign, and elected a "manager" who would be accountable to the popular will. The MCA is a space for popular political participation, comprising more than 200 delegates from local assemblies. Decisions are made by consensus in support of popular sovereignty, human-centered development, and peace through social justice.

The events of November 1997 catalyzed Mogotes' organization, but the inspiration was based on three factors: prior work with the Catholic Church's Social Ministry; Article 3 of the Colombian constitution, which states that "sovereignty rests exclusively in the people, who are the source of public power"; and Mogotes' own history of initiating Colombia's liberation process from Spain in 1780. These factors helped the people of Mogotes to declare autonomy in the midst of a war that aimed to force everyone to choose sides.

The people of Mogotes discovered that conflict could be countered by participation and organization. They have demonstrated that violence and armed actors can be countered nonviolently, and that corruption and injustice must also be challenged simultaneously. One of the first peace zones, and the recipient of the first National Peace Prize in 1999, Mogotes has inspired communities across Colombia to deepen their own participatory processes.

Despite popular and international support, the process in Mogotes attracted opposition as it began to challenge the status quo. Under the region's new bishop, the Catholic Church began to criticize the MCA, forbidding the Social and Ministry to visit, discouraging local people from participating in it.

Despite all this, many are still committed. The Social Ministry is still training new leaders, and local people believe that they can overcome current difficulties with solidarity and hard work. Other challenges include recent paramilitary incursions, which create the need for new forms of self-protection. The community struggles to to meet its basic needs. Nevertheless, Mogotes continues as a shining example of community resistance and participatory democracy.

Protectors of Life: The Indigenous Guard

In the mountains of Colombia's department of Valle del Cauca lie the traditional lands of the Nasa (also known as Paéz), to whom the constitution of Colombia promised sovereignty. In order to defend their territory and protect their communities, the Nasa created the Indigenous Guard in 2001. A special group of men, women, and young adults armed only with a ceremonial rod of office, the Guard is responsible for stopping any armed actor from entering Nasa territory.

The Indigenous Guard began during the years of colonization, when the people defended themselves against invasions of their lands. With the creation of indigenous reservations in the 1600s and 1700s, the Nasa formed a group that was responsible for protecting their communities. But they lost their autonomy at the time of Independence and became indentured laborers on their own ancestral lands. In the early twentieth century they regained some territory through largely unarmed mass occupations. Throughout the process of recovery, a special group of Nasa protected the communities against attack.

With the escalation of war from the late 1990s, the Nasa began to discuss creating a permanent civil defense force. The Indigenous Guard was formally established in March 2001. Today each Nasa village has ten members of the Guard, forming part of progressively larger units that together patrol the borders of Nasa territory twenty-four hours a day, seven days a week. When they need to alert others to an intruder, they communicate by walkie-talkie radio. A local coordinator of the Indigenous Guard explained:

> We don't look for security through weapons: we carry sticks. Now public authorities recognize us. Some still ask: "Why do you carry

that?" But most of them recognize our authority. We know our sticks don't shoot. We're here to defend our communities—but not with lead. With traditional medicine, our sticks are mediating forces. We purify them; then people see us as friends, not enemies. This protects us. Many people say they don't believe in the power of traditional medicine. But we do; it strengthens our culture and it strengthens us.

(Interview with the author)

Since the 1970s, the army, paramilitaries, and guerrillas have killed more than 400 Nasa leaders and organizers. Although the Indigenous Guard has not been able to put a complete stop to these assaults, the nonviolent protection strategy has allowed the Nasa to face down conflict and show how autonomy is possible, even under threat of violence. The Indigenous Guard's tenacity and success have earned recognition in Colombia and beyond. The Nasa People were awarded the National Peace Prize in 2000.

The Nasa face many of the same challenges as other communities practicing nonviolent resistance. They are trying to find viable economic activities that permit them to remain in and strengthen their communities. The specter of aerial fumigation is a constant concern. Land issues continue to be at the forefront of their struggle. There is particular concern about the future of young people. The community faces manipulation by armed actors who want to co-opt the population.

ANALYSIS OF CASE STUDIES

The prevailing political context is largely hostile to dialogue and to negotiated solution to Colombia's war. The US-led "war on drugs" has been absorbed into the GWOT and defines how the conflict is perceived and portrayed. The continued use of military force has tended to weaken national peacebuilding efforts, and the violent conflict and its fallout hit the poorest hardest.

With this bleak outlook for peace in Colombia, the development and expansion of grassroots peace communities is particularly encouraging. Such communities can shape a robust and sustainable future peace and hold the line on peaceful gains when the wider context appears hostile to peace. However, these initiatives—geographically isolated and the frequent targets of all the armed actors—are fragile.

Nurturing communities in nonviolent resistance can save lives and encourage peaceful solutions to armed conflict. These communities offer a new paradigm of grassroots protagonism that will be essential in reconstructing Colombian society. Nevertheless they face many obstacles in maintaining their resistance, and it is here that NGOs can lend support. This can be done well only by understanding the factors that generate and support grassroots resistance and protagonism as a basis for deciding how best to enhance their protection and strengthen their commitment to nonviolence.

Peace communities tend to emerge in areas that have traditionally been marginalized—also areas in which most of the armed conflict has been waged—and they are largely inhabited by people who suffer the structural violence of such marginalization, as well as suffer the added factor of discrimination based on class and ethnicity. Each community has its own characteristics of marginalization and thus experiences violence differently; each will therefore develop its own mechanisms of self-protection and resistance. Nevertheless, comparing experiences across different communities can lead to a better understanding of the processes, barriers, and challenges that they all share.

Becoming a peace community seems to include five important phases:

- Background events that raise people's awareness of their marginalization within the larger sociopolitical context
- A defining violent or traumatic experience that acts as a catalyst for community cohesion
- External support at the point of opting for nonviolent resistance
- Further violent or traumatic experiences that consolidate the community's resistance
- Internal and external factors that enable (or prevent) their resistance to survive

In each of the four cases examined, community members were aware of their socioeconomic position in relation to larger society *before* they experienced a "defining event." The process of settling the area of San José was based on a need for land and the impossibility of surviving elsewhere. Later on the settlers' situation encouraged them to create communal action groups. A history of slavery among Afro-descendant people in Colombia has resulted in their low status in almost every aspect of society, and again this is what created the cohesion of the Congal community. The people of Mogotes were participating with the Catholic Social Ministry in a process of education based on the principles of liberation theology. The Indigenous Guard and the Nasa consider themselves part of a centuries-long process of resistance against acculturation and extermination. All are examples of "critical consciousness," the concept developed by the Brazilian educator Paulo Freire and central to the development of civil society in Latin America and beyond.

Traumatic events were catalytic in all four examples: consecutive assassinations in San José; forced and uncompensated displacement for the families of Congal; violent guerrilla incursions in Mogotes; and the difficult recovery of traditional lands by the Nasa. In each case communities discussed cooperatively how to proceed. External support became important at this moment—whether it came from the Catholic Church (particularly in San José and Mogotes), from other NGOs (San José, Mogotes, and the Indigenous Guard), or from other local communities (the Indigenous Guard and Congal). The combination of strong internal foundations and an outside presence supported these communities in their decision to resist nonviolently.

Today, although they remain committed to nonviolent resistance, many peace communities are struggling to survive. The challenges confronting them all could potentially shatter their peace processes. Most important are the constant threats to people's physical safety. Opting for neutrality draws false accusations and both threatened and actual physical attacks by those who believe that these communities are supporting the "other" side. This is why it is vital to create and strengthen protection mechanisms, which both enable people to survive and provide space for community organization and planning. This is where NGOs have a real opportunity to assist in keeping these processes alive.

Widespread NGO-initiated protection mechanisms include raising a community's public profile by maintaining an international presence, ensuring the swift spread of information about human rights abuses that trigger national and international reaction. However, few peace communities enjoy the permanent presence of NGOs, whether national or international (of the four cases, only San José has permanent accompaniment). Moreover, the reaction to actual or potential abuses often depends upon how well known the community is—and few Colombian peace communities enjoy a broad reputation. It is therefore important that NGOs focus on ways to enhance the communities' own self-protection mechanisms.

The lack of economic opportunity and access to markets is another major threat to peace communities, as it is to many other rural communities across Colombia. They struggle to find sustainable production projects and other reliable sources of income. When people cannot make ends meet, they have four main options: tightening their belts; migrating in search of work; joining armed groups (paramilitaries tend to pay the best); or participating in growing or processing illicit drugs. All but the first contravene the vision of the peace communities. Improving self-sufficiency is one way to meet their daily needs. However, living is not about just surviving, but also about having the resources to plan ahead. Over time, acute poverty and economic hardship will test the determination of the peace communities.

A third threat is the absence, or weakening, of internal organization and cohesion. This may occur because of stress and lack of protection, income, or prospects, and it can create disagreements about community management. Community members may legitimately want to evaluate the whole process, but this can lead to a breakdown of consensus and the consequent weakening of organizational structures.

External sociopolitical dynamics are another threat to peace communities, as illustrated in the case of Mogotes, where dynamics within the Catholic Church are testing the strength of—and may yet destroy—the MCA. Important counters are the solidarity offered through a US-based sister-city program, and the relatively high levels of recognition and publicity that Mogotes has received in the national and international arenas.

When communities unite and find ways to confront conflict and defend themselves and their ways of life, it is legitimate to ask whether there are unique internal factors that support this kind of action. The role of a critical consciousness at the community level has already been mentioned. Another common characteristic is a shared cultural identity that encourages communal action. This is certainly the case in the Afro-descendant community of Congal and with the Indigenous Guard, two communities with a long history of identity-related action. However, it also appears true of both San José and Mogotes, although these communities have shorter histories (San José) and lack a cultural identity that differentiates them strongly from the majority (Mogotes). In these cases the binding force has been the necessity to join together to survive and progress—that is, the experience of having successfully worked together.

At the same time, the emergence of cooperation and communal defense in Colombia, which are very similar to initiatives elsewhere in

Latin America, begs the question of whether there are underlying enabling factors that are unique to this region. Although examples of nonviolent action and withdrawal of consent are found around the world, there are few known examples of initiatives like the peace community outside Latin America.

A deeper understanding of the process of forming peace communities, of the threats such communities face in developing and maintaining their option of resistance, and of the internal prerequisites that enable community members to make these decisions all present opportunities for national and international NGOs to work beside them to help protect them and strengthen their process of resistance, protagonism, and grassroots peacebuilding. The lessons that can be drawn from this understanding could inform other work in Colombia and Latin America, and be shared with other communities. In this way, the communities and the NGOs that support them will be better able to confront and transform armed conflict and build peace.

CONCLUSIONS AND RECOMMENDATIONS

NGOs have encouraged and supported peace communities in Colombia in collaboration with local partners by working within the communities, engaging with the national and international context, and being committed to learning. They may play a role in the community's initial decision and/or provide support if it opts to become a peace community. For the most part, it is the national NGOs—such as Colombia's REDE-PAZ (National Network of Citizen Initiatives for Peace and Against War) (www.redepaz.org.co) and the Catholic Church—that have become involved in the decisionmaking phase, whereas those providing subsequent support have included the international NGOs, including the American Friends Service Committee (AFSC), Fellowship of Reconciliation (FOR), Peace Brigades International (PBI), and Witness for Peace (WfP).

Both national and international NGOs involved in such initiatives are largely faith-based and/or pacifist in orientation. The distinction between the two is somewhat artificial because many national NGOs have ties to the international community, whereas many international NGOs have a local presence. The important point is that they are supporting grassroots nonviolent peace movements, irrespective of their background or provenance.

Working with Communities

Protection is the immediate need of communities in resistance. Without it, these communities are targets, lives are lost, and processes are dismantled. NGOs can support communities in developing and strengthening self-protection capacities by creating safe spaces in which to discuss existing and potential safety and emergency procedures. Learning about mechanisms used elsewhere can generate more ideas.

Strengthening their organization and identity is also vital in enabling communities to protect themselves and resist. This helps them before a crisis strikes and prepares them to react quickly and collectively when they need to do so. NGOs can encourage community organization through activities focused on themes such as culture, youth, gender, and ecology. Armed actors may be less likely to misconstrue this as rebellion. NGOs also protect themselves by promoting activities that are not overtly political.

Economic opportunity is central to the sustainability of communities' resistance. Without basic nutrition and health care, this is seriously compromised. This implies a direct link between humanitarian and development work: supporting the lives of peace-community members calls for help in developing sustainable production projects. NGOs can also focus on commercial activities that follow the objectives of fair trade and solidarity marketing. There is a particular need to focus on young adults who wish to enter the formal labor market. A lack of realistic opportunities within their communities has led many young people to migrate and even to join armed groups. The latter has serious implications for the individual as well as for the family and community: all become targets of threats and aggression.

To build confidence and grassroots protagonism, NGOs could get involved in activities that help communities to analyze their position within a wider economic, political, or environmental context. Gaining insight into what is happening and why can enable communities to see themselves within the bigger picture and ultimately recognize ways to protect themselves. This process will also help NGOs to find ways to support the communities' self-protection efforts. Another possibility is to provide people with safe spaces in which to analyze and express their emotions in relation to what they are experiencing. Their mental health and emotional well-being are central in enabling community members to feel empowered to assert themselves as subjects of their own destiny.

There is a critical need to focus on peace communities that do not have the sustained presence of international NGOs or humanitarian agencies. NGOs might consider providing accompaniment for these undefended communities. Organizations already working in Latin America that undertake this form of accompaniment—PBI, FOR, WfP, and Nonviolent Peaceforce—might expand their operations. Other organizations, especially faith-based groups with experience in Colombia, might also consider providing permanent presence.

In any engagement with local communities, NGOs must clearly state their own needs and limitations. For instance, NGOs need to provide certain results to their donors, and open discussion with peace communities can support cooperative action in meeting such needs. NGOs should also be clear about their limitations. Lack of transparency can cause misunderstandings and raise false expectations within the community, which risk weakening the process, doing more harm than good.

Working Nationally and Internationally

NGOs that are concerned about the viability of peace communities can support the continued linking of grassroots initiatives through existing national networks such as REDEPAZ. Such networks help to keep grassroots initiatives on the national and international radar screen— itself a form of protection—and attract moral, political, and economic solidarity. Similarly, NGOs can support international exchange visits among peace-community leaders and members. The opportunity to share and learn from other experiences could strengthen local resistance and psychological resilience.

NGOs can urge diplomatic action to deter further abuses of human rights and violations of international humanitarian law. Challenging abuses in national and international forums brings attention to the severity of the situation and is another means of helping to protect people and peace communities.

An assembly of human rights and peace organizations working in Colombia would be an opportune space to discuss the particular needs of both official and unofficial peace communities. Similarly an international forum for exchanging experiences of leading and supporting community-led protection mechanisms could fertilize and strengthen peaceful grassroots protagonism as a safeguard in the midst of conflict.

Developing strong connections with local, national, and international journalists is another way to sustain the peace communities. Positive reporting about peace communities can keep these initiatives within the public and political eye. At the same time, it is important to consider the risks of exposing currently unprotected peace communities because publicity could attract the hostility of those forces who are fearful of grassroots organizations.

Continuous Learning

There is a need for continued research into the processes and experiences of peace communities and their members. Some work is being done in Colombia to collect lessons and best practices, but there is little investigation of the undeclared peace communities, which tend to be the least protected. This is important, given the evolution of Colombia's conflict, and the fact that many peace communities are currently struggling to sustain their processes. Compiling detailed examples of the self-protection measures used in Colombia and other regions that have suffered prolonged wars can help peace communities develop and strengthen appropriate protection mechanisms.

Finally, NGOs and scholars alike can analyze peace communities for their value as the framework on which to build sustainable peace in Colombia, and as useful models for protecting lives and pursuing peace around the world.

NOTES

[1] The names of some places and individuals have been changed to protect anonymity.

REFERENCES

ABC Colombia (2005) "Colombia This Week," available at http://www.abcolombia.org.uk/previews_weeks.asp?id=130#bottom (retrieved May 18, 2007).

Amnesty International (2003) "Fear for safety," Urgent Action AT Index AMR 23/052/2003, available at http://web.amnesty.org/library/Index/ENGAMR230522003?open&of=ENG-300 (retrieved May 18, 2007).

Falla, Ricardo (1994) *Massacres in the Jungle: Ixcán, Guatemala 1975–1982*, Boulder, CO: Westview Press.

García Durán, Mauricio (2004) "Colombia: Challenges and Dilemmas in the Search for Peace," *Accord* 14, available at www.c-r.org/accord/col/accord14/searchforpeace.shtml (retrieved March 6, 2004).

Global Security (2007) "Plan Colombia," available at http://www.globalsecurity.org/military/ops/colombia.htm (retrieved May 17, 2007).

Hernández Delgado, Esperanza (2004) "Compelled to Act: Grassroots Peace Initiatives" *Accord* 14, available at www.cr.org/accord/col/accord14/searchforpeace.shtml (retrieved March 6, 2004).

Hernández Delgado, Esperanza and Marcela Salazar Posada (1999) *Con la Esperanza Intacta: Experiencias Comunitarias de Resistencia Civil no Violenta,* Bogotá: Oxfam GB.

Human Rights Watch (2002) *Colombia Human Rights Certification IV,* New York, NY: Human Rights Watch available at http://hrw.org/backgrounder/americas/colombia-certification4.htm (retrieved May 18, 2007).

Latin America Working Group Education Fund (LAWGEF), Center for International Policy (CIP), Washington Office on Latin America (WOLA) and US Office on Colombia (USOC) (2005) *Blueprint for a New Colombia Policy,* Washington, DC: LAWGEF, CIP, WOLA, USOC.

Lederach, John Paul (1998) *Construyendo la Paz: Reconciliación Sostenible en Sociedades Divididas,* Bilbao: Gernika Gogoratuz.

Misión de Observación (2002) "Misión de Observación a la Situación de las Comunidades Afrodescendientes en Colombia: Desplazamiento Forzado Interno y Violaciones al Derecho Internacional Humanitario," unpublished report, Colombia: Misión de Observación.

Parcomún and Diakonía (2002) *Enlaces y Rupturas: Experiencias de Participación Representativas de una Década en Colombia,* Bogotá: Parcomún.

Paul, Diane (1999) "Protection in Practice: Field Level Strategies for Protecting Civilians from Deliberate Harm," Relief and Rehabilitation Network Paper No. 30, London: Overseas Development Institute.

Sanford, Victoria (2003) "The Moral Imagination of Survival: Colombian Peace Communities and Guatemalan Communities of Populations in Resistance," paper delivered at workshop on Obstacles to Robust Negotiated Settlements at the Universidad Javeriana, Bogotá, May 21–23.

Sharp, Gene (2002) *From Dictatorship to Democracy: A Conceptual Framework for Liberation,* Boston, MA: The Albert Einstein Institute.

Sharp, Gene (2003) *There Are Realistic Alternatives,* Boston, MA: The Albert Einstein Institute.

Thompson, Martha and Deborah Eade (2004) "Women in War: Protection through Empowerment in El Salvador," in Haleh Afshar and Deborah Eade (eds.) *Development, Women and War: Feminist Perspectives,* Oxford: Oxfam GB (reprinted from *Social Development Issues* 24(3): 50–58), and in this volume.

First published in *Development in Practice* 16(3&4): 278–291 in 2006.

SEVEN

Women and War: Protection through Empowerment in El Salvador

MARTHA THOMPSON AND DEBORAH EADE

CHAPTER SUMMARY

Contemporary debate on the protection of civilians in times of war focus on the role of aid agencies, but contrast with the authors' experience of working with Salvadoran refugee and displaced populations during the 1980s. This chapter outlines some critical policy and practice lessons from how peasant women in particular developed their own protection capacities and leadership potential, even in the face of their aggressors.[1]

THE PORTRAYAL OF WAR

The human cost of war is something with which most readers of this book are probably familiar, albeit vicariously. The international media bring the images of war right into our own homes. The protagonists in these representations are almost exclusively male—soldiers, diplomats, politicians. By contrast, women are assigned one of two supporting roles: either the helpless victim caught in the crossfire, or the pillar of strength in adversity. The men do the talking and strategizing; the women suffer and struggle in the background. The implicit message of this narrative is clear. When conflict breaks out, men prosecute war to defend the homeland, while women bind the social wounds and keep the home fires burning. The statistics are well known, and may no longer have the power to shock:

> "contemporary wars are fought out not on demarcated battlefields, but in the towns, villages, and homes of ordinary people. The fact that 90 percent of today's war casualties are civilians, and the fact that four out of five refugees and displaced persons are women and children . . . are so often quoted that we hardly stop to think about what they mean."
>
> Deborah Eade 1996:5

To these, we can add that one-fifth of humanity survives on less than a dollar a day, and that two-thirds of the world's poorest people are women, as are two-thirds of adults who cannot read and write. Women perform most of the unremunerated work in the "hidden economy," and are disproportionately represented among the world's working poor, with lower average earnings than men in every country in the world, significantly so in some. It goes without saying, then, that most of those who become homeless, stateless, and penniless as a result of armed conflict, are women.

Recent years have witnessed renewed interest in the protection of civilians in war, which parallels increasing efforts to contain war-affected populations and prevent them from crossing borders. International humanitarian law (IHL) does, however, afford protection to internally displaced people who are in refugee-like situations, and although there is no agency with explicit responsibility for such people, both the United Nations High Commissioner for Refugees (UNHCR) and the International Committee of the Red Cross (ICRC) have both played that role. Indeed, the ICRC has played a leading role in both the discussion and the conceptualization of protection, which now encompasses a variety of activities formerly undertaken by human rights bodies, solidarity organizations, UN specialized agencies, humanitarian aid workers, and the ICRC itself.

In its 2001 publication (ICRC 2001), the ICRC defines the three areas of activities to strengthen protection for displaced persons:

1. **Responsive actions**—Any activity that puts a stop to a specific pattern of abuse and/or alleviates its immediate effects, including disseminating information, pressuring or dialoguing with authorities, and pursuing legal assistance.
2. **Remedial actions**—Any action that restores people's dignity and ensures adequate living conditions through reparation, restitution,

and rehabilitation, including pressuring authorities by public disclosure, helping bring about repatriation and resettlement, and providing direct services by being present.

3. **Environment-building actions**—Any action that fosters an environment conducive to respect for the rights of individuals in accordance with the relevant bodies of law in their broadest sense. This includes any activity aimed at implementation of international law, any activity that documents human rights abuses, and humanitarian activity whose ultimate goal is to protect people.

Frequently these protection activities are ascribed to outside actors, not to the affected population itself. However, the experiences of El Salvador in the 1980s and 1990s show that displaced persons themselves developed a whole strategy for protection based on these three types of activities long before they were articulated in the above form. Reviewing this experience can provide a new perspective, and take forward current thinking on protection issues by bringing two unique elements to the debate. First, the measures that most increased protection for civilians during the brutal eleven-year civil war were developed by organized communities of civilians displaced by the conflict, whether on their own or through their relationship with international NGOs and solidarity organizations. The primary actors therefore moved from being victims of war to building strategies for their own protection. Second, and what we focus on in this chapter, is that it was Salvadoran *campesinas* [peasant women] who played a major role in building and developing these protection capacities for themselves and their communities.

Nobody would suggest that standard "protection recipes" can be replicated across vastly different cultural and political realities. But we do believe that the main ingredients of the Salvadoran experience are relevant to other settings. In particular, we shall look at how people usually characterized as victims and aid beneficiaries moved to influence their environment; at what factors in the relationship between them and international agencies fostered their empowerment; and at what made it possible for women to play such a key role.

It is well-documented that women are particularly vulnerable to the depredations of war. (For an annotated bibliography of the contemporary literature that is analytical, testimony-based, and policy-focused, see Afshar and Eade 2003.) All too often, however, this knowledge fails to inform humanitarian policy and practice. Existing inequalities and gender imbalances are characteristically heightened by war, as women continue in highly adverse circumstances to combine their domestic and other roles, often assuming those of absent husbands and sons as well. Basic supplies run short, normal services are disrupted or suspended, sources of income dry up, and displacement becomes the key to survival. Fear is omnipresent, both of the known and of the unknown. Terror is a deliberate tactic of war, and includes the constant threat of attack as well as actual violence. The social fabric begins to unravel as trust is undermined. Yet it has become an aid agency truism that social disruption can sometimes create new opportunities for women, enabling them to break out of restrictive gender norms. Precisely because of this, it is worth looking more closely at what took place during the war in El Salvador.

THE 1980–1992 CIVIL WAR IN EL SALVADOR

By 1980 some of the most dramatic social and economic inequalities in Latin America were evident in El Salvador. The whole system was shored up by state violence and the brutal repression of dissent or democratic reform. The 1980-1992 civil war was the eighth armed uprising in 200 years to tear apart this small agricultural country. It was a particularly cruel war for the civilian population. The government maintained a system of structural violence that targeted any organized opposition to the status quo. Human rights groups estimate that of a population of 5 million, some 80,000 people—mainly noncombatants—were killed.

When this polarized situation exploded into civil war in 1980, the Frente Farabundo Martí para la Liberación Nacional (FMLN), had won widespread support from economically marginalized groups, particularly those influenced by liberation theology, as well as labor unions and peasant organizations. The military targeted all civilians it viewed as supportive of the FMLN. In the cities the armed forces arrested, "disappeared," tortured, and killed tens of thousands of people—professors, union organizers, health workers, slum dwellers, students, lawyers, and church workers. By 1984, the popular movement had been wiped from the streets; almost an entire generation of civil society leaders had been assassinated.

In the countryside, the military undertook a scorched-earth policy to depopulate the zones in the north and east of the country held by the

FMLN. They razed homes, massacred entire communities, destroyed crops and livestock, and carried out carpet bombing. By 1985 the FMLN-held zones were largely depopulated, and one in five Salvadorans was displaced within the country or had sought refuge abroad. For those who sought refuge outside El Salvador, at least there was the possibility of applying for refugee assistance and protection. The internally displaced were more vulnerable in terms of both security and livelihood.

Yet by 1986, in spite of the war and major US military and humanitarian aid designed to "win hearts and minds," groups of organized displaced persons within the country were beginning to agitate for the right to return. The new rallying cry of "Repopulation"—signifying the organized return of community members to their places of origin in the conflict zone—entered the popular lexicon. By 1988, the popular movement had reorganized and was protesting against the government; and repopulation of the conflict zones was well underway. This recovery is doubly impressive because it happened in the very teeth of war, and was carried out by the same people who had been military targets. The repopulation movement was characterized by strong, decisive action by the victims of the war. They were the actors in this movement and collaborated with international agency workers in ways that enabled them to work for their own protection.

Significantly, women were at the fore of the two most audacious initiatives of this movement. It was a women's organization, the Co-Madres [Mothers of the Disappeared], that led the public recovery of the popular movement, and women were prominent in organizing the repopulation of the conflict zones. In fact, 80 percent of the leaders of the National Coordination for Repopulation (CNR in its Spanish acronym), which spearheaded the repopulation movement into the conflict zones, were women under thirty years of age.

WOMEN IN PRE-WAR EL SALVADOR

The women who were prominent in the leadership of the repopulation movement and the many others who organized to confront the military in the conflict zones were people who had always been at a disadvantage. Campesino culture was intensely patriarchal, and machismo reigned in the household. Women were under the control of their husbands; they had little access to education, and the concept of women's rights was unknown. Gender roles were fixed—women gathered firewood and water, looked after the children, cooked for the household, cared for small animals, and supported men in the production of basic grains. Motherhood was women's major claim to dignity and respect, but that dignity was sentimentalized and devoid of economic rights and any legal claim.

Not surprisingly, rural women did not have high self-esteem. The absence of strong role models for them (apart from wealthy men's wives, almost universally portrayed as uncaring and lacking in compassion) deepened this lack of self-worth. In addition, El Salvador was a country of profound economic and social inequities buttressed by deep prejudice against the poor that cast them as ignorant, undeserving rabble. An exception to this general picture was in the gradual incorporation of women as "delegates of the Word" in the Christian base communities organized by priests who promoted liberation theology. This unique venue provided poor rural women a chance to learn, build self-worth through religious faith, and assume leadership.

Thus the women who became involved in building civilian protection had overcome major obstacles to play the significant roles that they did. The opportunity to act was also the opportunity to act politically. Every public civilian action in the counterinsurgency war was heavy with symbolism, and repopulation of the conflict zones was perhaps the most symbolic of all of acts of resistance. Repopulation was pivotal in changing how the war was fought, because the military strategy depended on separating the civilian population from the FMLN and penning in the FMLN up in the mountains. Furthermore, the low-intensity warfare practiced by the military relied upon state-sponsored violence and on terrorizing the civilian population. The repopulations were an open defiance of the armed forces, and the measures the returnees took to defend themselves were a remarkable illustration of this civilian challenge—a challenge that *attacked* the very root of the fear through which the military depended to exert social control.

THE DEVELOPMENT OF PROTECTION STRATEGIES

By 1983 there were about 20,000 refugees in camps in Honduras, and several thousand in twenty-seven camps of internally displaced persons run by the Catholic Church in El Salvador. These victims of war had a unique opportunity to develop protection skills in an environment that, although far from secure, was less dangerous than what they had been through. They learned how to develop responsive actions to build their own protection capacities. In doing so, they gradually became protagonists rather than victims. There were a number of specific reasons for their success: a cohesive political project that had popular support, the concept of a new society, and growing external political pressure on the Salvadoran government. There remains a great deal to be learned from the refugees' experience about how aid agencies can interact with civilian populations.

Telling Their Stories

In their respective camps in Honduras and El Salvador, the refugees and displaced were able to tell the steady stream of visiting journalists, human rights workers, international delegates, and agency representatives the stories of what had happened to them. Because the conflict zones were "no-go areas," the best way to learn about them was to listen to these stories and hear the news from the most recent arrivals. The only ones to witness the many rural massacres were the survivors. And only in the church-run camps in El Salvador or in the refugee camps over the border did those survivors feel safe to tell their story.

Women who had seen their houses destroyed; seen their own and their neighbors' children hanged from eaves, wounded by gunfire, or dying of disease and exposure as they fled; seen their men chopped up; and seen other women bayoneted felt the despair of abandonment. They believed the military could do this to them with impunity because they were poor. Often, the women in the camps formed mothers' groups to find comfort in shared despair. Their awful loneliness was somewhat alleviated as they felt each other's understanding and pain.

From Telling Stories to Reclaiming Human Rights

From these mothers' groups came many of the testimonies that began to paint for the outside world a picture of what was happening in the war zones, accounts that belied what the official sources were saying about military operations there. For the refugees and the displaced, testimony first meant simply telling their stories. But in the process of doing so for various audiences, they began to understand that what had happened to them was important, and that it horrified people. As one man said: 'We began to learn about this thing that they call human rights, we wanted to hear more about it." What they learned is that there were people around the world who believe that campesinos have human rights and who felt those rights had been violated. They learned there were people who had no intention of letting the official version of events erase the atrocities, and that there was power in the victims' testimony.

The displaced and the refugees slowly began to understand the legal framework of international humanitarian law through which they could articulate their experiences as victims of military attacks. In the capital city San Salvador, Tutela Legal, the legal office of the Catholic Archdiocese, helped people recall dates and names—the details that would turn a story into a legal denunciation. The women's groups were repositories of so many stories, and from these came our understanding of the war in the rural areas.

Once they grasped the idea of framing their experience in the context of human rights, a transformation process began. From feeling that they had no rights as victims and that no one cared about what happened to them, they moved to learning about and articulating their rights, and then to demanding that those rights be respected. Through the human rights workers in El Salvador, the priests who ministered to them, and the aid agency workers in the camps, the refugees learned about the 1997 Second Protocol of the 1949 Geneva Conventions, which delineates the rights of civilians in situations of armed conflict.

Becoming Human Rights Reporters

Initially, it was international workers and visiting delegations who would record the stories and translate the testimonies into denunciations of human rights violations. Later, agencies and human rights workers trained the refugees to take down the details needed in human rights reporting. When people returned to the conflict zones, they were already aware that reporting human rights violations was a way of enhancing their protection. If the military captured someone, the community leaders would send a delegation to report it to Tutela Legal, the Salvadoran Human Rights Commission and/or America's Watch Human Rights office. This became increasingly dangerous, however, because the offices were under surveillance and the delegations were not too hard to identify.

In order to minimize the risks, the returnees began to produce written reports for the human rights offices. At first, men seemed the obvious choice to make the long trip past the military checkpoints to get the reports to the capital. Soon, however, communities realized they could manipulate cultural gender stereotypes to their advantage. The military viewed women as less important and less intelligent than men, and were less likely to stop and search them. So women were increasingly chosen to carry the information, folding the written report into a tiny triangle and braiding it into their hair. With a basket of fruit balanced on her head, the courier would approach the checkpoint and humbly ask permission to go and sell her wares. Once through, she would take the bus, and from there get the report through to the human rights office.

Over the years, people in the conflict zones came to delegate community members to serve as human rights workers. These individuals would visit people who had suffered military attacks and record the incident, analyze the overall situation, and later work with internationals from NGOs or church organizations based in the area to send information out by computer. Young women were often chosen for these tasks because they were literate, had fewer household responsibilities, and—because the soldiers took them less seriously—they could move around more easily. This is not to say they were not vulnerable to rape or abuse if soldiers caught them alone on the road. But women found that adopting the guise of a simple campesina often enabled them to escape notice and blend into the crowd without drawing the soldiers' attention.

Organization

The refugees and the internally displaced learned a great deal about community organization during their time in the refugee camps. The lack of traditional authority figures, coupled with NGO encouragement, enabled them to accept new responsibilities. The preponderance of women in the camps meant they had to take on new roles. In Honduras, the refugees formed self-governing structures with refugees in charge of health, education, child day care, agriculture, sanitation, construction, and production workshops. These structures worked closely with the NGOs in the camps, allowing the refugees to develop leadership and organizational skills in a relatively protected environment. In addition, the constant pressure from the Salvadoran military, together with UNHCR's presence, gave real impetus to the refugees' will to defend themselves. They faced real adversity but also had recourse to an international organization whose role was to protect them—a combination that helped them develop a strong communal organization against military harassment based on a human rights discourse. This in turn led to highly organized communities with the real capacity to carry out their own political project.

In Honduras, the most dramatic change in women's roles may have occurred by virtue of the camps' social organization. Women increasingly took on roles of leadership, gaining valuable experience, providing role models, and challenging old stereotypes. When the camps were first established there were no women section leaders, but by the time the refugees returned, women held many positions of leadership, right up to highest level. The collectivization of domestic tasks and the provision of water and firewood were what made the women's transformation possible (Cagan and Cagan 1991).

In the camps for the displaced in El Salvador, women gained a degree of training and opportunities to accept new responsibilities and leadership positions. These camps were overcrowded and afforded little freedom of movement, but the fact that food and water, as well as child care, were provided generally freed women's time for literacy classes, training, meetings, and so on. In 1984, the Catholic church in El Salvador decided that the overcrowded camps were inadequate, and proposed incorporating the displaced in existing cooperatives and on lands that it had purchased. Four hundred people from the various camps met and formed their own organization, the Christian Committee of the Displaced (CRIPDES in its Spanish acronym). Over the next two years CRIPDES represented the displaced, negotiated with the church, and helped organize people in their new sites (Edwards and Siebentritt 1991).

When the displaced were relocated to cooperatives, the women lost ground. The cooperatives were run along traditional gender lines, and women's time came to be largely taken up with individual household duties. When the displaced set up their own communities, there was more funding, more collective practices were instituted, and women tended to fare better.

Despite these setbacks, CRIPDES was increasingly led by single young women without children. Many of them had spent time in the camps and had experienced military aggression firsthand, and most came from families with a history of organizing. As CRIPDES moved into the dispersed communities in the central and southern regions of El Salvador, these young women traveled by bus around the country organizing, exhorting, and building a movement.

Audacity

The strongest leaders among the young women who cut their political teeth in CRIPDES went on to play a prominent role in the next stage of the struggle. In 1986, when few of the male labor union or campesino leaders occupied prominent public positions, these young women led one of the most audacious movements of the war—the repopulation, or return to their places of origin.

This audacity was a creative response to the desperate situation of the displaced. In December 1985 and January 1986, the armed forces launched Operations Phoenix and Chávez Carreno, offensives aimed at forcibly displacing civilians from war zones in four provinces. As part of these campaigns, the military took more than 1,500 civilians off the Guazapa volcano, only 19 miles north of San Salvador. Times had changed: international pressure about the massive human rights violations had by then produced some limited effect. The government felt too much international attention was focused on El Salvador to allow these civilians to be killed, so they were turned over to the ICRC and many ended up in the church camps. Here they met others who had learned about framing a human rights discourse, about agency resources, and about the potential for and protection of church support. This proved a combustible combination. In May 1986, CRIPDES called a national conference to discuss the problems of the displaced—in particular the lack of land for their relocation—and concluded that the only durable solution was return to their places of origin. They formed the National Coordination for Repopulation (CNR) to facilitate a movement of organized returns to the conflict zones, in spite of the war (Thompson 1996, 1997).

There were several lessons to be gleaned from these experiences, and the refugees and displaced learned them all. They saw that reporting their testimonies had helped build a body of legitimate information about the massive violations of human rights during the war. They saw that this information could be used to build a case against the government, and that it was a key factor in increasing and maintaining the pressure that had forced the government to realize that the military could no longer act with such blanket impunity. The Guazapa incident was the first time the government recognized it could not afford a massacre, and decided instead to forcibly remove civilians from a conflict area. The major lesson drawn from this was that the rules of survival in a conflict zone may have changed for the better.

Building Legitimacy for a Political Project

Initially neither the military nor the government took the call for repopulation seriously, Perhaps the fact that the CNR was led largely by young women made the group easier to dismiss, as they were not perceived as powerful actors in wartime. But these young women had done their homework. Their essential building block for the creation of a safer environment was to have built legitimacy for the return to the conflict zones. CNR leaders insisted that the repopulation consist of high-profile, collective, organized events—and that these be recognized as *civilian* communities whose residents would have the right to live in their place of origin, free from attack, detention, or removal (Edwards and Siebentritt 1991). As the repopulations gained momentum, the returnees couched their demands for return, protection, and assistance in the framework of the Second Protocol, to which El Salvador was a signatory. Together with agency workers and human rights organizations, they hammered out the main tenets of their rights as returnees (Thompson 1995:129):

- The right to be in their places of origin, and carry out daily life (including the right to not be bombed or militarily harassed)
- The right to access to the supplies and materials needed to carry out their daily lives (rendering military checkpoints unacceptable)
- The right to humanitarian aid from NGOs and international agencies (and the right of access by NGOs and agencies)

The refugees in Honduras had no intention of returning, only to become internal refugees (Weiss-Fagan and Yudelman 2001). They used the above arguments in 1987, 1988, and 1989 to justify their collective repatriations to the conflict zones. By claiming legitimacy under international law in establishing human rights benchmarks against which any violations can be measured, the victims of war can enlist allies to advocate for them. The repopulated communities did exactly this. The Catholic, Episcopal, and Lutheran churches in El Salvador provided funds and ministry to the communities in the conflict zones.

National NGOs and the national popular movement also supported the repopulations with their presence, solidarity, and project assistance. Because the repopulations were based on an IHL discourse, these outside groups could legitimately claim that they had a mandate to work with them. Ten international agencies in El Salvador developed their work on this basis. Founded on a relationship of mutual trust and respect, the agencies and the communities developed complementary roles in constructing protection. The agencies provided funding, presence, and projects, but any advocacy was conducted in conjunction with the communities. They employed a person to investigate and report on violations of human rights and problems with humanitarian work in the repopulations (Thompson 1997). That information, along with analysis and recommended action, was sent on a regular basis to a network of agencies and human rights organizations in North America and Europe.

Building Visibility

The major massacres had taken place hidden away from international eyes and the cameras and notebooks of the press. However, returnees were clear that they had to build a safer environment if they were going to return to conflict zones while the war was still on. They had to reduce the military's sense of impunity in killing and torturing people in these areas. Once they established their legitimate right to return, the displaced had to increase the political cost of any military attacks against returnees. This meant raising the communities' visibility.

The first CNR caravan of buses that carried returnees back to Chalatenango in July 1986 arrived at the army checkpoints in the company of a lively medley of journalists, church leaders, humanitarian NGOs, and solidarity delegations. Bewildered by this bold move, the military actually allowed them to pass up the dirt roads into the weed-grown ghost town of San José de Las Flores. All the repopulations followed suit with highly visible caravans accompanying people back to their homes, as if to emphasize that these communities were in the public eye. The church and the humanitarian agencies demonstrated that they intended to have access to them, and internationals linked to the agencies were placed in each community to establish a visible international presence. The communities themselves conducted a program of communication outreach, cultivating relationships with journalists, embassy representatives, and human rights groups. Meanwhile, the agencies sought official funding, bringing in diplomatic representatives when the communities were attacked or projects destroyed.

The communities were also helped to send their human rights reports out to an international rapid-response network of individuals who had agreed to advocate on their behalf. These individuals would send telegrams, faxes, e-mails, or letters to the President, the head of the military, and the military barracks responsible for those specific violations—and this increased visibility aided the protection effort in very tangible ways. A community leader from Morazán recalls:

> "After I was in my cell for two days, they took me to see the colonel. He was very angry, throwing some papers at me, 'Who do you know in the USA?' he was shouting. 'How is it that all these people know you are captured? They are sending these faxes here.' He was very angry at me, but after four days he let me go; he said that they were making too much fuss."
>
> (Thompson 1997:53)

Collective Action for Access

By 1990, ninety-four repopulated communities had been reestablished in northern Morazán and northern Chalatenango. Access was the key to their survival. The communities needed to get materials and supplies past the military checkpoints, and they needed to ensure that outsiders could visit in order to guarantee their visibility.

An early struggle over access was won by women in Morazán (Thompson 1996: 329). The church had sent two trucks of dried milk for children in the war zone but the military wouldn't allow the trucks out of the provincial capital, San Francisco Gotera. Several mothers' associations got together and sent delegations on five separate occasions to make the seven-hour trek down to the military barracks to request the milk. Unexpectedly, after the fifth visit, the colonel gave in and let the trucks through. The women claimed their legitimacy as mothers and quietly insisted on their right as mothers to feed their children, again using a cultural gender stereotype to their advantage.

Women were extremely effective in persuading soldiers to grant access, and were chosen to intercede for this reason. Men went along but it was often the women who did the talking. Esperanza, a leader from one of the Chalatenango communities, would accompany supply trucks up to the conflict zones. She argued them through the checkpoints well into her eighth month of pregnancy.

The women also used a gender stereotype to confront military incursions into the communities. Together with their children they would quickly surround the soldiers, and scold them as mothers and grandmothers: "How can you take action against us, we could be your mother or your grandmother. You are peasants like us, so why do you try and hurt us? Would you do this to your sister, your mother?" Salvadoran custom has it that to strike a woman with child in her arms is unmanly. In testimonies of the massacres, some survivors would repeat unbelievingly, "they would even shoot women with children in their arms," an unusual spin on Susan Mackay's 'womenandchildren' nexus (cited in Kasam 2001). Some recounted that the soldiers would yell at the women to put the children down so they could shoot them. The image of mother with child in arms is a powerful one in El Salvador, and the women in the repopulations constantly used it to plead with the soldiers, asking that they leave them alone and rebuking them for harming members of the community. They chose their society's one powerful image of women to protect themselves and their communities.

WHAT ENABLED WOMEN TO PLAY
SUCH A MAJOR ROLE?

Almost all of the women who played leadership roles in the repopulation movement had spent time in the refugee camps in Honduras. This experience gave them tools to address the triple obstacles they faced as poor peasant women.

- As we have seen, the mothers formed mutual support groups where they could share their stories, take comfort from each other, and reflect on what had happened in terms of justice and rights. This broke down the tendency to isolation and despair. When delegations started coming to hear their testimonies, the women learned that their experiences were important, and this in turn began a process of reaffirming their self-worth.
- The camps, particularly in Honduras, gave women the means and opportunity to develop leadership and acquire new skills, including literacy. With the domestic burden reduced through simple technology and collectivization, the women were able to take advantage of the training and education offered. Firewood and

water were provided, and they organized communal child care. Health and education were available at no charge. In one refugee camp, meals for everyone were prepared in communal kitchens. Although the situation to which they returned provided less practical support for women, they still had child care, a nearby water supply, community corn mills, food for the vulnerable population, and health and education facilities. These factors reduced some of the class obstacles that had always kept women back. Because women and children had been sent to the camps for protection, in the camps, women outnumbered men. But this gender imbalance created the space and opportunity the women needed to change their conventional roles, as the absence of traditional authority figures removed some of the cultural constraints on their active participation in public life. Once women took on greater responsibility and moved into leadership posts, they became new role models for other women.

- The young women who led the CNR drew great strength from each other and their common status as single childless women who nonetheless had a strong community. They were able to discuss with each other the merits of having children, getting married, and so on, and figure out what would be best for them. These women were extraordinary role models for other young women who saw them up onstage at rallies, rebuking the military and being defiant. Their lack of family responsibilities and their political commitment gave them both freedom and a social structure. Although most of them had been held in military detention at one time or another, and some had been tortured and raped, they continued their work nonetheless.

- Women took strength from collective action and from playing an active part in a wider political project. This community strength was palpable. It enabled women to shake off the image of victim and at the same time, their sense of belonging gave sense and meaning to their suffering. Women saw that by working together to confront the armed forces, they had actually advanced. This was not a linear journey. Sometimes they were successful and sometimes the soldiers ended up achieving what they set out to do, capturing someone or refusing to let goods through the checkpoints. They did not win all the time, but they won enough to see progress and to draw strength from each victory.

- Women were shrewd in exploiting the culturally prejudiced assumption that women are less intelligent than men, and so were not watched as closely as men.
- They were able to build on and exploit the only source of dignity accorded poor women in El Salvador—motherhood. They used it to protect themselves, to justify their defiant actions, and to pressure young soldiers.
- As people strengthened their capacity to protect themselves, they also made it more likely that the wider community could participate in creating that protection.

Conventional understandings of conflict pay rather scant attention to grassroots political agency, and to the capacity of ordinary people to act for the common good in pursuit of what they consider a just society. We hear much more about civilians as innocent and helpless victims, or even as cynical and manipulative aid-grabbers, than we hear about their acts of courage, their capacity to bring about and respond to positive change, or their own ideas about building a new society. Jenny Pearce observed that "a real appreciation of how gender relations affect the ability of poor and powerless women to play their full role in the post-conflict situation (as opposed to a knowledge of the *discourse*) is essential. In my experience, few of the professional men involved in external assistance programmes . . . have that real appreciation" (Pearce 1998:85)

VICTIMS OF SOCIETY, OR SOCIAL ACTORS?
A CONCLUDING REFLECTION

Women frequently *are* victims of violence, of gender-inequitable public policies, and of discrimination. To take but one example, one in two women in the world has experienced some form of male violence, usually in the home. This so-called domestic, or culturally condoned, violence remains largely invisible: too mundane, too shameful, or too frightening for the survivors to talk about in public; and too private or intimate for outsiders to get involved (Pickup 2001). But to regard women simply as victims of patriarchal social forces, never able to challenge and overcome them, would be to further wrong them (and us). There is a critical difference between experiencing injustice and being defined by one's victimhood.

The use of rape as an instrument of war seeks to undermine the victim's personal and social identity and the integrity of her person by torturing and humiliating her. The practice of "political disappearance," used extensively throughout Latin America, seeks to terrify and paralyze the victims' families, their communities, and everyone known to them. Both mechanisms are immensely effective in sowing terror and a sense of moral chaos. What is truly remarkable is the way in which, as shown in this chapter, the intended victims can together grow through such brutality and find the strength to denounce and fight it. That former Chilean dictator Augusto Pinochet came as close as he did to facing trial for the atrocities committed during his rule, for instance, owes more to the resolve and courage of human rights groups and the families of the disappeared than it does to international law. That rape is now formally recognized as a crime of gender in indictments of suspected war criminals owes more to the collective bravery of women in speaking out than it does to the judicial system. Once they have broken the silence, survivors of rape may well move on to question the prevalence of male violence against women *outside* the context of war, and so to challenge gender-power relations within their own societies. Similarly, once they lost their fear, Salvadoran campesinos were able to challenge the structural violence that had oppressed them for generations, and to develop their own protection capacities. The real question, in both cases, is whether the shift from victim to social actor will give women the capacity to take their newfound confidence from the conflict to the development agenda, and whether international agencies are ready to help them to do so.

NOTES

[1] This chapter is based on the authors' extensive experience in Central America and has been shaped by their collaboration with agency colleagues and by their own involvement in local organizations throughout the region. The views and interpretations expressed are those of the authors alone and should not be attributed to any agency for which they worked. The chapter was originally commissioned as an article for a special issue of the journal *Social Development Issues* on Women in Conflict and Crisis: New Issues in an Insecure World (24(3): 50–58, 2002). We are grateful to editors Mary Ellen Kondrat, María Juliá, and Cathy Rakowski, and to the Inter-University Consortium for International Social Development, for allowing us to reproduce the article.

REFERENCES

Afshar, Haleh and Deborah Eade (eds.) (2003) *Development, Women, and War: Feminist Perspectives,* Oxford: Oxfam GB.

Cagan, Beth and Steve Cagan (1991) *This Promised Land, El Salvador,* New Brunswick and London: Rutgers University Press.

Eade, Deborah (ed.) (1996) Editor's preface to *Development in States of War,* Oxford: Oxfam UK & Ireland.

Eade, Deborah (1997) *Capacity Building: A People-Centred Approach to Development,* Oxford: Oxfam.

Eade, Deborah (2001) "Mujeres y conflictos armados," *Papeles de cuestiones internacionales,* Número 73, Invierno: 15–22.

Edwards, Beatrice and Gretta Tovar Siebentritt (1991) *Places of Origin,* Boulder, CO and London: Lynne Rienner Publishers.

ICRC (2001) *Strengthening Protection in War: A Search for Professional Standards,* Geneva: ICRC.

Karam, Azza (2001) "Women in War and Peace-building: The Roads Traversed, the Challenges Ahead," *International Feminist Journal of Politics,* 3(1): 2–25.

Pearce, Jenny (1998) "Sustainable Peace-building in the South: Experiences from Latin America," in Deborah Eade (ed.) *From Conflict to Peace in a Changing World: Social Reconstruction in Times of Transition,* Oxford: Oxfam GB.

Pickup, Francine, with Suzanne Williams and Caroline Sweetman (2001) *Ending Violence Against Women: A Challenge for Development and Humanitarian Work,* Oxford: Oxfam GB.

Thompson, Martha (1995) "Repopulated Communities in El Salvador," in Minor Sinclair (ed.) *New Politics of Survival: Grassroots Movements in Central America,* New York: Monthly Review Press.

Thompson, Martha (1996) "Empowerment and Survival: Humanitarian Work in Civil Conflict" (Part 1), *Development in Practice* 6(4): 324–333.

Thompson, Martha (1997) "Empowerment and Survival: Humanitarian Work in Civil Conflict" (Part 2), *Development in Practice* 7(1): 50–58.

Thompson, Martha (1999) "Gender in Times of War," in Fenella Porter, Ines Smyth, and Caroline Sweetman (eds.) *Gender Works: Oxfam Experience in Policy and Practice,* Oxford: Oxfam GB.

Weiss-Fagan, Patricia and Sally Yudelman (2001) "El Salvador and Guatemala: Refugee Camp and Repatriation Experiences," in Krishna Kumar (ed.) *Women and Civil War,* Boulder, CO and London: Lynne Rienner, pp. 79–95.

First published in *Social Development Issues* 24 (3): 50–58 in 2002.

PART 3

Between a Rock and a Hard Place:
Examples of Humanitarian Practice

EIGHT

Everyday Practices of Humanitarian Aid: Tsunami Response in Sri Lanka

UDAN FERNANDO AND DOROTHEA HILHORST

CHAPTER SUMMARY

This chapter underlines the importance of grounding the analysis of humanitarian aid in an understanding of everyday practice. It presents ethnographic vignettes illustrating three aspects of aid response in Sri Lanka following the tsunami disaster in 2004. The first deals with the nature of humanitarian actors, the second explores how different kinds of politics intertwine, and the third considers humanitarian partnerships. The authors discuss the need for a shift in current academic approaches, in which discussions on humanitarian aid usually start from the level of principles rather than practice. They argue that accounts of the everyday practices and dilemmas faced by NGOs help to correct blind expectations, expose uncritical admiration, and put unrealistic critiques into perspective.

INTRODUCTION

In this chapter we underline the importance of grounding the analysis of humanitarian aid in an understanding of everyday practice. We do this by presenting and discussing three ethnographic vignettes that illustrate three aspects of disaster relief. The first deals with the nature of humanitarian actors, in particular the role of private initiatives. The second prompts a discussion of how different kinds of politics play a role and how these roles intertwine. The third raises the issue of humanitarian partnerships. Although each vignette presents a unique angle, they all form part of the same picture, revealing the need for detailed analysis of everyday practice as the starting point for understanding humanitarian aid. Although this may sound simple, it would require a shift in current academic approaches, in which discussions on humanitarian aid usually start from the level of theoretical principles.

We use the response to the 2004 tsunami in Sri Lanka to illustrate our arguments. The tsunami was a globalized event: a disaster that manifested the processes of globalization and was shaped by them. We therefore assume that readers have some knowledge of the disaster, which gives a common frame of reference for the vignettes that we present.

Like the tsunami, this chapter is also the product of processes of globalization. Udan Fernando is a Sri Lankan national and is preparing his doctorate in the Netherlands, where Dorothea Hilhorst is based. When we met several years ago, we found that we had a lot in common. We are both academics with one foot in the university and the other in civil society. We both work *with* and *on* NGOs, and both share a passion for organizational ethnography. When we met again in Sri Lanka after the tsunami, we compared notes over a couple of beers and worked out the basic idea of this essay. It could be written at a distance from the hectic realities of the tsunami response, during one of Udan's periods of study in the Netherlands in April 2005.

Like many contemporary ethnographies of globalized processes, the chapter draws on material from various sites and sources, incorporating research experiences from both of us. Udan has been involved in the response to the tsunami from Day 1. Like every other Sri Lankan, he roamed around parts of the affected areas in search of friends, relatives, and bodies. Soon he was caught up in the "second tsunami" of aid agency responses and became active as a consultant, facilitator, and researcher. For instance, in April 2005 he conducted a real-time evaluation in Sri Lanka, commissioned by Action by Churches Together (ACT) International, a worldwide humanitarian network of churches and related agencies. Dorothea went to Sri Lanka in January and March 2005 for two one-week visits. The first concerned real-time research,[1] and the second involved a mission to assist the Consortium of Humanitarian Agencies to formulate a proposal on behalf of Novib/Oxfam Netherlands. During these two weeks she interviewed around fifty people, individually and in groups, and attended several meetings.

In addition, the chapter uses interview material collected in the Netherlands from funding agencies, NGOs, and private humanitarians. Apart from interviews, the article draws on newspapers and other media sources, as well as an analysis of e-mail correspondence. Because we did our research separately, "we" does not always refer to the two of us. When this is the case, it is specified in the notes.

THE IMPORTANCE OF GROUNDED RESEARCH

Humanitarian aid appears to be dictated by principles, policies, and intervention models. However, fieldworkers construct their own inter-pretations of principles and priorities in response to demands posed in the field. The translation of principles into practice happens through the combined actions of staff members and other involved actors. It is there-fore not enough to discuss principles and policy because understanding how they work requires looking at the everyday actions in the field. Recognition of the importance of everyday practices for understanding aid in situations of conflict is founded theoretically and methodologi-cally on the premise that social actors have agency (Long 1992, 2001). People reflect upon their experiences and what happens around them, and they use their knowledge and capabilities to interpret and respond to their environment. Humanitarian aid, in this perspective, is the out-come of the messy interaction of social actors struggling, negotiating, and at times guessing to further their interests (Bakewell 2000). An ethnography of humanitarian practice can illustrate the ways in which humanitarian actors give meaning to and act upon their mission.

Actor-oriented research also focuses on the multiple realities of NGOs. Humanitarianism prides itself on delivering principled aid that is needs-based, neutral, and independent. These principles are meant to forge the trust that is necessary in order to get access to people in need, while protecting the safety of the aid workers (Slim 1999; Hilhorst 2002, 2005). In practice, however, humanitarian aid comes about through an amalgam of different "drivers," and humanitarian aid is pro-foundly political. It often constitutes an uneasy mix of principles, for-eign policy, and military doctrine, as well as the everyday realities of organizational politicking and rivalry (see also Kerkvliet 1991:11). At the same time, humanitarian actors are geared toward seeking to legitimize their work. In order to mobilize support, they have to convince stakeholders of their appropriateness and trustworthiness (Bailey 1971). These different kinds of politics are entangled (Hulme and Goodhand 2000; Uvin 1998), and the resulting dynamics play out in everyday practice.

Grounded research is also necessary for revealing and analyzing the diversity of humanitarian response. The ways in which humanitarian aid is delivered have become increasingly complicated. The number of development NGOs and humanitarian agencies operating in crisis areas has grown, and many different approaches to aid can be found in the field, including those of international NGOs (INGOs) with their own operational capacity, INGOs working through local partners, and diverse local NGOs. The various aid modalities set different parameters for discussions of each agency's principles, humanitarian policy, and decisionmaking space. International discussion seems to focus mainly on operational INGOs, and neglects the wealth of other experiences.

Finally, a focus on everyday practices allows one to analyze the power processes within humanitarian communities and in their relations with wider domains. In the wide perspective of human suffering, humanitarians may appear as idealistic aid workers who help people in need, often at great risk to their personal security. But if we zoom in on the situation, the power differentials become apparent. International NGOs, for example, have been uncomfortably associated with a desire to impose a set of Western humanitarian values on the world. There are also questions about the power differentials between INGOs and their local implementing partners, and between humanitarians and the recipients of aid. These differences are hidden under the rhetoric of partnership and participation, but they are being played out in the realities of everyday interaction.

GLOBALIZING DISASTERS: KEES AND ANNETTE VERSUS THE AID AGENCIES

In 1968 the Biafra war was the first humanitarian crisis that was televised and had a real-time impact on people living on the other side of the world. Barely forty years later, the tsunami response shows how disasters have now become globalized. The processes of globalization collapse time and space, so that people all over the world can be immediately connected to the site of a disaster, whether via satellites that transfer information through the mass media and the Internet, or by getting on a plane. (This is not, of course, the same for everybody and every disaster: many people are beyond the reach of the media, and sadly, too many disasters fail to attract globalized attention.) Globalization can result in strands of affectionate identification stretching across the world. Among the many e-mails received by Udan after the tsunami from friends in the Netherlands was one that read: "Dear Udan, can you please go and check out if K.A.G. Ajith Priyashantha, Tharanga Siriwardana, Noel, Punchihewa, Padmini, Ama and Dilrukshi are still alive? These people worked in the Dayawasa hotel in Galle, where I spent my holidays several years ago. We have always stayed in touch and I am very worried about them."

Globalization has also led to greater informality. Increasingly knowledge and action have been taken out of the exclusive realm of experts and are now within everyone's reach. Post-disaster rescue, survival, and rehabilitation have always depended first and foremost on the informal help of neighbors and community members, with the professional agencies only coming in later. After the tsunami, however, for the first time the event appeared to be everybody's disaster. All over the world individuals assessed the damage, identified needs, and expressed opinions on the progress and quality of aid delivery. Members of the Sri Lankan diaspora came in huge numbers to help their people. Not only that, but many other people—whose only relation to the tsunami was having spent a holiday in Sri Lanka—got on planes with loads of relief items and cash collected from their own personal, neighborhood, professional, or church networks. One of them was a person whom we shall name Kees.

Kees is a former employee of a public company in Amsterdam who took early retirement. After the tsunami he traveled to Sri Lanka with 130 kilograms of relief assistance, including a heavy box of nails— which he thought would be handy to repair the damaged houses and boats—and a thick wad of euros. Kees is active in his local church, both as a religious lay worker and in its social work. His church is connected to an umbrella body, Kerkinactie, which deals with development and humanitarian assistance. Despite Kerkinactie's fundraising campaigns, Kees wanted to travel to Sri Lanka and do the work on his own. He went to the south, where he often spends his winter holidays. Together with friends there he started to build four houses in the tsunami-affected village of Habaraduwa. Two women from his church later came to assist him. The construction was to be completed in June 2005. Kees returned to Amsterdam in late March, having completed the initial work, and examined his weekly bank statements with the details of transfers to his account. He was surprised to see that he had received a total of € 17,000 from 214 different people, and he did not even know 77 of them.

There were many people like Kees who came to Sri Lanka. Their confident belief that they knew what to do and how to do it is related, we believe, to the way in which globalized news is packaged: as brief items stripped of complicated details, generating a sense of intimate knowledge and proximity—as if the world were indeed a global village. Their response shows the strength of informal networks and a personal approach, but it also illustrates the fact that although globalization can create bonds, it is certainly no equalizer. It is hard to miss the implicit sense of superiority among people like Kees. Equipped with nails and cash, they automatically assume they have something to offer to Sri Lankans. However, not a single Dutch person traveled, to the United States after the attacks of September 11, 2001, to help to clear the rubble, rightly assuming that the Americans could do this job themselves.

What about the relations between people like Kees and the official humanitarian agencies? Why did Kees not want to channel his assistance through such organized and formal agencies as Kerkinactie or Icco, which are linked to his church? These agencies claim some expertise in relief work and have their own networks of partner organizations in Sri Lanka that work at the grassroots level. Would it not have been more effective and efficient for Kees to use these agencies to channel the money he had raised from his own personal network? The response of people like Kees suggests a growing dissatisfaction with professional agencies and their expertise in relief and humanitarian efforts. They are wary of the agencies and the money they need to maintain their bureaucracies. This became increasingly clear when a Dutch woman named Annette (who went to do relief work in the eastern region of Sri Lanka) said: "[One] hundred percent of the money that we collected is given to the needy. I do not even deduct the bank commission as administration costs, and I paid my own ticket and hotel."

The humanitarian agencies, on the other hand, have difficulty with people like Kees and Annette. Although many agencies welcome volunteers working through their own channels, they tend to dislike the "loose-cannon initiatives" of private individuals, whom they regard as amateurs who get in the way of professional help. Interestingly, however, the case of Kees does not corroborate this view. Although Kees had never heard of the Sphere Code of Conduct, life experience had given him an implicit and not dissimilar set of principles. Clearly he is motivated by the idea of "humanity," and is eager to work on the basis of needs. He and Annette have their own form of professionalism. The impact of the work they did is yet to be assessed. But Kees and Annette hold themselves accountable to their own *achterban,* or con-stituencies. In an e-mail sent to his friends who donated money, Kees wrote: "Upon my return to the Netherlands I will send all of you a complete and detailed account of the expenses." He is also keen to avoid the adverse effects of aid and proudly announces that "Not a single penny was paid on bribery." Kees may have his *eigenwijze,* or idiosyncratic ways of doing things, but at the same time he also has his own logic—for instance, concerning accountability. Of course, the complexity of the individual networks defies generalization, because they each represent different interests, colors, and shades, but the case does point out that the difference between the professional and the "amateur" humanitarian may not be as straightforward as is often assumed.

While the amateurs and the professionals grapple with each other, the question that we wish to address is how to deal analytically with the phenomenon of a globalized disaster? To our minds the case underlines that there is no such thing as a humanitarian system, in the sense of an assembly of parts with clear complementary roles and responsibilities. Humanitarian aid comes about through diverse and geographically dispersed actors. Key players are the implementing agencies, their recipients, and the local institutional environment. Other relevant actors are foreign policy actors, donors, UN agencies, peacekeeping forces, the media, and a range of local institutions. Together they form a humanitarian complex consisting of shifting actors, diffuse boundaries, partly conflicting interests and values, a high diversity of organizations and work styles, and unpredictable outcomes (Hilhorst 2002). Analytically it would be unwise to attempt to draw a boundary between professionals and such other humanitarians as the military, private businesses, and the tsunami "amateurs." Instead one must analyze how different actors emerge and relate to one another in the everyday practice of providing humanitarian aid. Rather than making assumptions about what particular actors have to offer, we must establish how the differences between professionals and other brands of humanitarian or nonhumanitarian come about in practice.

THE POLITICS OF AID

After a brief moment of respite immediately after the tsunami, political differences and conflict resurfaced almost immediately, strongly affecting the way in which aid was organized. The long-running conflict in Sri Lanka is complex and multidimensional, made up of intertwining ideological, religious, and ethnic differences (Frerks and Klem 2004). Mutual allegations abound, claiming that the political factions of the government, the Liberation Tigers of Tamil Eelam (LTTE), and Janatha Vimukthi Peramuna (JVP) hijacked relief to distribute under their own names, favored their own followers, or withheld aid from areas not under their control.[2] This does not necessarily mean that the everyday organization of aid is always dictated by these differences. In a country of long-standing conflict such as Sri Lanka, conflict inevitably becomes ritualized while people find ways to accommodate their differences on the ground.

A case in point is the attempt of a Buddhist monk and a Christian clergyman to work together in a village close to the southern city of Galle. The church and vicarage were not affected by the tsunami because those buildings were located on high ground. But the temple, lower down, was almost submerged by the inundating waters. The clergyman through his network of churches was quick to receive loads of relief and money, which he sought to disburse through what he called "interreligious" work. The temple was turned into a relief camp. When we visited Galle,[3] the Buddhist monk told us: "Whenever there's a problem we [the temple] always get involved. When we need money we ask [for] money from the fathers [i.e., the Christian priests] because we know that the coffers of God are with them." Apparently this monk was resigned to the fact that Christian churches have an advantage in tapping into Western resources, owing to their networks. This does not mean the monk could afford to explain this fact to his people. When we asked a fisherman who had received food, medicine, clothing, and cooking vessels from the temple whether he knew where the aid had come from, he replied that it had come from Japan and Thailand! When asked how he knew this, the fisherman said that the monk had told him so. The monk had diplomatically concealed the Western/Christian source, which he knew would be unacceptable to his constituency, and instead attributed the relief to acceptable Eastern/Buddhist sources.

Even though conflict may not always be manifest, there is no doubt that the aid is subject to political pressures. One particular field of tension that intensified after the tsunami is the relation between the state and civil society, in particular the NGOs. On March 27, 2005, *Silumina,* the Sunday newspaper of a government-owned publishing house, carried an extra-large headline: "NGOs Have Taken Nine out of the Ten Billion Foreign Aid" (*videshaadaara biliyana dahayen namayakma engeeo aran*). The message was clear: the NGOs had snatched the money that would rightfully have come to the government. Indeed, many donors refused at that moment to channel funds through the government, unless the authorities reached an agreement with the LTTE for its joint management. The state's frustration in collecting limited funds, or none at all, from those who pledged support was vented when the president declared at a mass rally in the south that the government had not received even a *thamba doithuwak* [one cent].[4] Under different governments the Sri Lankan state has had a series of love–hate relationships with NGOs since the latter became a notable phenomenon in the late 1970s. Although there have been collaborations between the two sectors, NGO-bashing has been a favorite pastime of respective governments. The state has sometimes been vocal in the anti-NGO lobby, joining forces with some odd allies, who represent such ultranationalist groups as Sihala Urumaya, Jathika Hela Urumaya, and the Patriotic National Movement (Fernando 2003). When decrying the role of NGOs, respective governments have used two types of argument. First, they claim that NGOs snatch money that would otherwise be available to the state. Second, they ascribe a conspiratorial role to NGOs, whom they accuse of promoting Western interests. History was thus perpetuated when the deputy minister of foreign affairs said:

> After the tsunami disaster several hundreds of NGOs entered the country as "saviours" of the people. This sudden growth in the number of NGOs is a reason for concern. Some NGOs had developed into an organised network associated with the country's ethnic question, which is a dangerous trend. I need to tell you that all these NGOs have a political agenda. I would like to dub them as organisations which are servile to the West. Some NGOs openly display their servility to their neo-colonialist masters.[5]

> (*Asian Tribune,* June 4, 2005)

One can understand the frustration of a government that was seeing most official aid channeled through NGOs, in addition to the millions of euros in private donations that were also finding their way into the country through NGOs. What is interesting for our purpose, however, is to see how different kinds of politics intertwine with the dispute.

Institutional envy is coated in a sauce of ideological conspiracy theory. Hence, what appears to be an ideological dispute may hide underlying organizational politics. Similarly what appears to be straightforward organizational competition may be complicated by clashes of real values. Our point is that humanitarian politics constitutes a mix of different kinds of politics. It combines ideological politics, humanitarian principles, and everyday organizational politicking and rivalry. Stating that aid is political is simply a tautology. The real questions are what kinds of politics are involved, how they interrelate in practice, and how people's perceptions of these politics color their interpretation of what happens around them. Such questions can be tackled only by detailed analysis of everyday practice.

COORDINATION: INTERNATIONAL AND NATIONAL NGOs

Commenting on the overwhelming international response to the tsunami, one Sri Lankan NGO director observed: "There has never been so much money available, which is creating unique opportunities." Although the potential benefits were astonishing, the downside was also immediately visible. One experienced international humanitarian worker commented that he had never been in a situation of such fierce competition among the aid agencies. The Sri Lankan government was slow to register the influx of international agencies, but the numbers were estimated at around 250 in March 2005.[6] These agencies arrived in addition to the dozens of international agencies that already had a presence in the country, focused on either conflict-related or development programs. Many of them have signed the humanitarian Code of Conduct and are committed to working in partnership with local organizations and coordinating their work. Nonetheless, local organizations found it hard to find a place of their own in the implementation of tsunami-related activities. The case of X illustrates the problem.

NGO "X" had ten years' experience in supporting development projects in the district of Batticaloa. Naturally it wanted to be involved in tsunami response. When the NGO presented a proposal to one of its two core European funders, X was told it would be best to "leave the tsunami work to the international agencies and concentrate instead on continuation of [its] work in the nonaffected areas." X had no intention of abandoning the nonaffected areas, but nonetheless felt it should also be involved in the reconstruction effort. Fortunately its other core funder was more responsive, and the NGO was invited to present a proposal. During one of the district coordination meetings, X successfully registered a project to construct temporary shelters for two villages in Vaharai. During the preparation process, X discovered that the government itself had signed a memorandum of understanding with an international agency to construct new shelters in one of the villages. Although the district officials assured X that its project could still proceed, and provided a signed statement to this effect, after a few weeks X wrote to the funding agency that it was being "pressured by the government to withdraw from both villages." It was hoping to be granted permission to work in another village.

The case of X is not unique to local NGOs. International NGOs also encountered difficulties in planning their work because they found other agencies "taking over" designated areas. However, local NGOs felt they had unequal access to the post-tsunami rehabilitation effort, although they were frequently sought out to become partners in the international agencies' programs. And they often found that their best staff were attracted by the high-salary job offers extended by the agencies. Many international agencies are serious in saying they want to engage in partnership with local agencies and capacities. But what do they mean by the concept? What does partnership constitute in practice?

"Partnership" is the term most frequently used for relationships in which INGOs fund local NGOs to implement humanitarian work. The term "partner" is often misleading because it suggests a relationship of equality (Smillie 2001). In discussing international aid and development, some have argued that, given the asymmetrical relationship between funders and implementers, partnership should not be understood in a legal sense, but more appropriately in terms of the partnership of marriage, involving complementary and different identities: "as with most marriages, the relationship is as much a site of struggle as a cause of harmony' (Stirrat and Henkel 1997). The nature of partnership and the roles and decisionmaking discretion of the partners are always under negotiation, and the way in which the partnership evolves reflects the power struggles taking place (Hilhorst 2003).

In addition, the term "partnership" is used to refer to a wide variety of arrangements. Extending the metaphor of marriage, we can distinguish partnerships in humanitarian aid that range from close and exclusive partnership to tendered contractual arrangements. These are summarized in Table 8–1.

Table 8–1. Partnership: Different Types of Relations

Type of Partnership	Metaphor
Family networks, such as IFRC, in which local partners are determined by corporate policies	Family
Long-term equal relationship, two-way accountability, and two-way policy advice	Marriage
Long trajectory, including capacity building and/or institutional support	Adoption
Incidental support on the basis of specific project	One-night stand
(Tendered) subcontracting	Prostitution

Source: Developed by Udan Fernando and Dorothea Hilhorst.

The metaphors imply no moral preference for one type of partnership over others. Rather, we would stress that each type of relationship may be useful for good humanitarian practice. However, we would make two qualifications. First is the need to be more explicit about the nature and the type of partnership in which organizations engage. Second is the need to examine how partnership is shaped in practice. As the following case illustrates, this defies simple definitions of working arrangements.

Let us consider an agency using the pseudonym "Dutch Co-Financing Agency (DCFA)." The agency has regional departments for long-term development aid, as well as a separate department of humanitarian assistance. Its partners in Sri Lanka include, according to the scheme presented in Table 8–1, family relations, adoptions, and one-night stands. Partners are engaged in development, health, peacebuilding, and human rights. The dozens of partnerships are mainly arranged through e-mail and reports, with an occasional visit by a project officer from The Hague.

When the tsunami struck, DCFA immediately dispatched one of its staff members to Sri Lanka. This person—let us call him Paul—used to be responsible for Sri Lanka but had recently been moved to a different desk. When Paul arrived, three days after the disaster struck, he first traveled around the country to meet DCFA's partners and assess needs, and then settled in Batticaloa, base of DCFA's program. When we met Paul two weeks later, he had set up a program worth around € 5 million. While other organizations were occupied with distributing food, nonfood items, and first aid, and were setting up temporary shelter (some of which DCFA had funded), DCFA had almost immediately moved in to restore people's livelihoods. In the course of ten days, discussions were held with local fishing cooperatives to establish needs, contracts were established with local wharves, and the first fifteen boats were already afloat. The program aimed to provide 2,800 canoes for the lagoon and 3,843 boats of different sizes for sea fishing within five months, to cover the livelihood needs of three districts. On January 22, less than one month after the tsunami, DCFA celebrated the official launch of the one-hundredth boat, complete with an international press conference. To develop the program, which was directly implemented by DCFA, the agency gathered considerable support from a group of medical doctors who had formed an environmental protection organization. One of them was a surgeon from Argentina who had been hired by DCFA and had worked for two years in the local hospital. Although this group of doctors did not belong to the standard DCFA partner network, Paul felt they were better suited to help organize the large-scale and logistically demanding project than were DCFA's other local partners.

Soon after our visit, we heard that problems were beginning to emerge.[7] Other agencies in Batticaloa thought that DCFA should work in a more coordinated way, rather than launching an ambitious program covering the entire fishery sector of three districts. The local DCFA partners complained that their role in the program was too limited. The head office in The Hague questioned some aspects of the program; for instance, whether the boats should be distributed free.

It seems that Paul and his local colleagues had become carried away with the program. Several factors played a role here. First, Paul was very much affected by the situation. Knowing the environment from his previous visits, he was shocked by the extent of destruction. He moved into the guesthouse in which he had always stayed: a gesture that was highly appreciated by the owners. This was the only building still standing on its entire block, and he was literally surrounded by reminders of the tsunami. Second, due to the spontaneous public response in the Netherlands, DCFA had some € 27 million for tsunami-affected people, an amount almost equal to the annual budget of the humanitarian aid department. As a result, Paul felt under pressure to devise a substantial program. Third, the feverish and competitive claim-staking was fairly generalized among the INGOs, which seemed highly adrenalin-driven over this period. Like many aid workers, Paul had hardly taken time to eat and had visibly lost weight under the pressure of getting a program running. Finally, he and his colleagues were caught up in the enthusiasm of getting a big job done and finding local fishermen extremely happy to have their boats restored within one month of the disaster. After the problems occurred, DCFA decided to trim the program down and focus more closely on coordination and further dialogue with their existing partners to define their respective roles in implementing the program.

The point here is that partnership is highly fluid and changes with circumstances. Before the tsunami, DCFA partners had little day-to-day involvement with DCFA, which mainly acted as a funding agency. During the first post-tsunami weeks, DCFA became an implementing agency that set up a program under the felt pressure of time, while disregarding and to some extent alienating a number of their local partners. To its credit DCFA is a learning organization that has built-in checks to adjust programs as they evolve and has engaged in the kind of meaningful dialogue with its partners that may result in a far more equal relationship than before.

All INGOs in different ways and to different extents act as funding partners to local NGOs. The ways in which partnerships evolve do not translate from good intentions straight to the field. Partnerships depend on the history of engagement, the demands of the specific situation, the constellation of actors in the humanitarian response, and especially on the ways in which these actors interpret and negotiate their relationship in practice. A meaningful discussion of partnership should therefore, in our opinion, be grounded in analyzing real partnerships as they develop on the ground, rather than being based on an ideal image of partnership.

Although some INGOs may abuse the notion of partnership to mask highly unequal relations, it is also true that there are many risks involved in engaging in partnership in the context of a major emergency. Working with local partners means working with organizations that have their own historically developed patterns of work, which may or may not be appropriate to the task at hand. An NGO's local ties may enhance its effectiveness, but such ties can also have adverse and harmful consequences, especially in situations of armed conflict. The influx of international organizations in emergency situations may also have a profound impact on the local organizational field. Such risks are real, and international organizations should invest in finding out about these realities, rather than relying on an idealized notion of what constitutes a "typical" local partner. How can INGOs ensure that partnership—in the sense of ownership, participation, and equality—is a reality rather than an illusion, serving only to legitimize the humanitarian enterprise? How can they ensure that partnerships can indeed live up to their promise and contribute to building more resilient and capable societies?

CONCLUSION

From three different angles we have argued for the importance of research grounded in the everyday practice of humanitarian aid. The case of Kees and Annette concerned the identity of humanitarians. Although humanitarian organizations have a tendency to defend the boundaries around themselves, invoking their principled approach as their main distinction, this case tells us that differences between those who deliver aid cannot be predetermined, but have to be empirically established. The case of the joint Buddhist/Christian project concerned the politics of aid. Although it is a tautology to say that aid is political, the degree to which different kinds of politics intertwine and inform each other in practice is often understated. As a result, what appears to be a principled discussion may veil organizational politicking or attempts to establish legitimacy. The final section of this chapter dwelled on the issue of humanitarian partnership and showed how the concept of partnership can hide diverse meanings that are subject to change and social negotiation. What is agreed upon on paper may be very different from the way the partnership evolves in practice.

Starting from practice also has ramifications for the way in which we talk about humanitarianism. Discussions and fundraising campaigns relating to international aid conjure up a world of professionals who are motivated by high principles, bidding for the admiration and respect of the public at large. Media representations of agencies in tsunami response portray a different reality, often presenting humanitarian organizations as mainly self-interested and competitive. By relating the "petty normality" of humanitarian aid, as we have tried to do here, it is possible to counteract distancing discourses about humanitarian actors. Humanitarians are not heroes. Neither are they selfish vultures. Nor indeed do they correspond to any other stereotype concocted by their friends or foes. Accounts of everyday NGO practices and dilemmas correct blind expectations, expose uncritical admiration, and put unrealistic critiques into perspective.

NOTES

[1] This research was conducted together with Marijgje Wijers Tangalle, who did fieldwork on the tsunami response in Sri Lanka from late December 2004 to the end of March 2005. We thank Marijgje for sharing her insights and field observations.

[2] Although one speaks of three factions, JVP is currently represented in the government.

[3] The visitors, accompanied by Udan Fernando, were a group of foreigners who represented the aid agency that sent the money; the visit occurred on January 8, 2005.

[4] At Tangalle on March 16, 2005, (www.colombopage.com/archive/March16123144JV.html). Soon the Presidential Secretariat announced that "The Sri Lankan government has categorically rejected media reports quoting President Chandrika Kumaratunga as saying that the government had not received even a cent in tsunami aid. The Secretariat reported that what the president had said was: "The international assistance pledged as tsunami aid did not consist of cash and [the] cash funds received were only those remitted to the President's Fund and the Prime Minister's Fund" (www.colombopage.com/archive/March21123438JV.html).

[5] "Sri Lanka Accuses NGOs of Ethnic Bias and Political Agendas," *Asian Tribune,* June 4, 2005, available at www.asiantribune.com/show_news.php?id=13943 (retrieved November 8, 2005).

[6] Estimate based on various interviews.

[7] After a joint visit by Dorothea Hilhorst and Marijgje Wijers in January 2005, Marijgje stayed in touch with the program, while Dorothea conducted several follow-up interviews at DCFA headquarters in The Hague.

REFERENCES

Bailey, F.G. (1971) *Gifts and Poison: The Politics of Reputation,* Oxford: Basil Blackwell.

Bakewell, O. (2000) "Uncovering Local Perspectives on Humanitarian Assistance and Its Outcomes," *Disasters* 24(2): 103–116.

Fernando, Udan (2003) *NGOs in Sri Lanka: Past and Present Trends,* Colombo: Wasala Publications.

Frerks, G. and B. Klem (eds.) (2004) *Dealing with Diversity: Sri Lankan Discourses on Peace and Conflict,* The Hague: Netherlands Institute of International Relations "Clingendael."

Hilhorst, Dorothea (2002) "Being Good at Doing Good? Quality and Accountability of Humanitarian NGOs," *Disasters* 26(3): 193–212.

Hilhorst, Dorothea (2003) *The Real World of NGOs: Discourse, Diversity and Development,* London: Zed Books.

Hilhorst, Dorothea (2005) "Dead Letter or Living Document: The Code of Conduct of the Red Cross and Red Crescent Movement and NGOs in Disaster Relief," forthcoming in *Disasters.*

Hilhorst, Dorothea and N. Schmiemann (2002) "Humanitarian Principles and Organisational Culture: The Case of Médecins Sans Frontières, Holland," *Development in Practice* 12(3&4): 490–500.

Hulme, D. and J. Goodhand (2000) "NGOs and Peace Building in Complex Political Emergencies: Final Report to the Department for International Development," Peace Building and Complex Political Emergencies, Working Paper Series, Paper No 12. Manchester: IDPM, University of Manchester.

Kerkvliet, B. (1991) *Everyday Politics in the Philippines: Class and Status Relations in a Central Luzon Village,* Quezon City: New Day Publishers.

Long, N. (1992) "From paradigm Lost to Paradigm Regained? The Case for an Actor-oriented Sociology of Development," in N. Long and A. Long (eds.) *Battlefields of Knowledge: The Interlocking of Theory and Practice in Social Research and Development,* London and New York: Routledge.

Long, N. (2001) *Development Sociology: Actor Perspectives,* London/New York: Routledge.

Slim, Hugo (1999) "Future Imperatives? Quality, Standards and Human Rights," report of a study to explore quality standards for the British Overseas Aid Group (BOAG), Centre for Development and Emergency Practice (CENDEP), Oxford: Oxford Brookes University.

Smillie, Ian (ed.) (2001) *Patronage or Partnership: Local Capacity Building in Humanitarian Crises,* Bloomfield, CT: Kumarian Press.

Stirrat, R.L. and Heiko Henkel (1997) "The Development Gift: The Problem of Reciprocity in the NGO World," *Annals of the American Academy of Political and Social Science* 554:66–79.

Uvin, Peter (1998) *Aiding Violence: The Development Enterprise in Rwanda,* West Hartford, CT: Kumarian Press.

First published in *Development in Practice* 16(3&4): 292–302 in 2006.

NINE

Aid Partnership in the Bougainville Conflict: The Case of a Local Women's NGO and Its Donors

JONATHAN MAKUWIRA

CHAPTER SUMMARY

This chapter documents lessons learned from a study of aid partnerships in post-conflict development and peacebuilding in Bougainville. It examines how donor agencies, in this case the Australian Agency for International Development (AusAID) through the International Women's Development Agency (IWDA), contributed to the successes and failures of the Leitana Nehan Women's Development Agency (LNWDA). Although the donors contributed to the organizational development and capacity of the LNWDA, the balance of power remains unequal. Furthermore, the deployment of an intermediary body in the partnership exerts considerable pressure on the LNWDA, because it has to deal with multiple demands for accountability, which affect the impact of its own work on the ground. It is argued that in order to enhance the impact of their assistance, donor agencies need to develop a framework in which partnerships are sustained through mutual and less demanding accountabilities.

INTRODUCTION

Recent writers on conflict, peacebuilding, and development[1] have focused not only on the causes and prevention of conflicts but also on the role of aid and aid agencies in facilitating development and peacebuilding. The theme of maximizing the effectiveness of aid by establishing partnerships for peace and developing collaborative mechanisms, both within the international community and in the affected country, dominates current debates on post-conflict peacebuilding and development. While considering both short-term and long-term solutions to conflicts, the debate has also focused on ways in which donor agencies can strengthen the capacity and governance of states, and also how post-conflict states can recognize the roles that civil society actors, local community members, and the international donor community play in building sustainable peace and development. Prominent in this process is restoring trust, building accountable and transparent structures, and reinforcing the rule of law.

This chapter documents the lessons learned from a study of aid partnerships involving a donor agency, an intermediary organization, and a recipient organization engaged in post-conflict development and peacebuilding in Bougainville. The paper critically examines how donor agencies, particularly the Australian Agency for International Development (AusAID) through the International Women's Development Agency (IWDA), contributed to the successes and failures of the Leitana Nehan Women's Development Agency (LNWDA). It charts the dynamics of partnerships among the three organizations and examines the following four topics:

- How the partnership between LNWDA and AusAID/IWDA has changed over time
- The influence that each of the three organizations has had on the others
- The factors that enhanced or inhibited partnership
- How the organizations dealt with both opportunities and challenges in their partnership to promote development and peacebuilding

The study explores some fundamental issues concerning aid—for example, the dynamics of ownership, mutuality, trust, and power or control. It also examines how donors' changing agendas affect their relationships with partner organizations, particularly given their different points of departure and the tensions between them; and it considers how aid partnerships can facilitate or hinder development and peacebuilding.

THE BOUGAINVILLE CONFLICT

The island of Bougainville lies approximately 1,000 kilometers northeast of Port Moresby, the capital of Papua New Guinea (PNG), of which it is an autonomous province. Conflict was triggered in 1998 by a combination of social and environmental effects of the open-pit Panguna copper mine situated in the center of the island (Denoon 2000). The mine was managed by Bougainville Copper Limited (BCL), a subsidiary of the British–Australian mining giant Rio Tinto Zinc/Conzinc Riotinto of Australia (now known as Rio Tinto), with the PNG government as a minority shareholder.

The copper mine was a strong contributor to PNG's economy (Böge and Garasu 2004). However, a decade before the beginning of the conflict, landowners were increasingly resentful of the copper and gold mine in Panguna. It had been established against local wishes and was seen to disrupt the people's way of life. Bougainvilleans have been forced to share a cultural and linguistic identity asserted by outsiders, and the influx of workers from elsewhere in PNG gradually alienated and marginalized the indigenous Bougainvilleans. Their sense of being exploited and deprived of the benefits of the mining revenues, coupled with PNG's disregard of the environmental implications of the mining industry and the refusal to compensate for land loss, resulted in separatist demands (Böge and Garasu 2004). There followed a period of secessionist conflict between the Bougainville Revolutionary Army (BRA) and the PNG Defence Force. Australia's support for PNG was largely intended to protect its interest in the mining industry, as well as its colonial legacy. However, when a ceasefire (the Burnham Truce) was reached in October 1997, the political landscape was reconfigured, and Australia's role, along with that of New Zealand, became that of brokering a peace deal (Regan 1998).

BACKGROUND TO THE RESEARCH PROJECT

Through the Australian Agency for International Development (AusAID), the Australian government has provided essential financial assistance to Bougainville. This has focused on peacebuilding activities, social development, and resolution of conflict through support for peace and negotiation processes and for post-conflict reconstruction efforts to restore stability. Eagles (2002) claims that AusAID has been the largest donor, with $A 134 million (approximately € 82,270,000) earmarked for various development and rehabilitation programs. There is a considerable range of international NGOs and donor agencies in Bougainville, but the Australian development NGOs constitute the second largest contingency after those based in New Zealand.

Most of these international NGOs and donor agencies, such as AusAID and New Zealand Aid, work through or with local NGOs, the majority of which continue to engage in activities such as literacy and numeracy education, reproductive health counseling, small business training, capacity building, and human rights and peace education.

A number of organizations have participated and continue to participate in the peacebuilding processes, including a reconciliation process initiated by various local NGOs. The Leitana Nehan Women's Development Agency (LNWDA) was established in 1992 by a group of women from northern Bougainville who wished to contribute to the restoration of peace by promoting nonviolence and women's rights, and the empowerment of women as agents of social change (Carl 2000:10). LNWDA is one of the few local NGOs in Bougainville with a reputation for securing funding from overseas donors, its largest donor being AusAID. Although LNWDA enjoys a relatively stable partnership with various donor agencies, there are many concerns about the role of aid agencies in Bougainville's development programs.

Eagles (2002) observes that many international NGOs (INGOs) operating in Bougainville have been criticized by local NGOs and community-based organizations for setting up programs that cut across or bypass existing local initiatives. In particular, international aid agencies and development organizations are believed to have failed to realize or appreciate Bougainvilleans' resourcefulness and their desire to control their own development destiny. Furthermore, Eagles reports widespread local criticism of aid programs that create dependency on outside funds and/or follow a development model that many Bougainvilleans believe was the cause of the crisis in the first place. Other commentators (AID/WATCH 2004) have pointed out that many of the development programs are designed, developed, implemented, and monitored by managers appointed by AusAID. This raises the question of whether such aid packages really benefit the recipient organizations or countries. In other words, whose agenda does the aid serve?

THEORETICAL FRAMEWORK

The research derives its theoretical focus from two major themes in development—namely, development aid and partnership building. There is heated debate on the reality of aid, both in conflict and in stable states, particularly when it involves more than one partner. Commentators on the foreign aid industry (Martinussen and Engberg-Pedersen 2003; Hughes 2003; Fowler 2002; Anderson 1999) have questioned its effectiveness. They ask, for instance, why is aid given, and how is it justified to the recipient countries? How is development cooperation carried out, and to whose benefit; and what is the future of aid? Critical to these questions is the issue of donors' motives, goals, and strategies and also how aid should be governed (AusAID 2003; Singh 2003). The issues of donor conditionality and control over aid have also dominated the aid debate (Stokke 1995; Sogge 2002). On the side of the recipient country or organization, the debate has largely centered on the notions of accountability, transparency, and good governance as mechanisms that engender positive results. Much of the literature on this topic has sought to provide a clear framework for what exactly donors and aid recipients should do. In part these concerns reflect the complexity of the aid industry in the twenty-first century, particularly in countries ravaged by conflict. The current study, which was conducted in a state that is gradually emerging from conflict, examined and unraveled some of the critical issues pertaining to the role of aid agencies in building local capacity and empowerment.

The debate on partnership had also attracted international commentary, much of it critical of the types of partnership practised in the aid industry (Bennett and Gibbs 1996; INTRAC 2001; Fowler 2000b, 2002; Hughes 2003; Anderson 1999; Martinussen and Engberg-Pedersen 2003; Makuwira 2003). Although NGOs have been drawn to the concept of partnership as an expression of solidarity that goes beyond financial aid, there has been little empirical research on what NGOs actually mean by partnership, how they put it into practice, who benefits from it, and the challenges that they face in developing and managing effective partnerships. Absent from the discourses on partnership building is the aspect of engaging intermediary organizations as conduits between donor agencies and recipient organizations. Various partnership models have been developed (Fowler 1997, 2000b, 2002; INTRAC 2001; Leach 1997), but none reflects the tripartite nature of the current study. INTRAC (2001:3), for example, identifies three different types of partnerships:

- Funding-based, from a funding-only partnership at one end of the spectrum to one based on policy dialogue without funding at the other
- Capacity-based, in which a Southern partner with limited capacity requires support from the Northern partner, as opposed to a partnership with a strong, autonomous organization that contributes from its own experiences
- Trust-based, ranging from control over a Southern partner to unconditional trust in it

Leach (1997) identifies six models of collaboration among local development NGOs and INGOs that act as donor agencies:

1. In the contracting model, the INGO pays an independent NGO to provide a well-defined service package under conditions established largely by the INGO.
2. In the dependent franchise model, a formally independent NGO functions as a field office of an INGO that provides most or all of its direction and funding.
3. The spin-off NGO model—along with the contracting and the dependent franchise models—is expected over time to become organizationally and financially independent of the INGO.
4. In the visionary patronage model, the INGO and the local NGO share a development vision and jointly agree on goals, outcome measures, and reporting requirements for a program that the NGO implements and the INGO supports with funds and other resources.
5. In the collaborative model (closely related to the visionary patronage model), the INGO and NGO share decisionmaking power over planning and implementation of joint programs that are implemented by the NGO with funding and technical support from the INGO.
6. In the mutual governance model of collaboration, the INGO and the NGO have decisionmaking power—or at least substantial

influence—over each other's policies and practices at both the organizational and program levels (Leach 1997:3).

The kind of partnership model that NGOs adopt may depend on three fundamental principles: the effectiveness of the work on both sides, the quality of their relationship, and clarity about the purpose of their partnership. This study examines which of these partnership models was adopted by the LNWDA and AusAID/IWDA. Particular emphasis is placed on the processes of starting, maintaining, and ending partnerships, as well as examining issues of accountability, transparency, and shared governance (indirect power and implicit influence), and their implications for the partnership.

SIGNIFICANCE OF THE STUDY

The study reported in this chapter seeks to contribute to the ongoing debate about the roles that NGOs and aid agencies play in peacebuilding and post-conflict recovery processes. It adds to a fairly limited pool of empirical data in relation to Bougainville and also provides some insights into the broader literature on the role of aid and aid agencies in development and post-conflict recovery, expanding on Mary B. Anderson's (1999) work in *Do No Harm,* which shows how aid can support not only peace or war but also sustainable development. Finally the study seeks to enhance the work of the LNWDA in Bougainville, particularly in its quest to develop an understanding not only of dilemmas inherent in aid partnerships but also of related issues such as accountability and the governance of aid, and how these issues affect LNWDA's obligation to its constituency.

METHODOLOGY AND LIMITATIONS

The methods used were purely qualitative, in the sense of being "a situated activity that locates the observer in the world" (Denzin and Lincoln 2000:3), drawing on documentary evidence and individual interviews. Fieldwork was undertaken in Bougainville for a period of two weeks, during which semistructured interviews were conducted with staff of LNWDA and other members of the community closely associated with the organization. Some interviews were also conducted with staff in IWDA and AusAID, although with limited success in the

latter case. The documents consulted related to AusAID-funded programs in Bougainville and were mainly project proposals, annual
reports, evaluation reports, and memoranda of understanding between
AusAID/IWDA and LNWDA. Content analysis, in which both the content and the contexts of documents are analyzed (Robson 2002), and
policy and evaluation analysis, which examines the contexts for social
policies and programs and the effectiveness of their delivery and impact
(Ritchie and Spencer 1994), were used to identify the various ways in
which both LNWDA and AusAID/IWDA conceptualized and opera-
tionalized their aid partnership, and to identify tensions, contradictions,
and ambivalences in the partnership.

The study was constrained by the unavailability of some of the key
staff in both IWDA and AusAID who had overseen the establishment of
the tripartite partnership. This led unavoidably to an overreliance on
documentary evidence. However, although this study does not make
strong generalizations, the results do provide some lessons and raise
some questions for further research and analysis of development aid and
partnership building.

FINDINGS AND DISCUSSION

The basic theoretical principles governing any sustainable partnership
stipulate that "authentic partnership implies . . . a joint commitment to a
long-term intervention, shared responsibility for achievement, reciprocal
obligation, equality, mutuality and balance of power" (Fowler 2000c,
quoted in Brehm 2001:11). Broadly speaking, partnerships describe a
wide variety of institutional arrangements, designed not only as a means
of sharing information and resources but also to produce results that one
partner working alone could not achieve. As a process, partnerships are
dynamic as goals, abilities, and relationships change. How these principles are reflected in aid partnerships remains a challenge, and the findings
of this study were replete with claims and counterclaims, contradictions,
and ambivalences underlying the complexity of aid partnership.

THE DYNAMICS OF PARTNERSHIP BUILDING

Both documentary evidence (Carl 2000; Cox 2004) and interview data
strongly suggest that the Leitana Nehan Women's Development Agency
commands major respect for its building of relatively meaningful

partnerships with aid agencies based mainly overseas, such as Community Aid Abroad (now Oxfam Australia), Oxfam New Zealand, the British Embassy, and World Vision International. LNWDA's partnership with AusAID through the International Women's Development Agency (IWDA) is both in practice and in theory founded largely on a shared vision, reflecting Leach's (1997) notion of visionary patronage and the collaborative model. In addition, the findings reflect a capacity-based difference model, as suggested by INTRAC (2001). There are significant overlaps between the three models. The conflict in Bougainville had a profound impact on women, and LNWDA's initial contact with IWDA at the 1995 Fourth Global Conference on Women in Beijing provided an opportunity to share the experience of the role of women in this conflict. Although this marked the genesis of information exchange and research sharing, both formally and informally, the unbalanced collaboration persisted because of Bougainville's poor infrastructure.

Although LNWDA's partnership with AusAID can be described as "indirect," the visionary relationship is clearly reflected in the three organizations' desire to improve the well-being of women as well as that of the wider community. A critical analysis of the respective visions of the three organizations shows links in their emphasis on poverty alleviation and facilitating participation of the marginalized people in the development process. Table 9–1 summarizes the visionary partnership. Two points relating to Table 9–1 need to be highlighted. First, Australia's overseas aid has strategic implications. Although the focus is on poverty

Table 9–1. Three Mission Statements

Organization	Mission Statement	Source
AusAID	Advance Australia's national interests by assisting developing countries to reduce poverty and achieve sustainable development	AusAID 1997: 3
IWDA	Support women's efforts to improve their lives and choices and those of their families and communities, and to advance women's human rights, with emphasis on women who are particularly marginalized or suffer poverty or oppression.	IWDA
LNWDA	Meaningfully contribute to the restoration of peace [in] Bougainville by promoting non-violence and women's rights and empowering women as agents of change to improve their social status	Carl 2000:10

alleviation, there is a strong realization that high levels of poverty can increase the risk of violent conflict. Conflict and instability tend to undermine efforts to reduce poverty and achieve sustainable development. Moreover, instability in Bougainville might ultimately pose a threat to Australia's security, hence the need to implement aid programs that are "determined and implemented in partnership with development countries" (AusAID 1997:3). Although we acknowledge the strength of visionary partnership as based on a joint agreement to work collaboratively to achieve a common goal, in practice there is a significant contradiction, highlighted in the following.

THE LOCUS OF INFLUENCES IN THE PARTNERSHIP

Contemporary rhetoric on development aid implies a significant shift in control and distribution of power between donors and recipient NGOs. However, the gap between words and action continues to widen. As an IDS Policy Briefing (2001) observes, although partnership implies collegial equality, donor agencies will always call the shots.

The partnership between LNWDA and AusAID is markedly unbalanced in favor of AusAID and IWDA. There are two underlying reasons for this. First is the emphasis on the local NGO's accountability to IWDA, which in turn is accountable to AusAID. Second, the strength of LNWDA's partnership with AusAID is measured by how far the intended outcomes are achieved. In other words, it is a performance-enhanced partnership, the dynamics of which are significantly influenced by LNWDA's dual accountability to IWDA (directly) and to AusAID (indirectly). The fact that the two women's organizations share a common vision entails an important degree of understanding and trust, as has been shown through their history of association. As one participant observed:

> The partnership started out of common concern over issues that women faced and was based on friendship, trust, and information exchange. Eventually, the partnership evolved into working together on projects. As the aid industry has changed, IWDA has faced greater constraints, such as greater competition for funding and a greater focus on outcomes. This has impacted on the nature of the partnership between the two organizations to become more focused on a project delivery.
>
> (Participant 1)

Containing the donors' influence on an organization's vision is a skill that many local NGOs have yet to develop. LNWDA's experience in working with other donor agencies, albeit on project-specific funding, seems to have helped it to hone negotiating skills that have resulted in developing its own institutional capacities. It was clear from talking to a number of staff members that LNWDA has strongly resisted being pushed into donor dependency. Of course, compliance with donor conditionality cannot always be avoided. "Throughout this time, LNWDA's loyalty to IWDA was a major factor in maintaining the partnership" (Participant 2). Despite this, we found very little negative influence from the donor in its development and peacebuilding activities. We judged that this was due to LNWDA's ability to mobilize local resources and volunteers, as well as its familiarity with donor practices,

OWNERSHIP AND CONTROL OF AID

Peter Uvin (1999) argues that all aid, at all times, creates incentives and disincentives for peace or for war. An extensive literature indicates that ownership has a positive impact on the outcome of aid. The nature of partnerships among the three organizations suggests conflicting concepts of who controls the financial resources and, in essence, who owns the aid package.

According to AusAID, when funds are disbursed to intermediary Australian NGOs, the emphasis is on promoting the *Australian identity* of the activity in an appropriate manner. Furthermore, the role of the intermediary NGO is to be "responsible for the design, delivery, monitoring, and evaluation of the activities, submission of reports and acquittals, and for fully accounting for funds provided by AusAID" (AusAID n.d.) AID/WATCH (2004) recorded that IWDA received $A 529,785 (€ 326,000) for the project with LNWDA. Contrary to the rhetoric about ownership by aid recipients, this fact runs counter to the claims made by some participants in the study. More importantly, it highlights what is not said by recipient organizations that are reluctant to criticize the sources of their funding. For example, one of the officials in the intermediary organization hinted that ownership is a shared responsibility. Although this statement sounds sympathetic, it sharply contradicts AusAID's policy on who is in charge between the intermediary NGO and the recipient NGO, whereas the interview data suggested that overall responsibility and ownership rests with AusAID. For instance, in response to the question of who decides how aid resources are used, one participant observed:

> Everyone [decides how aid resources are used]. Ultimately AusAID has the final say on how resources are used, and resources have to be directed within AusAID's strategic framework. IWDA influences how resources are used by assessing the local situation, applying learning from other IWDA projects, and working within the context of the IWDA and AusAID strategic framework. Leitana Nehan provides the local knowledge and determines where to direct resources and sets priorities for their programs.
>
> (Participant 1)

One official in LNWDA reaffirmed that *"the organization decided where to go because we know the situation and it was really good."* However, this individual was quick to depart from such a simplistic view, pointing out that "now we are finding it difficult because AusAID and other donors are dictating. But at the beginning it was us, we dictated where the funds should go" (Participant 3).

Although these sentiments reveal a significant division of responsibilities, there are also contradictions, in the sense that no power is ultimately given to the local NGO to do as it sees fit, based on its own understanding of the local situation. This is not to say that donors do not have the responsibility to ensure accountability and transparency in the conduct of the work that it supports, but the *degree* to which this condition is applied can significantly interfere with development projects. Such practices contradict the fundamental principles that govern successful and authentic partnerships. They also raise questions about who benefits from aid and whose interests are being served.

CHALLENGES OF AID PARTNERSHIPS

The provision of development aid by the so-called developed countries has political and moral implications. It is political because donor agencies, as noted earlier, have to promote national interests. In the case of the Australian government, it is clearly stated that aid programs "will remain identifiably Australian—it is a reflection of Australian values and is a projection of those values abroad" (AusAID 1997:3). The discourse of "our national interest" essentially violates the principle of the "common good" that is invoked by advocates for social justice, because many of the developed countries have exerted control over—and have even encroached upon and siphoned off—the meager resources of very poor nations. This sharply contradicts the notion of "poverty eradication" and ultimately results in the ever-growing gap between the "haves and have-nots." Australia's moral obligation, expressed through its aid program, points to the gravity of this state of affairs. We will highlight a few of these major issues as they are exposed and experienced by AusAID/IWDA and LNWDA.

Poor Strategic Planning when Establishing Partnerships

As noted earlier, donors' responses to changing conflicts and post-conflict situations can have a damaging effect on seemingly smooth-running partnerships. Part of the solution is to ensure a clear long-term strategy when donors establish such partnerships. Some partnerships may be superficial and relate only to "project-specific collaboration." As one official noted:

> [D]onors need to do greater planning prior to working within countries as to what resources are actually needed and what can be coordinated with other donors. They also need to plan for withdrawals and be careful not to create NGOs as services that will not be maintained in the long term. (Participant 4)

In the case of AusAID/IWDA and LNWDA, changes in the donors' focus contributed to the fluidity of their partnership because there was no long-term plan in place. At the time of this study, LNWDA badly needed more funds in order to continue with its development activities.

Sustainability

The sustainability of development and peacebuilding programs is known to be problematic—in this particular case largely due to changes in AusAID's funding priorities. Although the project was thought to be good, such a change in AusAID's priorities would mean that the work would no longer be funded. This meant that the partnership became heavily focused on fundraising, a fact that in turn affected LNWDA's long-term outlook (Participant 2).

The outbreak of conflicts around the world and the occurrence of natural disasters like the 2004 Asian tsunami often result in donors shifting their attention from existing to immediate demands. Although this is to an extent inevitable, contingency measures have to be in place. At the same time, NGOs need to work on mustering local support in order to sustain their development activities in the event that donors' agendas shift. If the NGO is raising funds but is not committed to continuing its local-level work, there is bound to be resentment on the part of the intended beneficiaries, who may perceive the NGO to be using them for its own benefit. Post-conflict work is generally sensitive and highly politicized because beneficiaries participate in the development and/or humanitarian processes with high expectations. Tangible results therefore play a vital role in preempting a reaction that may serve to heighten the tensions and ultimately lead to further conflicts.

High Staff Turnover in IWDA

Linked to the lack of sustainability was the high staff turnover in IWDA at the level of leadership and senior program management. This meant that LNWDA had to adjust to new staff and often new administrative systems, which in turn affected its own collaborative mechanisms and strategic planning. Cox (2004) affirms this in her evaluation:

> The weaknesses of the relationship are associated with the tension and stress that arose out of very regular changes in IWDA staff and the pressures associated with increasingly bureaucratic and onerous project documentation and reporting. The staff changeovers meant that it was difficult to sustain the original quality and solidarity-based relationship. The relationship became more impersonal and based on LNWDA being held accountable to various IWDA representatives, who each had their own personality and way of relating and doing things.
>
> (Cox 2004:22)

In some cases the incoming IWDA staff relied on LNWDA to gain some understanding of the dynamics of the partnership.

Strict Accountability Deadlines

Another challenge was that of accountability deadlines. Interviewees in IWDA and LNWDA expressed concern about strict deadline demands, whereas the donor agency was oblivious of the lack of resources and infrastructure necessary to facilitate compliance:

> A major challenge was meeting accountability requirements that were set in Australia. Bougainville does not have resources or infrastructure . . . and everything takes longer to do. More consideration of these constraints would have been useful.
>
> (Participant 6)

Donors' Focus on Quantifiable Results

Linked to the challenge of strict accountability requirements was donors' disregard for one of the most important aspects in any post-conflict development and peacebuilding work—management of trauma. Because this partnership was result-oriented, activities related to training in the management of trauma (which were largely unquantifiable) were not counted as successes, thus underscoring a major weakness of donor agencies in aid partnerships.

As one interviewee observed, when you are working in an area where most people have experienced great trauma, where next-door neighbors may have raped or killed your sons or daughters, and where great community divides still exist, simply persuading people to meet and talk to each other, or persuading people to talk in public about violence, is a major achievement (Participant 1).

Without proper reconciliation and healing, post-conflict development and peacebuilding are daunting tasks. What makes the work even harder for implementing agencies is the fact that donors rarely visit the work that they are funding, or have the chance to interact with the intended beneficiaries, whose voices are rarely heard.

CONCLUSION AND RECOMMENDATIONS

Despite the rhetoric, it remains difficult to achieve partnership among donors, intermediaries, and local organizations in post-conflict development and peacebuilding because of the many layers of accountability demands that seem to obstruct local initiatives. As AusAID (1997:12) acknowledges, "the volume of aid spending will always be a difficult issue." In theory, there is a clear framework within which to implement long-term partnerships, based on the fundamental principles proposed by Alan Fowler (2000a, 2002). However, unless donors are willing to step out of their ivory towers to engage directly with their beneficiaries and learn from their mistakes, it is most unlikely that the political dimension of aid will shift the status quo. It is not surprising that many of the suggestions proposed, such as "allowing time for building trust and relationship, taking a long-term approach and planning for withdrawal, and putting great effort and time into reconciliation and healing" (Participant 2), were effectively recommendations for good practice.

Although this study focused on one NGO, it can be extrapolated that Australia's general approach to aid provision through NGOs and commercial companies is problematic, in the sense that when the focus is on commercial rather than altruistic relations, impact will be compromised. This mode of aid delivery also makes it difficult to monitor the impact of contracted NGOs and/or companies. For example, of the twenty-one AusAID contractors in PNG between January 2003 and March 2004, nineteen were Australia-based NGOs and companies (AID/WATCH 2004). How they are monitored in order to ascertain their impact remains debatable—a fact which underlines the question of who really benefits.

In the context of the post-conflict situation in Bougainville, Ahai (1999:135) provides a clear and succinct warning, which should serve as a lesson to many development and donor organizations:

> Donor countries as well as International NGOs will need to be sensitive to the development aspirations of Bougainvilleans, even within the political framework of PNG, and design the delivery of their support in ways that are mutually beneficial. The current practice in a few international NGOs . . . of bringing in outsiders will simply promote the "cargo development mentality" typical of pre-crisis development. The development tensions . . . and long-term sustainable peace may be mere rhetoric if donor countries [sic] support is coached by their own incipient interests.

In other words, the issues in Bougainville revolve around respect and autonomy. Donor agencies such as AusAID, operating through intermediary organizations and/or companies or otherwise, must realize that the right people to develop and build peace are the local population themselves. Technical support is what is needed.

Although many donor agencies operate according to the hidden agenda of their own "national interests" when they engage in partnerships with local organizations, the lessons drawn from the case of Bougainville call for coherent and responsive aid that recognizes the political, social, economic, and cultural needs of local contexts. That said, it would be unfair to place all the blame on the donor agencies. The governance of aid is a collective responsibility, and therefore all the parties involved must be committed to this aspiration. Recipient organizations also have a part to play in maximizing the donors' efforts. If they are to negotiate for greater flexibility on the part of donor agencies, then the recipient countries and/or organizations must also be willing to ensure that every coin of taxpayers' money is accounted for and used to benefit those communities that are most vulnerable.

ACKNOWLEDGMENTS

I acknowledge the University of New England's financial support through its Internal Research Grant. Many thanks to Peter Ninnes and Bert Jenkins for their support throughout the research process.

NOTES

[1] Anderson 1999; Boyce 2002; Patrick 2000; Galama and van Tongeren 2002; OECD 2001; AID/WATCH 2004.

REFERENCES

Ahai, Naihuwo G. (1999) "Grassroots Development Vision for New Bougainville," in G. Harris, N. Ahai and R. Spence (eds.) *Building Peace in Bougainville,* Armidale: University of New England.

AID/WATCH (2004) "Boomerang Aid: Australia and Papua New Guinea, Who Is Telling the Truth?" Briefing paper, December 2004, AID/WATCH, available at www.aidwatch.org.au. (retrieved January 10, 2005).

Anderson, Mary B. (1999) *Do No Harm: How Aid can Support Peace or War,* Boulder, CO: Lynne Rienner Publishers.

AusAID (1997) "Better Aid for a Better Future: Seventh Annual Report to Parliament on Australia's Development Cooperation Program and the Government's Response to the Committee of Review of Australia's Overseas Aid Program," Canberra: Commonwealth of Australia.

AusAID (2003) "Papua New Guinea and the Pacific: A Development Perspective," Canberra: AusAID.

AusAID (n.d.) "Overseas Aid," available at www.ausaid.gov.au/default.cfm (retrieved December 27, 2005).

Bennett, Jon and Sara Gibbs (1996) "NGO Funding Strategies: An Introduction for Southern and Eastern NGOs," Oxford: ICVA/INTRAC.

Böge, Volker and Lorraine Garasu Sr. (2004) "Papua New Guinea: A Success Story of Postconflict Peacebuilding in Bougainville," in A. Heijmans, N. Simmonds, and H. van de Veens (eds.) *Searching for Peace in Asia Pacific: An Overview of Conflict Prevention and Peacebuilding Activities,* London: Lynne Rienner Publishers.

Boyce, James K. (2002) *Investing in Peace: Aid and Conditionality after Civil Wars,* Adelphi Paper 351, New York: Oxford University Press.

Brehm, Vicky M. (2001) "Promoting Effective North–South NGO Partnerships: A Comparative Study of 10 European NGOs," INTRAC Occasional Papers No. 35, Oxford: INTRAC.

Carl, Andy (2000) *Reflecting on Peace Practice Project: A Case Study,* Cambridge, MA: Collaborative for Development Action.

Cox, Elizabeth (2004) "Strengthening Communities for Peace Project: Evaluation Report," Leitana Nehan Women's Development Agency, Buka: Bougainville.

Denoon, Donald (2000) *Getting Under the Skin: The Bougainville Copper Agreement and the Creation of the Panguna Mine,* Melbourne: Melbourne University Press.

Denzin, Norman K. and Yvonna S. Lincoln (2000) *Handbook of Qualitative Research,* 2nd edition, Thousand Oaks, CA: Sage.

Eagles, Julie (2002) "Aid as an Instrument for Peace," in Andy Carl and Lorraine Garasu Sr. (eds.) *Accord: Weaving Consensus–The Papua New Guinea–Bougainville Peace Process,* London: Conciliation Resources.

Fowler, Alan (1997) *Striking a Balance: A Guide to Enhancing the Effectiveness of Non-Governmental Organisations in International Development,* London: Earthscan.

Fowler, Alan (2000a) "Questioning Partnership: The Reality of Aid and NGO Relations," guest-edited issue of *IDS Bulletin,* 31(3) (July).

Fowler, Alan (2000b) "Partnerships: Negotiating Relationships: A Resource for Non-Governmental Development Organisations," INTRAC Occasional Papers No. 32, Oxford: INTRAC.

Fowler, Alan (2000c) *The Virtuous Spiral: A Guide to Sustainability for NGOs in International Development,* London: Earthscan.

Fowler, Alan (2002) "Beyond Partnership: Getting Real about NGO Relationships in the Aid System," in Michael Edwards and Alan Fowler (eds.) *NGO Management,* London: Earthscan.

Galama, Anneke and Paul van Tongeren (eds.) (2002) "Towards Better Peacebuilding: On Lessons Learned, Evaluation Practices and Aid and Conflict," Utrecht: European Centre for Conflict Prevention.

Hughes, Helen (2003) "Aid Has Failed the Pacific," *Issue Analysis,* No. 33, May 7, Sydney: The Centre for Independent Studies.

IDS (2001) "Policy Briefing: The New Dynamics of Aid: Power, Procedures and Relationships," Brighton: Institute of Development Studies.

INTRAC (2001) "NGOs and Partnership, NGO Policy Briefing Paper No. 4 for the NGO Sector Analysis Programme," Oxford: INTRAC.

Leach, Mark (1997) "Models of Inter-organisational Collaboration in Development," *IDR Reports,* 11(7), available at www.jsi.com/idr/web%20 reports/html/11-7.html (retrieved October 28, 2004).

Makuwira, Jonathan J. (2003) "Non-Governmental Organizations, Participation and Partnership Building in Basic Education in Malawi," unpublished Ph.D. thesis, University of New England.

Martinussen, John D. and Poul Engberg-Pedersen (2003) *Aid: Understanding International Development Cooperation,* London: Zed Books.

OECD (2001) *The DAC Guidelines: Helping Prevent Violent Conflict,* Paris: OECD.

Patrick, Stewart (2000) "The Donor Community and the Challenge of Post-conflict Recovery," in S. Forman and S. Patrick (eds.) *Good Intentions: Pledges of Aid for Post-conflict Recovery,* Boulder, CO, and London: Lynne Rienner Publishing.

Regan, Anthony (1998) "Case study: Bougainville," in P. Harris and B. Reilly (eds.) *Democracy and Deep-Rooted Conflict: Options for Negotiation,* Stockholm: International IDEA.

Ritchie, Jane and Liz Spencer (1994) "Qualitative Data Analysis for Applied Policy Research" in A. Bryman and R.G. Burges (eds.) *Analysing Qualitative Data,* London: Routledge.

Robson, Colin (2002) *Real World Research,* 2nd edition, Oxford: Blackwell.

Singh, Kuvaljit (2003) "Aid and Good Governance: A Discussion Paper for the Reality of Aid," available at www.realityofaid.org (retrieved October 20, 2003).

Sogge, David (2002) *Give and Take: What's the Matter with Foreign Aid?* London: Zed Books.

Stokke, Olav (1995) "Aid and Political Conditionality: Core Issues and State of the Art," in O. Stokke (ed.) *Aid and Political Conditionality,* London: Frank Cass.

Uvin, Peter (1999) *The Influence of Aid in Situations of Violent Conflict,* Paris: OECD.

First published in *Development in Practice* 16(3&4): 322–333 in 2006.

TEN

Art and Disarmament: Turning Arms into Plowshares in Mozambique

FRANK JAMES TESTER

CHAPTER SUMMARY

Following the Renamo/Frelimo conflict and the 1992 Rome Accord ending hostilities, the Christian Council of Mozambique undertook to remove arms from the civilian population by trading them for development tools. The weapons were given to artists associated with a collective in the capital, Maputo. The weapons were cut into pieces and converted to sculptures that subsequently focused international attention on the Tools for Arms project, or *Transformação de Armas em Enxadas* (TAE). Although it succeeded in drawing attention to the proliferation of arms among civilians, and collected a considerable number of arms and munitions, the project encountered difficulties in relating the production of art to the overall initiative. This chapter examines the aspect of the project that produced art from weapons, with insight and observations based on fieldwork conducted for the Canadian University Services Overseas (CUSO) and the Canadian International Development Agency (CIDA).

INTRODUCTION: THE RENAMO/FRELIMO CONFLICT

Disarming civilian populations following internal conflicts in countries that have been heavily armed is increasingly important, not only in order to minimize the chance of further armed conflicts erupting once peace has been achieved, but also to address the subsequent use of weapons—particularly small arms—in robberies, hijackings, and kidnappings (Rotfeld 2000; Angola Roundtable 1999). Mozambique's history of armed conflict is a long and tortuous one, commencing in 1962 with the formation of Frelimo (*Frente de Libertação de Moçambique*) and the initiation of an armed struggle for independence from Portuguese rule in 1964. No sooner was independence achieved in 1975 than further conflict erupted in a confrontation that has been characterized by some as a civil war and by others as an invasion. Mozambique's independence and support for similar liberation struggles in Rhodesia and South Africa were the most probable reasons for the creation of Renamo (*Resistência Nacional Moçambicana*—also known as the Mozambican National Resistance or MNR). This guerrilla army originated in an agreement signed by the Rhodesian Central Intelligence Organization and the Portuguese before the April 1974 coup that ended the military dictatorship in Lisbon. Renamo also recruited inmates who were freed in raids on Mozambican reeducation camps and former Frelimo soldiers who had been imprisoned for corruption (Hall and Young 1997). Renamo received backing from Portuguese expatriates and rightwing private US foundations opposed to the Marxist leanings of the Frelimo government.

Renamo set about destabilizing the Frelimo government. It conducted operations within the country aimed at destroying rail and water lines, roads, and bridges. It waged a campaign of terror against local populations who were not supportive of Renamo. It burned and looted villages and kidnapped children, who were then used as soldiers. Following Robert Mugabe's successful struggle against the Ian Smith regime, South Africa continued to provide support and a base for Renamo's operations. It also supported Renamo bases in Malawi and inside Mozambique at Gorongosa, an area where it is believed there are still significant buried arms caches. The war was bloody, killing more than one million Mozambicans.

Founded in 1947, the Christian Council of Mozambique (CCM) attempted—commencing in 1988—to bring both sides in the conflict to the negotiating table. Its efforts culminated in the 1992 Rome Peace Accord. Anglican Bishop Dinis Sengulane describes what happened after a woman from Nampula Province asked at a church seminar what

would happen to all the guns in the country, now that the armed conflict
had ended:

> So the following day, when the seminar was continuing, I thought:
> "Well, okay—we will implement a Biblical disarmament program that
> will consist of four operations—four steps. The first step is to
> persuade the people to bring in their guns. . . . The second step is
> making the gun unusable: to destroy it, if possible, to dismantle it com-
> pletely so that even if the same people who had given us the gun were
> to try to ambush us in order to get it back, it won't be useful at all to
> them. The third is to give to the people an instrument of production. It
> could be—we had the idea that it could be exchanged for a plow, or a
> bicycle, or a sewing machine. And the fourth step would be to turn that
> gun into an instrument of production."
>
> (Bishop Sengulane, interviewed in Maputo, July 3, 2003)

The project outlined by Bishop Sengulane was launched on October 20,
1995. A major, but not the only, weapon of concern was the AK-47
Kalashnikov assault rifle. There is no reliable information on the number
of weapons remaining in the country following demobilization. One
source (Smith 1996) reported that in 1995, six million AK-47s were
believed to be in circulation. The situation was complicated by the
caching of arms by former Renamo soldiers during the UN peacekeeping
operation known as ONUMOZ, who were distrustful of the peace accord.
About 100,000 combatants were demobilized. Among the accord's conditions was the holding of democratic elections. Renamo subsequently
became a political party, seeking power by democratic means.

Some insight into the extent of the arms problem can be gained
from an examination of weapons collected by the TAE project as well
as weapons and ammunition collected as part of a joint undertaking by
the governments of South Africa and Mozambique. Dubbed "Operation
Rachel," this annual military exercise uncovered and destroyed 611
weapons caches between 1995 and 2003, as shown in Table 10–1. The
number of weapons collected can be compared with the arms and munitions collected through the TAE project (shown in Table 10–2). The
figures are revealing. It is evident that, compared to government activity, the CCM efforts were of largely symbolic value. This suggests that
the manner and extent to which CCM was connected to the civilian population, and was able to use this relationship to raise the awareness of
Mozambicans, was at least as important as the number of weapons

Table 10–1. Results of Operation Rachel Weapons Collection, 1995–2003

Type	1995	1996	1997	1998	1999
Handguns	8	13	79	353	453
Submachine guns	91	68	980	735	1,874
Rifles	981	355	4,345	3,183	8,864
Light/heavy machine guns	47	52	279	467	845
Mortars	15	44	35	21	115
Ammunition	23,153	136,639	3,000,000	155,314	3,315,106

	2000	2001	2002	2003	Total
Handguns	18	372	101	45	1,442
Submachine guns	126	467	346	235	4,922
Rifles	2,205	2,943	2,072	1,302	26,250
Light/heavy machine guns	66	148	47	1	1,952
Mortars	70	32	5	0	337
Ammunition	83,276	486,000	2,004,018	2,200,000	11,403,506

Source: Leão 2003.

collected. The figures also indicate that there were probably considerably fewer AK-47s in the country than suggested by Smith (1996).

ARMS TO ART

The transformation of weapons into works of art began in 1997 with funding from the Canadian High Commission and assignment to the TAE project of a cooperant working for the Canadian NGO CUSO.[1] An

Table 10–2. Arms Collected by TAE, 1995–1999

Year	1995	1996	1997	1998	1999	Total
Firearms	280	543	465	867	338	2,493
Explosives	1,172	844	57	103	33	2,209
Ammunition	10,489	9,943	2,881	33,307	10,226	66,846
Accessories	147	128	371	187	22	855
Engineering matter	5	7	1	0	2	15
Bayonets	75	4	1	1	0	81
Totals	12,168	11,469	3,776	34,465	10,621	72,499

Source: Tester and Teves 2004:36.

experimental workshop, *"Transformação de Armas em Objectos de Arte,"* was organized by a *nucleo,* a core group of fifteen artists, to see what they could do with the material. This successful undertaking was followed by an exhibition of the work in Maputo. From the outset there were indications that future complications might arise with the trans- formation process. In Mozambique—perhaps more so than is charac- teristic of Northern countries—artists are not always taken seriously. The idea that artists "do art" for a living is not well understood. Artists are often seen as living in a fringe culture, and doing art is seen as a passion or hobby, not as a means of making a living. At the time, some artists indicated they wanted to be paid for their efforts.

One of the artists explained the origins of and his relationship with the project as follows:

> The project started in '97 and in the beginning, nothing happened. We just worked; there were not any exhibitions. After two to three years, we still worked. We had to find the money. We used our own money to buy the materials (welders, welding rod, saws, etc.). . . . When the project started, we had all the materials from the project. But after that, all the material is broken—you know—and we still work, and we continue to use our money to do—to work—because we are artists and we're interested to work with this project.

> (Interview with Gonçalo Mabunda, June 10, 2003, Maputo)

Prior to receiving US$ 35,000 in March 1997, the TAE project had received about US$ 60,000 from the German government, with which it had provided welding equipment and supplies. However, as the process of collecting weapons developed, this activity increasingly absorbed funds that might have been used to provide ongoing support for the artists. This is noteworthy not only because of the general attitude toward the artists' role, but because the number of weapons collected, their condition, and classification, were increasingly viewed as a quantitative and reassuring indicator of the project's success. Recognizing this, project staff rapidly began to focus their efforts and attention on weapons collection. The processes of transformation and providing civic education aimed at creating a culture of peace and rec- onciliation thus came to play secondary roles in the overall project. The CUSO cooperant attempted to formalize a working relationship between the artists and TAE, but quickly came up against the attitudes referred to earlier. Furthermore, as religious organizations, TAE and its CCM parent organization felt that the works of art should be a charitable donation to the project: a form of expression for which people probably should not be paid.

The role of the art and of the artists quickly became a source of controversy. In seeking further financial support for the TAE project, its founding director, Jacinto Muth, was inclined to take pieces of sculpture and offer them as gifts to individuals he was visiting. Such items subsequently found their way into the hands of church leaders and other potential funders. By some accounts, forty to fifty pieces of art produced in 1997 "went missing" (Tester and Teves 2004:49). The artists were not reimbursed for these items. The working relationship between TAE and the artists began to deteriorate.

The initial idea of transformation—melting down weapons and making them into plows, scissors, and other practical instruments—had local symbolic value. This can be attributed to the fact that the concept originated with a church organization that had a considerable community-based constituency in Mozambique, and because these implements had a local and practical use. The concept was retained, albeit by different means. Beneficiaries were to receive development tools (bicycles, sewing machines, cement, corrugated roofing, etc.) in exchange for weapons. The transformation of weapons into sculpture—something of symbolic but not practical value to local people—subsequently diminished the significance of conversion to the overall project. Although the sculptures gave the TAE project international attention, the pieces were rarely used in Mozambique for purposes of civic education. One reason given by TAE field staff was that rural people would not understand the artists' ideas and might even mistake the sculptures for magic charms (Faltas and Christian-Paes 2004). Whether this was a complete explanation or whether the TAE staff, who were focused on weapons collection rather than civic education, had little interest in lugging pieces of sculpture into the field for this purpose, is debatable. Photographs of the art (see Figures 10.1 and 10.2) were published on many occasions in local newspapers, and some pieces were exhibited in Maputo on November 5 and 16, 1998.

As the working relationship between TAE and the *Nucleo* artists continued to deteriorate, their art was starting to attract international attention. In May 1999 the sculptures were displayed throughout Maputo during an international Landmines Ban Treaty Conference. Between November 1999 and January 2000, CUSO organized a Canadian tour for one of the artists and the art. The tour included seven cities and included displays and talks in Canadian schools. The increasing attention

Figure 10.1 Examples of sculptures produced as part of the TAE project by artists working for *Nucleo de Arte*. (Photo credits: Frank Tester 2003).

given to the art and growing tensions between TAE and the artists gave impetus to a formal agreement that attempted to address their role in the project. Brokered by a CUSO cooperant, the agreement proposed giving 45 percent of sales to the artists, 45 percent to the TAE project, and 10 percent to *Nucleo de Arte*. The artists' collective was in difficulty. Electricity bills that mounted during the welding of weapons into sculptures and unpaid rent threatened to close the facility used by its members in Maputo.

Following the Canadian tour, pieces were shipped to New York for exhibition at the UN Conference on Small Arms held in June 2001. Thereafter pieces were sent to London and shown at the Oxo Tower Wharf Gallery in January 2002, in an exhibition sponsored by Christian Aid. More than thirty pieces of art were subsequently sold, some of which were displayed in prominent public places—the Imperial War Museum, the Commonwealth Institute, and the British Museum in London, and the Royal Armouries in Leeds. The sale raised $56,103, money that was reportedly to be used to support the TAE project (Satori 2002).

However, what was unfolding behind the scenes was considerably more complicated. Contrary to the agreement reached between TAE and the artists, the latter were promised only $4,500 from the sale, far short of the agreed 45 percent. To complicate matters further, the director asked the artists if he could borrow this amount from the artists to cover TAE staff salaries. Canadian government funding was officially to end on March 31, 2002, and no additional support had been confirmed at the time. The artists agreed to this, and the director provided a letter stating

Figure 10.2   Chair made of rifle parts displayed at the entrance to the Africa Arts Exhibit at the British Museum, London. (Photo credit: Frank Tester 2003)

that the amount would be paid back in full. One of the artists explains what subsequently happened:

> We work with TAE. It's a good project. We must respect [TAE's need for funds] because other people work under demands too. So, okay, no problem. We ask [the TAE director] for the money, and he says we must wait. Must wait. And we still wait. And then in December [2002] around Christmas, we ask for the money and he said: "I am going to give you 55 percent.". . . He said to come back Monday and we are going to give you 55 percent. Okay, when we get there on Monday, he says: "No. I don't have the money." He is just—like—joking with us. We have a family. We have a house. We are artists.
>
> (Interview with Gonçalo Mabunda, June 10, 2003, Maputo.)

The issue remains unresolved. What happened after the Oxo exhibition and sale appears to have fundamentally changed the working relationship between the *Nucleo* artists and the TAE project. It was becoming increasingly obvious to TAE that the art, whatever its symbolic importance might be, had commercial value that could benefit the project.

The TAE director then decided to hire several of the artists on salary to produce art that could be sold to raise funds for TAE operations. This divided the artists and created considerable tensions within the collective. Some of the artists strongly contended that artists don't work for a salary in this way, and that the arrangement undermined their independence and would affect the process of artistic production. At the same time, *Nucleo* artists needed the TAE project as a source of materials for their art. And, as for most artists, making a living in Mozambique, particularly by selling art, was a difficult undertaking. TAE also held equipment—welding machines and welding rods—needed by the artists. Necessity was ultimately to drive several of the artists to work directly for TAE.

When funds were given to the TAE project to produce a sculpture for a meeting of the African Union, held in Maputo in July 2003, two of the artists—after much debate and dissent among their ranks—agreed to work for TAE. They produced a large globe and a map of Africa for the conference, both made entirely of weapons. Others broke ranks entirely, producing and advertising their work on the Internet. Gonçalo Mabunda advertised twenty pieces for sale in a virtual gallery based in Amsterdam (Designserver 2004). Exhibitions of work by *Nucleo* artists have also been held in Barcelona at the Universal Forum of Cultures and in Paris at the Pompidou Centre. Artists, like other producers, need money to survive: to feed their families, to pay their rent. The lesson is this: addressing institutional attitudes toward visual and performing artists in relation to their potential role in development education is an essential to project planning and the successful integration of art with peacebuilding and community development work.

ART: SYMBOLISM AND SIGNIFICANCE

The role and potential of art in addressing the aftermath of armed conflicts has received only limited attention from the international community. The TAE experience suggests that both the potential and limitations of art require a closer examination in contributing to building cultures of peace and reconciliation.

It is not difficult to understand the international appeal of the sculptures produced by *Nucleo* artists from weapons handed in to CCM by people committed to the idea of a lasting peace in Mozambique. The idea of a menacing piece of metal, designed to destroy life, being transformed into a form suggesting play, whimsy, irony, and humor is appealing. For example, a miniature Eiffel Tower, one of the pieces made of arms by the *Nucleo* artists, is symbolic of the cultural achievements of Europe built on the exploitation of former colonies. It conveys in a glance many messages thoroughly grounded in a post-Soviet experience with international conflict. Far from addressing the horrors of armed conflict through silencing them in the name of national reconstruction, as Michael Humprey (2002) suggests is characteristic of post-colonial nation-building, the *Nucleo* art reminds the viewer of the more then one million people who lost their lives in the Renamo/Frelimo conflict. Simultaneously it suggests the "normal things" of life that point to the need for peace and reconciliation. These sentiments are captured by a review of an Oxo gallery exhibit held in January 2003:

> As I walked around the exhibition, I was struck by the technical virtuosity of the artists' work and their choice of subject. Birds, musical instruments, and chairs seem to reaffirm the everyday joys of peaceful life that most of us take for granted. . . . To see them forged from modern weapons seemed a triumph of the human spirit over adversity and of the artistic imagination over the dead hand of war.

> (Saunders 2003:1)

The reviewer very likely wants—and perhaps needs—to see what he has eloquently put to paper. The real social relations engendered by this artistic production—in this case giving rise to conflict and adversity, albeit of a fundamentally different order than that of the armed conflict inspiring the sculptures—are hidden from view.

Unfortunately, apart from the relationship of the artists to their own processes of production, the TAE art has contributed less than might have been possible in both processes of healing and in building a culture of peace and reconciliation. At the same time, the art has drawn a distanced—and aestheticized—attention to armed conflicts such as that experienced by Mozambique. Little has been written about artistic production as a form of catharsis, although "art as therapy" is a popular topic among Western academics. To the extent that art is cathartic, as illustrated by the following quote from one of the *Nucleo* artists, a much wider role for art and artistic production in building cultures of peace and reconciliation is suggested:

> There are some days that are difficult to work because I have memories.
> . . . These are of old situations because I lost school. It was a time of
> war. There are days when you get up and you are not feeling well. It is
> these things . . . you see something in the most destroyed state and your
> head doesn't support it. But there are days when I tolerate—I tolerate
> because, "OK, [the weapons] are cut and I can do something different
> with them."
>
> (Interview with Fiel Desantos, June 6, 2003)

This quote provides some insight into the implications of alienating the artists from the process of production by locating them and the production of art in a space (and presumably in a time—a working day) under the control of the TAE project. Placing the artists on a salary (presumably related to their ability to produce art of commercial value to the project) has additional implications and raises questions about whether art—the subject of often fleeting and unpredictable imagination—can be produced in this way. If so, what kind of "product" might be the result?

The mixed record of the role of art in the TAE project suggests that artistic production and expression as part of international development strategies and processes merit closer examination. The initial concept, articulated by Bishop Segulane, is reminiscent of ideas advanced by Theodor Adorno, Max Horkheimer, and Herbert Marcuse: the idea that art in a European romantic tradition can provide critical insight and act as "a last refuge for critical ideas as well as for the expression and experience of beauty and satisfaction, thus auguring a better society" (Agger 1998:90). The TAE sculptures appear to suggest such possibilities to an international community while regrettably not having played a significant and comparable role within Mozambique. As initially conceived, the TAE sculptures have a "conscious, methodological alienation from the entire sphere of business and industry and from its calculable and profitable order" (Marcuse 1964:58). Paradoxically this romantic appeal—for which there exists an international market— has given rise, within the project that conceptualized this conversion, to relations, dynamics, and tensions reminiscent of Adorno's lament about the absorption of culture into commodity relations (Adorno 1984). In this case the art retains its aesthetic and transformative potential—albeit restricted to ideas far removed from what needs to be a site where transformation to a culture of peace and reconciliation takes place *in practice.* However, the dynamics created within Mozambique among artists and others working to disarm the civilian population are far more reminiscent of commodity relations. Critical questions need to be asked about how such dynamics fit with developing a culture of peace and reconciliation.

These dynamics must also be understood within a larger structural context of poverty and unemployment. The official unemployment rate in Mozambique is about 21 percent. This figure must be interpreted taking into consideration that 80 percent of the population lives in rural settings where many Mozambicans are involved in subsistence and marginal agricultural production. Although Westerners may view the TAE project as primarily a humanitarian undertaking for those collecting arms (and church officials in the country apparently conceptualized it in this way), the TAE project was employment; a tenuous job dependent upon foreign donations. Paying staff (whose collection of arms is essential to measuring project success) comes up against paying artists whose contribution to overall funding may be important but amounts to considerably less than grants from foreign donors. It appears that in regard to funds raised from the sale of art, the TAE project director gave clear priority to paying the staff involved in arms collection.

The priority given to arms collection and the apparently peripheral role of art and artists in the delivery of the project in Mozambique is also tied to international funding priorities. Considerable attention was directed toward measuring the success of the TAE project. The most obvious and concrete measures of that success were the number and types of weapons and munitions collected. Questions about what was being collected, and in what amounts, were the most common inquiries directed at project officials by international dignitaries and other visitors. Furthermore, this information was quickly identified by project staff as important to international agencies in considering funding requests. Statistics on arms figured prominently in reports to CIDA, applying "results-based management" criteria to project reporting (Tester and Teves 2004). It was an emphasis that, as noted by the Bonn International Centre for Conversion, "diverted attention away from the impact on people's mentality and the effect on public security" (Faltas and Christian-Paes 2004:31).

What was initially conceived as a project in which the collection of guns was only one objective—the others being "reducing violence; educating the civil society to abandon violence; and build[ing] up a culture of peace" (Christian Council of Mozambique 1996:2)—quickly evolved into an exercise primarily in weapons collection. This was the most expensive aspect of the project, and one with particular appeal to the military experience of TAE staff. The emphasis also affected gender dimensions of the project, as potential roles for women were underplayed by the focus on arms collection.

CONCLUSION

The relationship of art to processes of peace and reconciliation has received relatively little attention in the international development literature. Pilar Riaño-Alcalá writes about the use of art and images collected in the Antioquia barrio in the Colombian city of Medellín. To address their history of violence, she documents a process in which the victims of violence assemble objects symbolizing their memory of people in the neighborhood (Riaño-Alcalá 2003). This exercise becomes an active one, involving the barrio in artistic production and a range of activities. The Antioquia neighbors display their artifacts in a bus that becomes a museum that moves around the city. Unlike the Colombian experience, the TAE project, although producing art with international appeal, did not actively involve Mozambicans in its production.

The TAE experience suggests that the potential and pitfalls of incorporating artistic production in similar processes deserve more attention. Are the dual objectives of drawing international attention and acclaim to a project and using art as a tool for community organizing compatible? In the case of TAE, it clearly was not possible for the average Mozambican to be involved in cutting and welding pieces of arms into sculpture, and the sculptures' role in generating discussion about peace and reconciliation was never fully appreciated. Furthermore, the role and importance of the artists was never fully developed or recognized. Of greater significance, the international image—the *idea*—of what was happening in Mozambique to build the culture of peace conveyed by the sculptures falls short of what actually transpired.

This is not to say that the TAE project was not partially successful in achieving its objectives, but to acknowledge that collecting arms, in and of itself, is largely a symbolic act. Building a culture of peace is an undertaking that requires more active public involvement. In this case, the sculptures might have been moved around the country and used to generate other activities: the writing of plays or poetry, the telling of stories, the use of other artifacts to complement the sculptures in addressing the fallout from years of violent conflict. The TAE experience suggests nonetheless that the symbolic and material roles of art in processes of peace and reconciliation are potentially considerable, and their incorporation requires careful consideration and design.

NOTE

[1] CUSO (originally known as Canadian University Services Overseas) is a Canadian NGO that sends volunteers—known as cooperants—to work with partner organizations addressing issues of social justice and working for sustainable alternatives to conventional forms of development. Its strength is its relationship with NGOs in the South and its role in supporting the development of this aspect of civil society. CUSO has had a presence in Mozambique since 1978.

REFERENCES

Adorno, Theodor (1984) *Aesthetic Theory,* London: Routledge & Kegan Paul.
Agger, Ben (1998) *Critical Social Theories: An Introduction.* Boulder, CO: Westview Press.
Angola Roundtable (1999) *Angola Roundtable Report,* Ottawa: Canadian Centre for Foreign Policy Development.

Christian Council of Mozambique (1996) Swords into Plougshares [sic] (TAE), The Culture of Peace, Maputo: CCM.

Christie, Iain (1989) *Samora Machel: A Biography,* London and New Jersey: Panaf.

Designserver (2004) "Arms into Art Exhibition," available at www.designserve.nl/nucleo2 (retrieved July 5, 2004).

Faltas, Sami and Wolf Christian-Paes (2004) *Exchanging Guns for Tools: The TAE Approach to Practical Disarmament,* Bonn: Bonn International Centre for Conversion.

Hall, Margaret and Tom Young (1997) *Confronting Leviathan: Mozambique since Independence,* London: Hurst & Company.

Humprey, Michael (2002) *The Politics of Atrocity and Reconciliation: From Terror to Trauma,* London: Routledge.

Leão, Ana (2004) *Weapons in Mozambique: Reducing Availability and Demand,* Monograph Number 94, Pretoria: Institute for Security Studies.

Marcuse, Herbert (1964) *One-Dimensional Man,* London: Abacus.

Riaño-Alcalá, Pilar (2003) "Encounters with Memory and Mourning: Public Art as a Collective Pedagogy of Reconciliation," originally published as: *Arte, memoria y violencia. Reflexiones sobre la cuidad,* Nedekkub: Corporación Región.

Rotfeld, Adam Daniel, Rolf Ekéus, Steven E. Miller, Zdzislaw Lachowski, Wuyi Omitougun, and Ian Anthony (2000) *Arms Control and Disarmament: A New Conceptual Approach,* New York: UN Department for Disarmament Affairs.

Satori, Peter (2002) "Art—A Farewell to Arms?" *Campaign Against Arms Trade Magazine,* April 2002.

Saunders, Nicholas J. (2003) "Swords into Ploughshares," review of the Transforming Arms into Art Exhibition, the.gallery@oxo, London, available at www.fish.co.uk/culture/arts/0102/swords.html (retrieved April 1, 2003).

Smith, C. (1996) "Light Weapons and the International Trade," in UNIDIR, *Small Arms Management and Peacekeeping in Southern Africa,* New York: UNIDIR.

Tester, Frank James and Sandra Teves (2004) *Turning Arms into Ploughshares: An Evaluation of the TAE Project,* Ottawa: CUSO.

First published in *Development in Practice* 16(2): 169–178 in 2006.

ELEVEN

Mission Impossible: Gender, Conflict, and Oxfam GB

SUZANNE WILLIAMS

CHAPTER SUMMARY

This chapter explores the terrain of the international NGO (INGO)—in this case Oxfam GB (OGB)—and some of its difficulties in integrating gender equity goals in the institutional structures and policies that govern its activities in conflict and its aftermath. The chapter looks at terrain that is divided into areas that are treated very differently. These are, on one hand, the field of humanitarian interventions in the throes of an emergency, and on the other, the "non-conflict" field of reconstruction and development. Historically these two fields of activity have been governed by very different ways of thinking and acting, often in conflict with each other. Gender analysis and gender-sensitive programming are central to these differences and are essential tools in the attempts to overcome them. In OGB at present, the differences in approaches to gender equity in these two territories are acknowledged, if not routinely addressed; but the importance of addressing gender equity in order to overcome some of these differences is more complicated and controversial.

INTRODUCTION

It is now widely recognized among international NGOs (INGOs) that working in the context of conflict and turbulence presents them with specific challenges in relation to delivering gender equity in both their humanitarian and development aid programs. INGOs in general accept the need for gender-disaggregated data, the fact that women and men have different needs and interests, that conflict and upheaval present women with opportunities as well as threats, and also the chance to renegotiate gender roles following their de facto assumption of male responsibilities in the absence of men. However, the analysis is rarely taken further or deepened. Gender is not identified by INGOs as a key defining factor of identity in relation to how war begins, what it is about, how groups are mobilized to fight, how ceasefires and peace agreements are reached, and what kind of peace can be said to have been achieved. For women, the end of war rarely brings peace and can in fact bring new levels of violence into their lives.

The power relations that define gender identity, the allegiances, beliefs, and behaviors that are gender-based, are seldom regarded as important for, and even more rarely built into, most INGOs' analysis of war and noninternational conflict, or the planning of interventions to address its consequences. The failure to do this can sometimes be attributed to lack of expertise or experience in gender analysis, and sometimes to a profound, often unformulated, resistance to incorporating it into the analytical framework for a number of reasons that will be examined later in this chapter. To address gender relations in the context of conflict entails entering highly contested terrain, not only within the war-torn society, but also within all the institutions intervening in the situation, including the INGOs.

In this chapter I will explore the mission of a large UK-based INGO, Oxfam GB (OGB), and some of its experience in addressing gender inequalities in the institutional structures and policies that govern its activities in situations of conflict and its aftermath.[1] I present some of the contradictions within OGB's organizational culture that have held this work back and continue to provide obstacles to it, in spite of substantial work on the issues within the agency over the years. I also examine some of the recent developments within OGB that are beginning to seek new solutions to the problem of gender blindness in its interventions, and look at some positive examples of gender-sensitive practice.

My perspective is that of a policy adviser in what is now OGB's Campaigns and Policy Division, with a brief to work on gender, human rights, and conflict. My principal role is to offer advice and support to OGB's programs at regional or country level, and to contribute to the development of OGB's global program policy on conflict, gender, and human rights, within which violence against women is a key priority. Although this chapter represents my own views and not those of OGB as a whole, I draw upon the experiences and concerns of many staff within the organization—indeed, all of us who believe in and work for the consistent delivery of gender equity in every intervention OGB makes. The next few years will reveal whether this is indeed a "mission impossible."

Having looked at some of OGB's institutional imperatives—in other words, its goals and aims, its mandates, policies, and guidelines—which govern its work during conflict and its aftermath, I will discuss some of the problems inherent in several conceptual and programmatic divides that make program implementation in this area complicated and difficult. These divides, which overlap each other, are the same divides that separate relief and development responses and technical and social approaches. Interwoven with them are different perceptions within OGB of the division between the public and private domains, and indeed different perceptions of these areas among those with whom OGB works in the North and the South. The critical feminist insight that the private/public divide has to be broken down, and the personal made political, in order to end discrimination against women and build gender equality is taking a long time to percolate through OGB; and there still remain both perceptual and actual obstacles to making the connections between gender relations in the private and public spheres. However, there is a growing area of work on violence against women in war and in peacetime, which has the potential to encourage new ways of thinking beyond these divides, and I look at some of the implications of this work at the end of the chapter.

The body of the chapter presents examples selected from OGB's program in Kosovo, Central America, South Africa, and Cambodia, where I look at some of the agency's experience in relation to integrating gender equity into its program goals for work in the aftermath of war. Both direct operational interventions, especially in Kosovo, and work with counterpart organizations, are considered. Although OGB's work is increasingly concerned with campaigning and advocacy, these areas are beyond the scope of this chapter. Nonetheless, it is true that many of the contradictions that make it so difficult for gender equity to be at the heart of OGB's direct interventions are equally problematic in its campaigning and advocacy initiatives.

OGB'S INSTITUTIONAL IMPERATIVES

Founded in 1942, OGB is based in Oxford in the United Kingdom, with a decentralized structure of nine regional offices around the world. Its mandate is to relieve poverty, distress, and suffering, and to educate the public about the nature, causes, and effects of these conditions. It describes itself as a "development, relief, and campaigning organization dedicated to finding lasting solutions to poverty and suffering around the world." OGB works principally with partner or counterpart organizations—international, national, and community-based—supporting them to achieve goals common to both. In the fields of emergency response and campaigning, OGB is also operational, employing its own staff to deliver relief programs in the field, or to lobby and campaign for changes in policy and public awareness, and working in conjunction with other INGOs and international agencies.

In recent years OGB has defined its purpose in terms of helping people to achieve their basic rights, loosely in line with articles related principally to social and economic rights within the Universal Declaration of Human Rights, and the two International Covenants. Thus OGB aligns its programs according to a range of basic rights, including health, education, freedom from violence, and a sustainable livelihood. Additionally political and civil rights are defined by OGB as the "right to be heard," related to governance and democratic representation, whereas the "right to an identity" refers to gender equity and discrimination.

OGB has had a corporate gender policy since 1993, but the implementation of this policy throughout the organization has been patchy, dependent upon the efforts of committed individuals and limited to its international program. This has meant that the profound transformations envisaged by the gender policy in human resources policy and the structure and culture of OGB as a whole have not taken place. Progress in implementing the gender policy within the international program was mapped in 1997 and pointed to several important lessons. These included that in the absence of clear criteria for measuring progress in implementing gender policies and practices, managers used very different standards, and there was no overall consistency in the integration of gender equity throughout OGB. Strengths revealed by the study were that OGB could demonstrate considerable success in working at the grassroots level with women's organizations and in OGB's own gender publishing program. There has been less success in relation to mainstreaming gender in large-scale emergency or development programs, and little to point to in relation to gender-sensitive advocacy and campaigning work (Oxfam GB 1998). The mainstreaming of gender throughout OGB and its program thus remains a challenge, but it is a challenge that the organization has prioritized and is beginning to take up in a systematic way through its new framework of objectives and accountability related to basic rights and gender equity.

OGB now has a number of sets of guidelines and standards relating to gender for its emergency programming, and these have been implemented successfully in some instances but are not routinely applied. OGB was a key collaborator in an interagency project known as the Sphere Project, which aims to "improve the quality of assistance provided to people affected by disasters, and to enhance accountability of the humanitarian system in disaster response" (Sphere Project 2000). The project's field handbook lays out a humanitarian charter and a set of minimum standards for the various technical sectors in disaster response—water and sanitation, nutrition, food aid, shelter and site planning, and health services. The 1998 trial edition was gender-blind; a gender review was called for, and OGB, among other agencies, submitted a detailed revision of the handbook from a gender perspective. The subsequent edition (Sphere Project 2000) has incorporated some of these revisions. The charter itself, however, makes no specific reference to gender or to any specific commitment to gender equity in the delivery of emergency relief, and there is still room for improvement in the guidelines themselves.

OGB is currently developing the concept of "net impact" or "net benefit" in relation to humanitarian relief. This has arisen as a result of the work—and the challenge—of Mary B. Anderson's Building Local Capacities for Peace project. The question addressed by Anderson's work is:

> How can international and local aid agencies provide assistance to people in areas of violent conflict in ways that help those people disengage from the conflict and develop alternative systems for overcoming the problems they face? How can aid agencies and aid workers encourage local capacities for peace?
>
> (Anderson 1996)

OGB, along with other international humanitarian agencies, has to ask difficult questions: when does our presence do more harm than good by exacerbating the conflict through diversion of aid, or inadvertent support to perpetrators of human rights violations in conflict, or perpetuation of the war through provision of humanitarian relief, thus enabling national resources to be allocated to arms and the war itself? What are the alternatives to providing immediate help to victims of violent conflict? How do we balance high-profile advocacy with the security of staff and counterparts? How do we continue to provide humanitarian aid within all these constraints and difficulties?

David Bryer, former director of OGB, writes:

> The future of humanitarian aid is now perhaps more in question than at any time since 1945. The providers question whether the abuse of their aid outweighs its benefits; while the donors, at least the official ones, reduce their funding. Yet the need for aid continues; the number of people who suffer needlessly for lack of it rises. Here, we consider some of the practical difficulties and ethical choices involved in judging the "net impact" of aid that is provided in armed conflicts, where its abuse has become a certainty.
>
> (Bryer and Cairns 1997:363)

This same question could well be applied to gender equity and the impact of external agencies on women and on gender relations. When do our interventions bring more harm than good to women? Are we exacerbating inequitable gender relations by intervening in ways that do not positively address gender inequality, and tackle male dominance? Are we inadvertently exacerbating male violence against women by acting without a clear analysis of gender power relations? Are we making it easier for male oppression to continue by focusing on women's projects that do not disturb the status quo? Are there times when we should be making a judgment and deciding to pull out of a direct intervention and focus instead on high-profile lobbying and campaigning for women's rights? In the context of conflict and in highly militarized societies, both of which can have extreme consequences for women, these dilemmas are particularly acute.

OGB had to address these issues in Afghanistan, when the Taliban took control of Kabul in 1998 and OGB's local female staff were prevented from coming to work. OGB had to scale down its operation and find a way to balance its presence in the country with a principled stance on the abuse of the rights of women under the

Taliban regime. There was considerable debate among those who thought OGB should take a very public position on what was happening to women rather than implicitly supporting an unjust system by working with "approved" women, and those who thought OGB should try to find ways of working with women wherever possible within the constraints. A 1999 internal OGB report states that gender remains a vital concern in the program, but in the absence of being able to address women's rights directly, health and education remain the most appropriate entry points to work with women. The report points to the dangers of adopting an approach that would aim for quick results and advocates building on the positive aspects in the situation of women in Afghanistan—for example, that women's voices in local communities are stronger than normally perceived, and that intra-household distribution is more equitable than in many parts of the world. In the end, it was judged that the net benefit to women of OGB staying and working with the opportunities that could be found were greater than radically changing its program approach and abandoning direct interventions. (See Clifton and Gell 2001:12–13 for further discussion of these issues.)

The judgment of whether we are doing more harm than good is not, however, routinely applied in OGB's work in conflicts, emergencies, or any other situations, and the tools to help staff make such an assessment are not yet developed. But the issue is regularly brought up in debate. A workshop to take forward its work on gender equity took place in Oxford in September 2000, attended by staff from all over OGB. Participants emphasized the critical importance of applying much tighter standards and developing much clearer systems for assessing OGB's impact on women and gender equity in the areas where it works—and for withdrawing support where it was either of no use to women or damaging to them. Much research and NGO experience over the last decades have shown how gender-insensitive development and relief interventions damage women and exacerbate their disadvantaged position. The concept of "net impact" or "net benefit" in relation to women's basic rights is an important overall guiding principle for OGB in all aspects of its work. Current work on impact reporting is beginning to formalize systematic procedures for asking questions related to the impact on gender equity of every project OGB supports. How this is to be measured and appropriately recorded is still a work in progress.

PROGRAMMING IN CONFLICT-PRONE AREAS:
THE HARD AND THE SOFT

"The thing about this program," one of the water engineers said to me in Kosovo when I visited in 1999, "is that it's the soft side of the program that is the hardest to do."

The categories of the "hard" and the "soft" run through the ways in which different forms of action taken in response to conflict and poverty are seen and thought about. Actions and interventions that are bound by the urgent, which show fast, quantifiable results, and which are predominantly technical in nature, are "hard." The inputs are "hardware." Those which are associated with more subtle and cautious forms of intervention, whose results are more difficult to measure and take longer to manifest, and which are predominantly social and cultural in nature, are "soft." The inputs are "software." This dichotomy is closely associated with stereotypical categories of the masculine and the feminine and runs through not only the ways actions and achievements are perceived in OGB—and indeed in most institutions—but also how they are valued and rewarded. The "hard," masculinized interventions, whether in policy and advocacy work or humanitarian relief, are generally more visible. The supply lines of the "hardware" and the context of much policy work, are male-dominated and masculinized. Visible results and high-profile actions carry a premium in NGOs that are struggling in the marketplace for funds and that are under pressure to show concrete and quantifiable results to their donors—many of whom, in their institutional structures and cultures, are subject to the same kinds of masculinized and feminized dichotomies in values. The less visible, "soft," feminized interventions do not thus attract the same attention or the same amounts of money and are not valued as highly, either inside or outside the organization. This, of course, becomes a self-perpetuating cycle of highly gendered systems of value and reward, which affects not only the nature of interventions but also the staff responsible for them.

Gender equity programming in conflict-prone areas is thus itself prone to conflict in quite complex ways—linked to the opposing categories of the hard and the soft. Other divides intersect or run parallel with this broad dichotomy, as outlined in the introduction. For although organizations such as OGB have theorized about the end of the "development–relief" divide, the division still persists institutionally and in field policy and practice.[2] The technical (hard) and the social (soft) approaches to program planning and implementation are also strongly associated with short-term relief and longer-term developmental approaches within the humanitarian intervention. Threading in and out of these issues, as was mentioned above, is the divide between the public and the private, and the implications for perceptions of violence against women in war and in "peace." Rape as a war crime is perceived as hard, a public crime associated with military strategy; rape as a domestic crime is soft, a private crime associated with social issues and intimate relationships.

The Impact of the Dichotomies

The short-term versus long-term divide is gradually narrowing but its persistence in both policy and practice means that the implications of the nature of emergency relief response for the rehabilitation and longer-term recovery and reconstruction work are not always appreciated. Or, to put it another way, the nature of the relief effort is often only peripherally influenced by the longer-term social and economic prospects for the victims of the conflict. The focus is on saving lives, which in OGB's case is principally through the provision of clean water, sanitation, and hygiene promotion. The importance of this aim and its achievements cannot be underestimated or undervalued. However, longer-term goals of addressing issues linked to gendered inequalities that sought, for example, to improve women's prospects through education, empowerment, training, or strategies to prevent further conflict, are secondary to the provision of immediate relief.

Often the aims of relief and recovery themselves thus seem to be in conflict—particularly if resources are limited. Achieving one set of aims may be seen to be at the expense of the other. Moral claims for one or the other raise the temperature. Staff focused on, and responsible for, delivering a quick, large-scale response, accuse those emphasizing the social complexities of the emergency of "fiddling while Rome burns." Although the technical staff are saving lives, the social staff are seen to work on non–life-threatening issues, complicating questions, and holding things up, or achieving nothing significant or measurable—or worse still, exacerbating social and political tensions they do not fully understand. Social development staff, on the other hand, accuse the technical staff of rushing in blindly, treating people like numbers and objects, potentially doing more harm than good by ignoring social and gender differences in the population, creating dependencies, and paying little attention to the long-term consequences of the relief aid itself.

Add gender equity to the mix and the environment may become explosive. It is common to find strong resistance to building gender equity goals into emergency response on the grounds that: (1) lives have to be saved quickly, information is not available, and there is no time for social surveys; (2) donors and the media are applying immense pressure to show that the measures already rapidly implemented have had an immediate impact, and the gender dynamics of society are of less concern, and certainly less visible; (3) although we know distribution is more effective through women, there is often not time to organize it this way, or there is local resistance to it that OGB should not challenge; (4) the height of an emergency is no time to challenge gender power relations; and (5) special attention should not be paid to women when everyone is suffering.

I have heard all these arguments in the field. They are arguments that frustrate practitioners on both sides of the debate, all of whom are trying to get the job done as best they can. These are complex issues that are not easily resolved in the clash between speed of response and the social, cultural, and political composition of groups that will determine the quality of that response.

OGB's response to the Kosovo crisis brought these issues out quite clearly, and program managers made real efforts to work across the relief–development and technical–social divides, and integrate the hard and soft elements into a single program. The process was fraught with difficulties, yet it seemed to have made a good start.

The Example of Kosovo

OGB had been in Kosovo since 1995, working closely with women's groups and associations in several regions in the country. OGB-Pristina had strong relationships with local counterparts and a strong local team. The focus was on long-term development initiatives aimed at the social and political empowerment of women, through capacity building of women activists. With the intensification of the conflict in 1998, OGB's work shifted focus to respond to the needs of displaced women and children. Women's centers were funded in Viti, Pristina, Obiliq, and Gjilan as relief distribution points, and as meeting places for psychosocial support. The program also included substantial work on the provision of water, sanitation, and public health.

At the onset of the NATO campaign in March 1999, OGB evacuated with other INGOs, and set up an office in Skopje with several of its staff from Pristina. The existing Albania program was rapidly expanded to take on the provision of humanitarian relief for the refugees flooding into the country. During the period of exile and displacement, OGB continued to work in Macedonia with its highly committed former Pristina staff and some of its Kosovar counterparts, principally in the refugee camps. With the continuity provided by the former Pristina staff, and program experience from several years in Kosovo, the chances of a well-integrated program building the relief response within longer-term strategies for recovery and return, with gender equity goals at its core, seemed to be high, if not optimal.

However, this integration did not happen for a number of reasons. A large-scale humanitarian relief program was mounted with an enormous budget raised by emergency appeals in the United Kingdom and in the limelight of the high media interest in the crisis. The pressure was on OGB to spend the money, and spend it fast. A large number of expatriate staff, mostly water technicians and engineers, flew into Macedonia to set up OGB's water program in the camps. Money flowed freely for the emergency response. But the dynamic between the social and technical responses, when I arrived to look at gender, human rights, and protection issues in April 1999, was difficult and competitive. Kosovar staff members, refugees themselves, were dealing with their own personal and family trauma, and with loss and uncertainty, as a result of the war. The problem was heightened by the fact that the new arrivals who arrived en masse to run the emergency relief response were all expatriates, some with no previous experience of the region. The former Pristina Kosovar staff felt overrun by the new technical "expats," misunderstood and alienated from a program that had been theirs and had now inflated beyond recognition.

Kosovar refugees—mostly educated young men and women—were taken on by the technical and social programs to carry out the work in the camps. There was a heated debate about payment of the young workforce. In the old Pristina-based program, much of the work was based on voluntarism. But in the refugee situation, many of the other international agencies were paying their local recruits. Initially the debate was played out in gendered terms—the young men working with the water engineers were paid, and the young women were not. This situation was subsequently adjusted.

The technical staff, running the water program (the "hard" side of the program), were almost exclusively male and were perceived by the almost exclusively female staff working on gender, disability, social development, and hygiene promotion (the "soft" side of the program) to have privileged access to the emergency resources. The technical aspects were thus perceived by those working on the other parts of the program to be valued more highly than the social aspects. In fact, as in any emergency, all staff, whether they were logisticians, engineers, managers, or social development staff, were clamoring for more resources. Where all eyes are on the crisis, and there is external pressure as well as pressure from the desperation of the refugee population, competition over resources is inevitable; and where other divisions exist, it is very difficult to manage.

As is often the case, strong feelings focused on access to vehicles as essential and desirable program resources. I traveled with staff from all three parts of the program and observed that indeed, the water program staff in each camp had access to their own new four-wheel-drive vehicles, whereas the hygiene promotion, disability, and social development staff had to share older vehicles, one of which was quite unsafe, with a cracked windscreen and a field radio that did not work. I vividly recall sitting on the dusty roadside at the exit from one of the Stankovic camps for some time, trying to hitch a lift back to Skopje because the social development program did not have its own vehicle. This put extra pressure on the "soft" teams and made it harder for them to accomplish all they had to do in the dispersed camps where they worked. There were other specific and more general problems regarding access to program resources that were not adequately resolved, and this exacerbated the divisions between teams responsible for different components of the program. This in turn militated against the integration of the social and technical aspects of the program.

I reported at the time that OGB's program was a three-pronged effort, comprising community development with special emphasis on women and people with disabilities, hygiene and public health promotion; and the provision of clean water. The program had many strengths—namely OGB's long and established reputation in the fields of emergency relief and development, and skilled and experienced staff to implement them. The report's recommendations included the following:

> For further development of Oxfam's response, its three elements need to be built into a single integrated program, with the three aspects based on a clear analysis of the needs and rights of women, men, and children. Data collection and appraisal methods sensitive to gender and

age are needed to provide the information Oxfam needs for planning of all parts of the program. Oxfam will then be well placed to make a significant contribution not only to the current crisis but to the future in Kosovo.

(Williams 1999)

Nonetheless, and in spite of not managing to achieve the desired program integration, OGB's program in Macedonia was respected for both its technical and social achievements, and some of the key issues were addressed. Specific needs related to gender and disability were taken into account by the technical team in, for example, the design of washing facilities in the camps. The work of the social development and gender team in providing separate tents for social spaces for women and men set the context for beginning to address the gender-related violence experienced by women and girls, and OGB lobbied UNHCR to fulfil its protection mandate and implement its own guidelines by providing better protection measures for women and girls in the camps.

One of the real difficulties, common to all humanitarian response, was the tension between the pace and style of work of quick-impact emergency relief, and longer-term social processes, and the substantial differences in scale and funding levels of these programs. Staffing patterns in humanitarian relief are based on rapid scaling up of numbers, high turnover, and short-term contracts. Induction processes for these staff members are usually sketchy, and the culture of "hitting the ground running" is not favorable to training in social and gender awareness in the field. In the Kosovo crisis the result was the running of parallel programs in Macedonia, which was carried forward into the post-conflict work of reconstruction and recovery after the refugees returned. The integration of gender equity into the program as a whole remains a challenge, although the social development program works with previous and new counterparts with the overall aim of the empowerment of women for gender equity in a future Kosovo.

The nature of the funding environment during a crisis and in its aftermath has implications for longer-term work. "Red" money is tied to specific donor-defined goals; "green" money is for programming and thus offers more flexibility. The "red" appeal money that sustained the Kosovo humanitarian program ran out in due course, and the OGB program had to fund its development and gender work under the Kosovo Women's Initiative (KWI), managed by UNHCR, but which came from an emergency budget line in the US State Department. Although the KWI project set long-term empowerment goals, the spending for this fund, totaling US$ 10 million, was short term. This created considerable pressure on Kosovar NGOs as well as on the INGOs, such as OGB, acting as brokers, or "umbrellas," for this fund, to get new projects up and running and spending money, often beyond the organizational capacity of the partner groups. Some women's groups set up in order to create activities the KWI could fund. The KWI was itself an example of the tension between short-term emergency funding demanding quick and visible returns, and developmental goals whose benefits are only measurable in the longer term. When the emergency money moves on to the next crisis, the gap left can be devastating to organizations that were mobilized, or created, in the plentiful funding climate, and which subsequently find themselves without support, and often collapse, amid their dashed expectations.

The importance of program integration was underlined again in OGB's September 2000 workshop on gender equity, referred to above. Joint planning between technical and social intervention teams was identified at the workshop as essential to programming, and it was established that *all* staff operating in emergency relief need to understand the social and gender dimensions of their work and have clear guidelines to help them. The integration of gender equity would help the planning and design of emergency relief measures to take into account the longer-term recovery and future development of the population involved and foster consistency with program goals designed for the long haul.

Gender assessments were carried out during the Kosovo crisis in both Macedonia and Albania. The consolidated recommendations drawn up by gender advisers for the response in both countries hold for OGB programming in general. These included:

- Gender and social development issues need to be fully integrated in the emergency response and future program development, with every aspect based on a clear analysis of the needs and rights of women, men, children, and disabled people.
- The social and technical aspects of the program should inform each other effectively for maximum impact. Social and community services must run hand in hand with distribution of non-food items; and water, sanitation, and health/hygiene planning must be as well resourced from the start, and should operate concurrently in Kosovo as soon as OGB has access to the designated sector.

- Unified program aims and objectives for social and technical interventions need to be set for the region within the framework of OGB's strategic change objectives, to which gender equity is central, and gender-sensitive indicators for success should be set.
- Setting up a new program in Kosovo presents an excellent opportunity for OGB to implement best practice in gender-sensitive program response in view of the above recommendations. Baseline data and indicators for gender equity should be set at the earliest stage in program planning for effective monitoring and impact assessment (Clifton and Williams 1999).

WORKING WITH COUNTERPARTS IN CONFLICT

OGB's success in integrating gender equity into programming in conflict and its aftermath depends critically not only upon how OGB's institutional dichotomies are resolved (or not), as we have seen above in the case of Kosovo, but also on the relationships with partner organizations and local/national NGOs, and their analysis of the situation. This section looks at some of OGB's experience in Latin America, where its programs have been notable for the quality of long-standing relationships with local counterpart organizations. Here I focus on the work with counterparts in the immediate aftermath of conflict, where OGB did not have the same level of operationality in its response, and thus the technical–social dichotomy is less evident. The hard and soft elements of the situation, and the program response through counterpart organizations, however, still had a key influence on the way gender equity was addressed.

In the 1960s and 1970s the country programs were characterized by intense counterpart relationships, many of which were built around a strong sense of solidarity with the political struggles against brutal military dictatorships and the social injustice and poverty brought about by these regimes. The emphasis was on the long-term transformation of society, by armed or peaceful means, by the real agents of change—the poor and oppressed people of the region. Because of the nature of the regimes, much of the work supported by OGB was initiated by the Catholic Church and took place under its umbrella. But the analysis of social injustice did not include an analysis of women's oppression by men.

In El Salvador, OGB's program focused before and during the war on the strengthening of popular organizations allied to the church and progressive Salvadoran NGOs. In common with many of the liberation struggles of the 1980s, however, gender equity was not seen as part of the liberation goal, and the analysis of gender oppression was often regarded as a special interest issue, potentially divisive to the aims of the movement. The liberation struggle was "hard," armed, macho, political. Women's specific issues were "soft," secondary, personal, and for women and men alike, diluted the toughness and authenticity of the armed struggle, whose goal was social justice for all. Moreover, despite the long history of popular feminism and women's struggles in Latin America, both counterparts and some of the OGB staff saw the analysis of gender inequity as having been imported from the developed countries as yet another example of cultural imperialism (particularly from the United States). Martha Thompson, deputy regional representative for Central America at the time, writes: "Most counterparts saw the inequalities based on gender relations as a Northern concern, and not one of their priorities" (Thompson 1999:48; see also Thompson and Eade's chapter in this volume).

Although OGB began to include elements of gender analysis into the El Salvador program in the 1980s, the extent to which it pushed its gender work was greatly influenced by the position of OGB's counterpart organizations. By 1995, however, OGB's gender policy began to require field programs to show evidence of pursuing gender equity in their work. Thompson outlines four basic mistakes made by OGB in trying to incorporate gender analysis into the program.

- Money was "thrown" at the issue. Counterparts could access funding if they attached "gender" to a project. Without a gender analysis, counterparts included projects with women, such as training or the development of microenterprises—some of which were effective, some of which were not. Funding agencies went along with this to gain the approval of the head office.
- Rather than fully explore the tension between a class and a gender analysis, an uneasy compromise was reached, whereby OGB and counterpart agencies basically continued working as before, but with the addition of specific projects with women and support given to some women's organizations in the popular movement. A broad discussion with counterparts and local women's organizations on gender should have taken place, and would have avoided OGB contributing to the distortion of the concept of gender equity.
- Aid agencies did not recognize the gains women had made during the war, where they gained visibility performing acts of courage

as combatants or in resisting the fighting. Nor did agencies understand how the transformation of gender roles could be integrated into social transformation. In the refugee camps, and later in the repopulated conflict zones, women began to take on leadership roles. But at the end of the war, they were expected to relinquish these positions, and strategies were not in place to deal with this.

- OGB was unwilling to risk prejudicing its relationship with counterparts by raising gender power differences because of their perceived potential to cause divisions (Thompson 1999:50–53).

In El Salvador, the popular movement had traditionally been dominated by men; during the war, women grew in strength and were able to challenge their traditional position after the fighting had ceased. A narrow political analysis, which did not take gender oppression and the value of internal democracy into account, held women back during the political struggle. Martha Thompson reflects:

> I am struck by a dichotomy: when the popular movement in El Salvador was strong, the development of gender work in member organisations was very weak; it became much stronger in the post-war period, when the popular movement was weaker.
>
> (Thompson 1999:57)

The experience of Salvadoran women in the post-conflict arena is reflected in countries such as Nicaragua, Mozambique, Zimbabwe, and South Africa. Once the war is over, women are sent back to resume being "barefoot, pregnant, and in the kitchen" while men make the political decisions about peace and reconstruction and fill the political positions in the new government order. Women are less likely to accept their subordination once they have experienced relative autonomy and respect during the war, but the obstacles to their advancement are exacerbated by militaristic constructions of masculinity and femininity. The overall message to them is clear: both the war and peace will be dominated by men and masculinist priorities and interests; and this will be maintained as long as women have no formal role in peacemaking and reconstruction. The message to INGOs is that they need to bring their global experience to bear on local and national politics and social relations, and to seek and strengthen counterparts locally, particularly among women's organizations and organizations working for gender equality.

In Central America, OGB supported Guatemalan women's organizations in exile in Mexico, planning the return of the refugee populations to Guatemala. The support included training and organizational strengthening, and women participated in some of the delegations identifying land for resettlement. However, according to Beate Thoresen, then OGB's program coordinator in Guatemala:

> After the return to Guatemala, there was a significant decline in the level of organization of women. This has to do with the dedication to immediate survival in the resettlement process as well as the need to reorganize as the return communities were dispersed and the groups that had lived together in Mexico returned to different places. It could also be observed that there was a change in the attitude of men, saying that things should get back to "normal" as they were now back in Guatemala. In some cases the leadership in the communities (men) resisted organisation of women after the return.
>
> (Personal communication)

A central element in this resistance is connected to access to resources, such as land. As women often only have land-use rights through men, widows and single women are dispossessed during and after war. In Guatemala land is allocated collectively, or in the majority of cases, through individual plots by family. The first post-war land allocations showed that women were not taken into account. Women are demanding joint property rights with men, and their right to become members of cooperatives to acquire land. In response to men's allegation that women have not contributed money or community work to the cooperatives, women are claiming that their domestic work should be accepted as their contribution to the community. On the southern coast of Guatemala, Madre Tierra is an OGB-supported returnee women's organization that developed in response to women's specific livelihood needs, such as for cooking stoves and for animals that generate income, providing food and milk. Tensions arose with men in the community over the success of the women's projects, but women opted to retain control of them outside the community cooperatives, which do not represent women's interests. Madre Tierra now employs men to carry out some of the labor for the project.

Although many in Guatemala assert that gender relations have not improved, there are considerable differences between one community and another, and women have gained skills and confidence in organization building and awareness. Thoresen reports help given by an

OGB-supported returnee women's organization, which assisted a neighboring women's group in preparing a project proposal that included gender training. When asked why they wanted training on gender awareness, "they said they wanted a better future for their children, and they had observed that the returnee women could dance with men other than their husbands at community celebrations!"

THE HEART OF THE MATTER:
GENDER VIOLENCE AND POST-WAR PEACE

> In Africa there is not a universal definition of peace. It is not the clichéd definition of not being at war. In South Africa today there is increasing domestic violence, an increase in child abuse. So we cannot say South Africa is at peace.
>
> (Thandi Modise, African National Congress Women's League)[3]

Peace does not come with the cessation of armed hostilities and the signing of peace agreements. High levels of social and gender violence are a feature of post-war societies. South Africa has experienced spiraling levels of interpersonal violence, with shocking statistics of sexual abuse of women and children. Violence, like war, is gendered. Its expression is inseparable from female and male gender identities, and the relations between women and men. Gender identities constructed, promoted, and sustained by armed conflict and the impact of militarization powerfully influence women's and men's attitudes and behaviors in the post-conflict environment.

This section looks at the significance of gender violence and the meaning of peace in the light of the contradictions described in this chapter. To address gender violence means overcoming the private/public divide, and bringing together issues commonly categorized as "hard"—those linked with war, arms, and high-profile, militarized peacekeeping, and "soft"—those linked to the personal experiences of violence of women, girls, and boys during and after war. It means making the connections between the violence perpetrated in war, within the ambit of relief interventions, and the violence perpetrated outside war, addressed by development programs. Policies for the construction of post-war peace must also embrace and ensure peace between women and men. In this sense, programming on gender violence goes right to the heart of the matter, bringing the issues described in this chapter into stark relief.

The wars in Rwanda and Bosnia brought rape and sexual violence in wartime to the public gaze through intense media coverage. These crimes were in the public domain, and thus became a legitimate focus for the attention of human rights organizations, and for the interventions of development agencies—although in fact research in Bosnia showed that the majority of rapes and sexual crimes against women were committed by men known to them. The crimes of domestic violence and sexual abuse in societies not at war, or recovering from it, do not attract the same attention, and international organizations show greater ambivalence in addressing issues still widely perceived as too difficult, too complicated, and too private.

Nonetheless, OGB has supported work on violence against women for many years, and in line with the new program objectives outlined earlier in this chapter, a global program on violence against women was being developed at the time of writing. The program seeks to overcome the analytic division between the public and the private, and to address violence within a framework of understanding gender relations and the construction of masculine and feminine identities in any sphere, in war and in peace. OGB's experience from all over the world—South Africa, Central and South America, the African Great Lakes, Eastern Europe, Cambodia, Vietnam, South Asia—show that gender violence carries on decades after a war is officially over; peace means different things for women and for men. A closer analysis of gender violence is beginning to inform OGB's work in post-conflict reconstruction and recovery, but gender violence has yet to be tackled strategically, and in an integrated way, as a central element of emergency response.

OGB has supported work by local and national NGOs that tackles violence against women in the aftermath of conflict, or where conflict is endemic, in many parts of the world—notably in South Africa, Rwanda, Bosnia, Indonesia, Cambodia, Guatemala, and Colombia. In Cambodia, for example, the Alliance for Conflict Transformation, comprising nineteen NGO and government workers, conducts training on conflict resolution for officials from the municipality of Phnom Penh, to be applied to disputes ranging from land issues to domestic violence. Domestic violence is widespread in Cambodia, the legacy of thirty years of war and brutalized relationships. The Project Against Domestic Violence in Cambodia (PADV) has been instrumental in raising awareness about violence against women through education and public campaigning with government support. A national survey of the incidence of violence against women in 2,400 households gained national and international media attention. These organizations make the link clearly between the violence of war and continuing violence against women after the war is over. A victim of violence is quoted in PADV's survey of domestic violence in Cambodia:

> After 1979 men changed. Nine out of ten men are broken, nasty ('Khoch'). During the Khmer Rouge period they had no happiness at all. So now that they are free, men do whatever they want.
>
> (Zimmerman 1994)

There are many examples of the brutalization of men by extreme nationalism and the experience of military action, and this has been well documented by women's NGOs and international organizations in Bosnia, Uganda, Sierra Leone, and other parts of the world. A chilling case is reported from South Africa, in which a township gang was formed to rape women as a way of bolstering or recovering male identity and status while at the same time getting back at political leaders by whom gang members felt betrayed. These ex-combatants replicate militaristic patterns of discipline and punishment and assert their dominance through acts of gendered violence—the sexual abuse and rape of women. The leader of the organization stated in a television interview:

> I was a comrade before I joined this organization. I joined it because we were no longer given political tasks. Most of the tasks were given to senior people. Myself and six other guys decided to form our own organization that will keep these senior comrades busy all the time. That is why we formed the South African Rapist Association (SARA). We rape women who need to be disciplined (those women who behave like snobs); they just do not want to talk to most people.
>
> (Vetten 1998)

Addressing masculinities and the forces that lead to, promote, and maintain male violence toward women as a defining feature of gender power relations will be part of OGB's mission to have a significant impact on gender equity through all aspects of its programs. To do this effectively, OGB—as any INGO or international agency—will have to examine closely its own gendered structures and cultures. This chapter has identified some of the key areas of difficulty in relation to delivering on gender equity in the context of conflict and post-war programming. The tensions show up at all levels in the institution. The core argument of this chapter is that the ways that OGB's organizational imperatives are both conceptualized and implemented are themselves gendered. The hard and the soft run through OGB's structure and culture as metaphors for the masculine and the feminine, and can bump up against each other in the heat of the moment in the highly charged context of emergencies and post-conflict interventions, and can generate tensions over priorities and resources, value, and reward. It is only by a thorough and profound commitment to gender equity in all aspects of its structure, culture, and programming that OGB—or any other organization—can begin to overcome these tensions and avoid the weakening of its effectiveness in fulfilling its mission to relieve human suffering and address its root causes.

ACKNOWLEDGMENTS

This chapter is based on a paper delivered in October 2000 to an Expert Seminar on gender relations in the aftermath of war. The seminar at the Humanist University in Utrecht, Holland, was convened by Cynthia Cockburn and Dubravka Zarkov. The paper subsequently appeared under the title "Conflicts of Interest: Gender in Oxfam's Emergency Response" in their edited volume *The Postwar Moment: Militaries, Masculinities and International Peacekeeping,* published by Lawrence & Wishart (London 2002), and was reprinted in Haleh Afshar and Deborah Eade (eds.) *Development, Women and War: Feminist Perspectives,* published by Oxfam GB (Oxford 2004).

NOTES

[1] In this chapter "Oxfam" refers only to Oxfam Great Britain (OGB), and not to the wider family of organizations known as Oxfam International.

[2] Many writers have emphasized this. Anne Mackintosh, OGB's regional representative for the Great Lakes region 1991–1994, writes: "Even agencies who recognize the inappropriateness of regarding 'relief' and 'development' as separate phenomena perpetuate this false dichotomy, through resourcing long-term and emergency programmes in different ways and having them managed by different departments and staff. This often leads to unhelpful tensions and rivalry" (Mackintosh 1997:468). Some of OGB's policies and protocols have evolved since the paper on which this chapter is based was first written. For up-to-date information, visit www.oxfam.org.uk.

[3] Cited in "Women and the Aftermath," *AGENDA* No. 43 (2000), a report on "The Aftermath: Women in Post-conflict Reconstruction," a July 1999 conference, held in Johannesburg.

REFERENCES

Anderson, Mary B. (1996) *Do No Harm: Supporting Local Capacities for Peace through Aid*, Cambridge, MA: LCCP/CDA.

Bryer, David and Edmund Cairns (1997) "For Better? For Worse? Humanitarian Aid in Conflict," *Development in Practice* 7(4):363–374.

Clifton, Deborah and Fiona Gell (2001) "Saving and Protecting Lives by Empowering Women," *Gender and Development* 9(3):8–18.

Clifton, Deborah and Suzanne Williams (1999) "Gender Assessment of Oxfam's Emergency Response to the Kosovo Refugee Crisis in Albania and Macedonia," unpublished paper, Oxford: Oxfam GB.

Committee on Women's Rights and Equal Opportunities (2000) *European Parliament: Draft Report on Women's Involvement in Peaceful Conflict Resolution*, Brussels: European Parliament.

Mackintosh, Anne (1997) "Rwanda: Beyond "Ethnic Conflict", *Development in Practice* 7(4): 464–474.

Oxfam GB (1998) *The Links: Lessons from the Gender Mapping Project*, unpublished report, Oxford: Oxfam GB.

Sorensen, Birgitte (1998) *Women and Post-Conflict Reconstruction: Issues and Sources,* War-torn Societies Project Occasional Paper No 3, Geneva: UNRISD.

Sphere Project (2000) *Humanitarian Charter and Minimum Standards in Disaster Response*, Geneva: The Sphere Project.

Thompson, Martha (1999) "Gender in Times of War (El Salvador)," in Fenella Porter, Ines Smyth, and Caroline Sweetman (eds.) *Gender Works: Oxfam Experience in Policy and Practice*, Oxford: Oxfam GB.

Vetten, L. (1998) "War and the Making of Men and Women," *Sunday Independent*, South Africa, August 16.

Williams, Suzanne (1999) *Gender and Human Rights in the Macedonian Refugee Camps*, unpublished report, Oxford: Oxfam GB.

Zimmerman, Cathy E. (1994) *Plates in a Basket Will Rattle*, Phnom Penh: PADV.

PART 4

Reviews and Resources

TWELVE

Women, Gender, and Conflict: Making the Connections

MARTHA THOMPSON

CHAPTER SUMMARY

This chapter explores the need to make the roles of women and men visible in order to understand the different ways in which they are involved in and affected by armed conflict; and also to examine the ways in which gender roles, the relations between women and men, are changed during and as a result of such conflict. The author reviews current literature on the political economy of conflict and feminist writing on women in conflict, noting that the former tends to be gender blind whereas the latter generally fails to take into account an understanding of the wider realpolitik. The author focuses on five recent feminist works that in attempting to do this, have contributed to moving the debate forward.

- Enloe, Cynthia (2004) *The Curious Feminist: Searching for Women in the New Age of Empire*, Berkeley, CA: University of California Press.
- Giles, Wenona and Jennifer Hyndman (eds.) (2004) *Sites of Violence: Gender and Conflict Zones*, Berkeley, CA: University of California Press.
- Mazurana, Dyan and Khristopher Carlson (2004) *From Combat to Community: Women and Girls in Sierra Leone*, Cambridge, MA: Women's Policy Commission, Harvard University.

- Mazurana, Dyan, Angela Raven Roberts, and Jane Parpart (eds.) (2005) *Gender, Conflict and Peacekeeping,* New York: Rowan & Littlefield.
- Nordstrom, Carolyn (2004) *The Shadows of War: Violence, Power and International Profiteering in the Twenty-first Century,* Berkeley, CA: University of California Press.

LIFTING EXPERIENCE UP TO THE LIGHT

Camilo Cienfuegos, a much loved hero of the Cuban revolution, is pictured on Cuba's blue 20-peso banknote. When you hold it up to the light, the face of Celia Sánchez appears behind him. Although she is a famous revolutionary hero in her own right, and widely believed to be Fidel Castro's most trusted advisor until her death, Celia is invisible until the light shines through the banknote. One way to classify the literature on gender and conflict is to divide it into that which makes women's and girls' experience of conflict visible by holding it up to the light; and that which analyzes the different gender roles that emerge in conflict, the changing concepts of masculine and feminine identities, and changes in the power relationships between men and women.

Both aspects of the gendered analysis of conflict are of fundamental importance. Practice has shown that if we do not understand the specific circumstances, experiences, roles, vulnerabilities, and capacities of men and women in war, we construct homogeneous strategies of response that do not address gender-based differences and generally tend to disadvantage women. Holding women's experience up to the light is also crucial: without doing this we cannot set that experience in the context of shifting gender identities, roles, and power relationships in situations of conflict. This is true whether you work in humanitarian relief, rehabilitation, peacekeeping efforts, human rights, disarmament, demobilization, or post-conflict reconstruction.

The literature on gender and conflict and on women in conflict has grown steadily over the last twenty years. This includes texts dealing with the ways in which war affects women and girls differently from men and boys, the particular vulnerabilities and capacities that women develop in conflict, and the different ways in which relief and other forms of assistance and the cessation of hostilities can affect men and women. (See, for example, Afshar 2004; Byrne 1995; Cockburn 2004; El-Bushra and Piza López 1984; El Bushra 2004; Enloe 2000; Kampwirth 2002; Korac 2004; Manchanda 2001; Mertus 2000.)

Despite this, there are still several important areas of the literature on conflict for which there is little or no gender analysis. As Cynthia Cockburn says, "Gender has a curious way of being both simultaneously present and absent in popular perception" (Cockburn 2004:25). Much of the current literature is still mainly about men's involvement in conflict, whether they are creating it, profiting from it, provoking it, supplying it, doing the fighting, directing it, or suffering from it. This gender blindness is perpetuated when writers specifically identify men as the main or sole actors in armed conflict, or fail to question the assumption that men's experiences and perspectives of war are universal.

In this review of current writing on women, gender, and conflict, I focus on the weakness of gender analysis in the current debates on conflict theory. Most of these debates are being conducted from a gender-blind perspective, and far too few feminists and gender specialists have engaged in them. This chapter first lays out some of the areas where I feel there is a need to apply a gender analysis to new conflict theories; then it identifies some of the writers who are trying to do this.

CURRENT DEBATES ON CONFLICT THEORY

Analysts across the political spectrum agree that the conduct and characteristics of war have changed since the end of the Cold War. Most wars are fought internally; ethnic divisions are prominent; no sides can any longer depend on support from the superpowers and must find their own forms of financing the war; civilians are widely targeted; and national sovereignty has been challenged by the growing use of armed humanitarian intervention.

However, much mainstream thinking about contemporary armed conflict is still dominated by outdated and questionable theories about the causes and mechanics of war. This is partly due to the dominant paradigm in the North that countries in the global South are all at different stages of progression toward states modeled on the democratic capitalist societies of Europe and North America. The underlying assumption is that democratic capitalism is the world's only viable political and economic model. Authors such as Robert Kaplan (1994) and Samuel Huntington (1998) go much further, popularizing the ideas that certain

countries and cultures are more inclined to violence, that "ancient ethnic hatreds" are the cause of many wars, that the combination of youth
and poverty in many countries in the South is combustible, and that the
perpetrators of the new wars employ an incomprehensible brutality.
Even more liberal authors base their analysis of conflict on a series of
"truths" that are accepted as self-evident. These include the idea that
war is largely fought by men, acting in formal roles as soldiers; that it is
defined and contained within the framework of state and seeks to acquire
or retain state power; that it is caused by conditions of poverty and frustration and failure of the state; and that although violence against civilians
is widespread, it is simply an unfortunate by-product of war.

The work of authors such as Alex de Waal (2001), Mark Duffield
(1994, 1996, 2001), Adele Harmer (Harmer and Macrae 2004; Harmer
and Cotterrell 2005), David Keen (2000), Joanna Macrae (2002), Nicola
Reindorp (see Macrae et al. 2002), and Hugo Slim (1998) challenges
these assumptions and compels us to question our own way of viewing
today's conflicts. The distinguishing characteristic of new conflict theory is that post–Cold War conflicts cannot be fully understood in terms
of the breakdown of systems—in other words, failures of the state, ethnic hatred, or resource conflicts—but should be analyzed as indigenous
strategies for adapting to globalization. Although they all write from
their own areas of specialization, most of these authors share the following observations about contemporary conflict:

- Many internal wars are not simply a failure of development
  policy: they represent new processes that seek to reshape political and economic power.
- The aim of many insurgencies is not to take state power, but to
  create parallel economic and political spheres of power that are
  linked into international economic systems.
- Many internal wars are partly or fully shaped by reactions to
  globalization and are linked into international economic and political networks.
- The resulting "network wars" have different nodes of influence
  and power, which can shift among countries, individuals, economic
  systems, and organizations.
- Ethnicity and religion do not cause war, but are used by elites as
  ways to mobilize populations into war.
- Many insurgents depend on terror as a means of controlling territory
  or populations, rather than relying on sophisticated weaponry and

well-trained troops. Thus, violence against civilians is not an unfortunate by-product of war but a deliberate strategy of control.

- Many governments employ militia or irregular forces as a cheap and easy way to reduce costs and circumvent international law. The number of non-state actors in war is growing, as combat is increasingly "privatized." These may include militia, paramilitaries, irregular forces, security companies, warlords, and private armies.

- It is essential to understand the political economy of war and the actors (at differing levels) for whom war is a viable or profitable concern.

- In the post–Cold War era, the principles of impartiality and neutrality have become increasingly blurred, as Western governments seek to apply the policy of "coherence," trying to line up political, economic, diplomatic, military, and aid actors into the same overall strategy.[1]

- Wars are not caused by widespread poverty and the failure of development, but by local and regional power elites who seek to maintain networks of patronage.

The authors cited above are exceptional analysts of conflict, and their work is essential reading for everyone who works in the fields of development aid, humanitarian relief, conflict resolution, and peace-building. However, their writing rarely mentions women and is largely gender-blind (Byrne 1995). The new theories of conflict have so far failed to bring to light the different ways in which such conflict affects the roles of men and women, or the relationships and power balance between them.

We therefore need a more gendered understanding of how and why contemporary conflicts are developing, what happens to the people involved in them, where the different poles of power lie, and who and what moves them. Below I outline three main areas in which a gendered analysis is most needed.

Causes of Internal Wars and Western Strategies to Shape their Outcomes

Duffield (2001) and Macrae (2002) question the "failed state" argument, which conveniently both circumvents the need for structural transformation or questioning of the international global system and prescribes a better application of the democratic capitalist model as the only logical way in which to organize a nation-state. Both authors analyze how insurgencies are developing strategies of economic and political power that are not centered on the state. Although there are many gendered analyses of state building (most notably Enloe 2000; Cockburn and Zarkov 2002; Afshar 2004; and Klein 2004), there is little gendered analysis of the increasing number of conflicts in which the state is disintegrating and new forms of power are being fashioned (Byrne 1995).

Duffield (1996, 2001) and Macrae (2002) also analyze Western geopolitical strategies to control and contain conflict in countries in the South. They develop the idea of coherence, explaining how Western democracies have sought to align diplomacy, political aims, economic policy, military actions, and international aid with security objectives as a way to contain conflict within the borders of other countries. Macrae focuses on the use of the doctrine of human security within the context of "coherence." Feminists have begun to bring a gendered analysis to this doctrine, particularly in the realm of peacekeeping (see, for example, Afshar and Eade 2004; Broadhead 2002; Hyndman 2001). Most feminist analysis, however, does not address current conflict in the light of these new theories.

Western states are using a range of measures, from sanctions to humanitarian intervention, to alter the internal governance of countries in the South (Macrae 2002). From the bombing of Afghanistan in 2001, after the attacks on the United States on September 11, 2001, as the "global war on terror" (GWOT) develops, the policies of Islamic countries in relation to women are increasingly being used as a justification for intervention. Mohammed Haneef Atmar (2001) presents an excellent dissection of Western governments' cynical concern for gender issues for reasons of their own political convenience.

Economic Systems and Conflict within the Global Framework

Keen (2000) examines the economic engines that drive and sustain conflict, arguing that these must be examined in order to understand the conflict's causes. An increasing number of studies, such as those by Philippe Le Billon (2000) and Sarah Collinson (2002), consider the political economy of war. Because neither insurgents nor governments can now depend on superpower patronage, they have had to find new ways to fund wars, including trading in drugs and arms, sex trafficking, and illicit resource extraction. These and other funding strategies are now embedded in international economic and financial systems (Duffield 2001; Keen 2000). Although there are good studies of how women develop livelihood strategies in situations of conflict (for example, Pain and Lautze 2002; El Bushra 2004), these largely country-specific studies have not been tied into a gendered analysis of the global economic systems that drive and sustain conflict.

New Types of Insurgencies: Their Objectives and Use of Violence

Although nation-states such as Afghanistan, Burundi, the Democratic Republic of the Congo (DRC), and Somalia appear to be weak or disintegrating, new spheres of economic and political power that depend on continual instability are being constructed within them (Duffield 2001). In such situations, and also in stronger states such as Uganda and Colombia, brutality is increasingly the central weapon of war. It is used both by rebel armies who use terror in place of manpower and sophisticated weaponry, and by paramilitaries deployed by governments in order to duck responsibility for war crimes and avoid giving grounds for humanitarian intervention. Max Glaser (2005) has produced a good up-to-date study on armed non-state actors (ANSAs) with matrices to help humanitarians figure out how to engage with them. However, because this study is gender blind, it will not help humanitarians to engage with the gendered reality of these non-state actors. Rebel groups such as the Revolutionary United Front (RUF) in Sierra Leone, the Lord's Resistance Army (LRA) in Uganda, and the various armed groups in the eastern Congo have kidnapped girls and women for use in sexual, military, and logistics roles. They have forced their combatants to commit horrific acts of sexual abuse and other atrocities that have become their key mechanisms for population control. Although there has been some good gendered analysis of the role of rape and sexual violence in ethnic cleansing and genocide, particularly in the cases of Bosnia, Kosovo, Rwanda, and now Darfur (Lorentzen and Turpin 1998; Turshan and Twagiramariya 1998; Mertus 2000; Rees 2002), there is far less gendered analysis of how the insurgencies in Uganda and armed groups in the DRC operate and successfully alter social relationships through the widespread violation of cultural norms and gender identities. The increasing role of non-state actors in war is a key element in new theories about conflict, but there are as yet too few gendered analyses of these actors' goals and how they build and wield power.

LITERATURE ON GENDER AND CONFLICT

You need to cast a wide net when looking for literature on gender and conflict. Apart from Cynthia Cockburn, Cynthia Enloe, Dyan Mazurana, and Sandra Whitworth, many feminists are either writing about conflict from their particular areas of expertise or focusing on a specific national or regional conflict rather than doing a global analysis. Authors on gender and conflict come from fields as diverse as anthropology, human rights, geography, gender studies, law, and political sciences, and many are actively involved in health, humanitarian work, conflict resolution, peacekeeping, and solidarity activism. However, they tend not to address the wider dynamic of conflict as global process; instead they concentrate their attention on the particulars of a conflict in a certain time and place and its effects on women, men, and their relationships. Although such specific studies are absolutely essential, this focus on the particular may be one of the main reasons that particular studies of gender and conflict are not tied into a more global analysis.

A plethora of good solid work on gender and conflict began to flourish in the 1980s. The report of an Oxfam GB workshop on "Gender, Development and Conflict" was a breakthrough from an aid perspective, demonstrating how conflict affected women differently from men (El Bushra and Piza-López 1984). From the Institute of Development Studies (IDS) at the University of Sussex, Bridget Byrne (1995) made the critical link from Enloe's gender analysis of masculinity in war to theories of conflict and issues in humanitarian work, although her analysis does not include enough of the new thinking on contemporary conflict. Julie Mertus (2000) is a valuable source on the effects of both war and humanitarian relief on women, but rather than examining why war has developed in these ways, she looks at how conflict is experienced by women. At the Catholic Agency For Overseas Development (CAFOD), Fiona Fox looked critically at the conditionality implicit in the "new humanitarianism" (Fox 2001). The volume edited by Haleh Afshar and Deborah Eade (2004) is an excellent collection of women's analysis of the impact of war and peacekeeping from different parts of the world, unique in its geographic breadth.

There are many examples of excellent place-specific work; the following lists only a few. Judy El Bushra (2004) offers a perceptive account of the gendered impact of war on women in five African countries, making women visible in the political economies of conflict in those societies. Judith Zur (1998), an anthropologist, has written an authoritative portrait of the gendered use of terror by Guatemalan paramilitaries as a form of social control over women, while Rita Manchanda (2001) illustrates women's experience in a spectrum of Asian conflicts.

Its high quality notwithstanding, I would argue that this work should be carried further in two regards. As stated earlier, most of the literature on gender and conflict seems to be written in parallel with the new theories of conflict, without either of the debates engaging with the other. Analyses of gender and conflict urgently need to intersect with and engage with new theories of conflict. There is a considerable volume of gendered analysis of traditional conflict theory, including women's experience in guerrilla movements in El Salvador, Sri Lanka, and Namibia during the Cold War (Kampwirth 2002; Manchanda 2001). However, with the exception of authors such as Cynthia Enloe, there is very little gendered analysis of the reasons that insurgencies are now fighting in different ways. And although some place-specific studies touch on aspects of political economy, there is little literature that links these ideas with the larger debates in order to give us a comprehensive gendered view of the dynamics of contemporary conflict.

GENDER AND CONFLICT LITERATURE AND NEW THEORIES OF CONFLICT

Although there is a great need for more gendered analysis of the new theories of conflict, a few writers have been doing seminal work in this area. Within the confines of this chapter, it is only possible to highlight the books and articles that I have found most helpful in bringing a gendered understanding to the three areas identified in the introductory section.

Causes of Internal Wars and The Role of the West

Dyan Mazurana's chapter, "Gender and the Causes and Consequences of Armed Conflict," in Mazurana et al. 2005 is the most comprehensive gendered analysis to date of the new theories about the causes of conflict.

Mazurana successfully weaves a gender analysis into the intersections of globalization and conflict, incorporating many of the key challenges to mainstream assumptions about war. The strength of this edited volume is both in bringing a gendered analysis to peacekeeping and human security and incorporating the new theories of conflict into a gendered analysis, particularly in relation to human security. The introduction to this edited volume also provides a comprehensive, gendered analysis of conflict. The chapter by Ruth Jacobson provides two gendered histories of the conflicts in Mozambique and Angola, with a focus on how the international community could have learned (but did not) from the good examples of gender sensitivity at the end of hostilities in Mozambique. Although Jacobson does not really relate to the new theories of conflict, the way in which she analyzes gender roles could easily be applied to them.

In *Sites of Violence: Gender and Conflict Zones,* Wenona Giles and Jennifer Hyndman, both in their introduction and in their concluding chapter, "New Directions for Feminist Research and Politics," give a gendered analysis of some aspects of conflict theory, touching on political economy and human security and gender. The chapter by Edith Klein examines the intersections between globalization, political violence, and social transformation in the former Yugoslavia. Klein develops a gendered framework tool for tracing the linkages among the politics of globalization, conflict, and the increased oppression of women (Giles and Hyndman:293), and provides a good gendered analysis of what she calls "coercive constitutionalism" and the geopolitics of intervention in the Balkans. Although it resembles the explanations given by Macrae and Duffield of why Western democracies use humanitarian intervention to reshape the landscapes of conflict, Klein does not draw on their work. If she were to tie coercive constitutionalism into a broader examination of the political underpinnings of globalization, her analysis would be brought into the wider debates on conflict theory.

This edited volume is meant to "analyze the gendered, nationalized, racialized and economic dimensions of violent conflict and the ways these phenomena shape the waging of contemporary war." Its primary focus is the impact of war-related violence on women, and many of the chapters are written by women who are conducting research in conflict zones. The editors also do an excellent job of pointing to future areas for feminist research. Again, however, the book seems to have been written in parallel with much of the new conflict theory, because the editors and contributors never really locate their work within the framework of the debates shaping the analysis of contemporary wars. This may explain the state-centric perspective adopted by most of the contributors. The exception is the outstanding and provocatively titled chapter by Audrey Macklin on the role played by Talisman, a Canadian oil company, in the conflict in southern Sudan.

How Global Economic Systems Intersect with Conflict

In her book *The Shadows of War,* Carolyn Nordstrom takes apart the complex scenario of people trying to sell tomatoes in a war zone and their links to the international economy, and lays out the pieces on the table so that we can understand how the links work. She does not give an explicitly gendered analysis of political economy of war, but provides all the essential elements for building up such an analysis because she brings to light so many things that usually remain hidden. She brilliantly links the experiences of men, women, and children both inside and outside war zones in Angola, and draws the lines that connect rural women surviving war, businesses and people engaged in smuggling goods, and the international centers of commerce. The chapter by Macklin referred to earlier is a good companion piece to Nordstrom's work: she offers a more gendered study of the linkages between displaced women from southern Sudan who were imprisoned in Khartoum for brewing beer and the practices of a Canadian oil company operating in their place of origin.

Political economy is crucial to understanding how wars are sustained — from the way in which elites manipulate resources, right down to the way in which villagers adapt their livelihood strategies in order to survive (Le Billon 2000). Women, as the majority of those displaced by war, both within borders and as refugees, are often the heads of their families. They spend a lot of time "diversifying their livelihood strategies." Women wash diamonds, smuggle drugs, farm crops for insurgents, are used as war slaves in resource extraction, sell food to insurgents and government forces alike, and act as porters for rebels. In other words, they are an integral part of the political economy of war and the financing of war. We need many more studies to help us to understand how women are affect and are affected by these shadow war economies.

Conflict analysts often "locate" women primarily in roles defined by humanitarian relief terms (i.e., as *refugee* or *displaced*). Arturo Escobar (1995) argues that "the power of the development apparatus to name women in ways that lead us to take for granted certain descriptions and solutions has to be made visible" (p. xx). Would not analysis of women in conflict situations also be different if women were primarily located as actors in the political economy of war? We cannot begin that kind of analysis unless we can make women's roles visible. Analysis that maintains women's invisibility contributes to the concept of "womenandchildren," the term that Cynthia Enloe so graphically uses to describe how we lump those populations together as faceless victims of war.

New Types of Insurgency

Contributors to Giles and Hyndman (2004) provide useful gendered analyses of the uses and construction of nationalist and/or ethnic identities as a tool for mobilization. They are, however, rooted in a state-centered analysis and illustrate the need for equally detailed gendered analysis of how identities are constructed in the new kinds of insurgency, new paramilitaries, and parallel spheres of power. When authors fail to look at new understandings of how parallel spheres of economic and political power are emerging in situations of conflict, they consequently fail to address the gender politics that shape and inform them.

Mark Duffield (2001) and David Keen (2000) both examine how insurgents who are fighting against the state have changed the ways in which they prosecute war since the end of the Cold War, and they identify fundamental shifts in the insurgents' relationships with civilians. Insurgents must now support themselves, and they do so by siphoning off relief supplies, controlling resource extraction, linking up with international markets, engaging in illicit trade, and controlling civilians in their areas of influence. Many such groups feel no need to build a political project with the civilian population in territory that they occupy. Rather than even paying lip service to it, in places such as Sierra Leone and Uganda, part of the modus operandi of the rebel groups is to use brutal terror in order to exercise control over civilians. These armed non-state actors depend on the widespread kidnapping of civilians for use as combatants, cooks, porters, workers, sexual companions, and spies, forcing them to comply by making them witness or participate in gruesome attacks on other civilians. As documented extensively by Human Rights Watch (2002, 2003) and Amnesty International (1999), rebels in Liberia, Sierra Leone, and Uganda found that forcing kidnapped civilians to beat other people to death or amputate limbs under the threat of torture proved a brutally effective way to control large populations with only a limited supply of weapons.

Neither Duffield nor Keen offers a gender analysis of how these rebel groups operate, but Dyan Mazurana and Kristopher Carlson do in their 2004 report *From Combat to Community: Women and Girls in Sierra Leone.* They render women in these rebel and paramilitary groups visible in analyzing how girls and young women participated in the war in Sierra Leone and showing how girl soldiers in Sierra Leone fared in disarmament, demobilization, and reintegration (DDR) programs sponsored by the United Nations and the World Bank.

Mazurana and Carlson show that the rebels needed captive "wives" and children in order to maintain their war systems and kidnapped young women and girls for that reason. Many of these women and girls also fought, as well as working as spies, cooks, health workers, or porters. Mazurana and Carlson pay close attention to the differences among these girls and women and find that forcibly abducted commanders' wives were key to the entire operation of the rebel forces. These women controlled the distribution of loot, supervised operations when their captor-husbands were away, and decided on fighting strategies. As captives themselves, some commanders' wives also tried to use their power to protect captive girls from sexual abuse by other male combatants. Much that is written about abducted women and girls in fighting forces simplifies the issue into male soldiers and kidnapped girls who are sexually exploited. Mazurana and Carlson provide insights into how rebel leaders manipulate and use gender in order to make their warfare systems viable, and the effects on those girls and women and their communities both during the conflict and in reconstruction.

The study is a good example of the kind of gendered analysis that needs to be done, and it demonstrates why such analysis is so necessary. Its detailed research reveals that the roles that women played in the rebel groups went far beyond being simple "sex slaves" or "camp followers," showing rather that they were essential to the functioning of the war systems. Mazurana and Carlson also reveal how little the females in the rebel forces benefited from DRR programs, compared with the males, precisely because there had been no gendered analysis of the fighting forces by those who planned and implemented the programs.

One very important way to make women's roles visible as the nature of conflict evolves is to identify and unravel the different gender policies of different actors in war. This means understanding the gender policies devised by the controlling group to ensure that women and men will be more effective in carrying out their roles within the war system. In this way, we can see that the Revolutionary United Front (RUF) in Sierra Leone, a group infamous for crude amputations, brutal violence, widespread sexual abuse, and kidnapping of children to serve as their soldiers, had a very clear gender policy. Although it was brutal and sub-jugated women, the RUF certainly had a gendered analysis of how to control civilian populations as well as a gender-specific policy on the kidnapping and use of children and women. Two excellent reports by Human Rights Watch (2002, 2003) on Eastern Congo and Sierra Leone give insights into a gendered analysis of the different roles and power relationships of men and women, civilian and combatant, in the insur-gencies, including the cultural norms and gender roles that are consis-tently violated by the fighters. These reports provide an excellent basis for building a more complex gendered analysis of non-state actors and their methods of waging war.

GENDERED VIOLENCE IN CONTEMPORARY WARFARE

It has been argued that violence against civilians is not an avoidable or neg-ative consequence of war, but a deliberate and necessary strategy of the conduct of contemporary wars (Duffield 1994, 2001; Mazurana et al. 2005). Although there is an important body of work on gender violence that examines rape, sexual abuse, and other types of violence against women in war, much of it focuses on rape as a weapon of ethnic warfare. Important literature on this subject came out of the collapse of Yugoslavia, and some focused on Rwanda and latterly on Darfur (see, for example, Abdela 2004; Copeland 1998; Turshan and Twagiramariya 1998; Manchanda 2001; and Gingrich and Leaning 2004). Only a few writers such as Mazurana et al. (2005) and Macklin (2004) take up the insights of Mark Duffield and others, who say that this type of violence is not simply a by-product of war but is an organic part of how war is waged. Nor is rape primarily a tool of ethnic warfare, although it seems to be a fairly universal and effective strategy of military, insurgent, and non-state armed forces for the control of territory and populations. This begs a gendered analysis of how combatants and those running today's wars see sexual violence as part of their strategy. Cynthia Enloe has consis-tently driven home the point that construction of masculinity matters in militarization. In her chapter, "All the Men Are in Militias, All the

Women Are Victims" (2004), she undertakes a thorough analysis of how Serbian militias used constructs of masculinity to make a twenty-one-year-old casual worker rape Muslim women as part of his war effort. Her work raises questions about how war leaders define gender relations and gender identities so that fighters accept rape as such a universal strategy, even when it violates cultural norms. To move from denouncing rape as a war crime to finding out why generalized brutal sexual violence is such an important weapon in modern warfare, we need more studies like Enloe's of the gender policies of armed forces that also engage with the discussion of new theories of conflict, particularly in challenging the "weak states" argument.

Parallel Spheres of Political and Economic Interests

What roles do men and women play in constructing the parallel spheres of political and economic interest in conflict zones in the South? What are the impacts of living in these parallel spheres for men and women at different levels of power? What are the gendered identities upon which these spheres are built, and how does the participation of men and women differ? Enloe (2004) addresses precisely these points when she examines the role of militarized masculinity in creating and maintaining one sphere of parallel power, by taking a careful look at the area controlled by the former warlord (now statesman) Ismael Khan in Afghanistan. Enloe's description of Khan's sexual politics and the role that militarized masculinity plays in the US military support for him underlines an urgent need to develop a feminist analysis of the warlord phenomenon. Given the Bush administration's incorporation of gender oppression into its rationale for bombing Afghanistan and for the war on Iraq, more thorough analysis of the role of gender relations in the mechanics of how warlords claim and maintain power is extremely important.

Chris Dolan (2002) has examined the links between violent masculinity and weak states in the Ugandan conflict, concluding that weak states do not allow alternative masculinities to evolve. This is an intriguing angle, but it needs to be far more developed. For example, Uganda is not a weak state in the sense that Somalia, the DRC, and Afghanistan are. However, Dolan's examination of the frustrations caused by men's expectations and experiences of masculinity in northern Uganda, and how those frustrations are played out violently in the larger political landscape, is a helpful lens for gender and conflict analysis.

CONCLUSION

Cynthia Enloe has always made the point that masculinity matters and must be taken into consideration when doing a gendered analysis of conflict. Such analyses are even more important in this New Age of Empire (Enloe 2004). The authors whom I have highlighted in this literature review are among those whose work is moving feminist insights into the field of new theories of conflict. A gendered analysis must now be brought into the new debates on how and why war is waged today.

NOTES

[1] Andrew Natsios, the director of USAID, gave a good illustration of coherence in May 2003 when he told the US aid agencies that their aims in Iraq were part of US government goals.

REFERENCES

Abdela, L. (2004) "Kosovo: Missed Opportunities, Lessons for the Future," in H. Afshar and D. Eade (eds.) *Development, Women and War: Feminist Perspectives,* Oxford: Oxfam GB.

Afshar, H. (2004) "Women and Wars: some Trajectories towards a Feminist Peace' in H. Afshar and D. Eade (eds.) *Development, Women and War: Feminist Perspectives,* Oxford: Oxfam GB.

Afshar, H. and D. Eade (eds.) (2004) *Development, Women and War: Feminist Perspectives,* Oxford: Oxfam GB.

Amnesty International (1999) "Sierra Leone," in *1999 Annual Report,* available at www.amnesty.org/ailib/aireport/ar99/afr51.htm (retrieved October 7, 2005).

Atmar, Haneef (2001) "Politicization of Humanitarian Aid and Its Consequences for Afghans," *Disasters* 25(4):321–330.

Broadhead, L. (2002) "Repackaging Notions of Security: a Skeptical Feminist," in S. Jacobs, R. Jacobson, and J. Marchbank (eds.) *States of Conflict, Gender, Violence and Resistance,* London: Zed Books.

Byrne, B. (1995) *Gender, Conflict and Development: Volume I: Overview,* BRIDGE, Brighton: Institute of Development Studies.

Cockburn, C. (2004) "The Continuum of Violence: A Gender Perspective on War and Peace" in W. Giles and J. Hyndman (eds.) *Sites of Violence: Gender and Conflict Zones,* Berkeley, CA: University of California Press.

Cockburn, C. and D. Zarkov (eds.) 2002, *The Postwar Moment: Militaries, Masculinities and International Peacekeeping,* London: Lawrence & Wishart.

Collinson, S. (2002) *Politically Informed Humanitarian Programming: Using a Political Economy Approach,* Humanitarian Practice Network Paper 41, London: Overseas Development Institute.

Copeland, R. (1998) "Surfacing Gender: Reconceptualizing Crimes against Women in Time of War," in L. Lorentzen and J. Turpin (eds.) *The Women and War Reader,* New York: New York University Press.

Dolan, C. (2002) "Collapsing Masculinities and Weak States," in F. Cleaver (ed.) *Making Men Matter: Men, Masculinities, and Gender Relations in Development,* London: Zed Books.

Duffield, M. (1994) "Complex Emergencies and the Crisis of Developmentalism," *IDS Bulletin* 25(4): 37–45.

Duffield M. (1996) "Symphony of the Damned: Racial Discourse, Complex Political Emergencies and Humanitarian Aid," *Disasters* 20(3):173–193.

Duffield, M. (2001) *Global Governance and the New Wars: The Merging of Development and Security,* London: Zed Books.

El-Bushra, J. (2004) "Fused in Combat: Gender Relations and Armed Conflict" in H. Afshar and D. Eade (eds.) *Development, Women and War: Feminist Perspectives,* Oxford: Oxfam GB.

El-Bushra J. and E. Piza-López (1984) *Development in Conflict: The Gender Dimension,* Oxford: Oxfam UK and Ireland.

Enloe, C. (2000) *Maneuvers: The International Politics of Militarizing Women's Lives,* Berkeley, CA: University of California Press.

Enloe, C. (2004) *The Curious Feminist: Searching for Women in the New Age of Empire*, Berkeley, CA: University of California Press.

Escobar, Arturo (1995) *Encountering Development: The Making and Unmaking of the Third World*, Princeton: Princeton University Press.

Fox, F. (2001) "New Humanitarianism: Does It Provide a Moral Banner for the 21st Century?," *Disasters* 25(4): 275–289.

Giles, W. and J. Hyndman (eds.) (2004) *Sites of Violence: Gender and Conflict Zones,* Berkeley, CA: University of California Press.

Gingrich, T. and J. Leaning (2004) "The Use of Rape as a Weapon of War in the Conflict in Darfur, Sudan," paper prepared for USAID/OTI under the auspices of the Harvard School of Public Health and the François-Xavier Bagnoud Center for Health and Human Rights, Boston.

Glaser, M.P. (2005) *Humanitarian Engagement with Non-State Armed Actors: The Parameters of Negotiated Access,* Humanitarian Practice Network Paper 51, London: Overseas Development Institute.

Guatam, S., A. Banskota, and R. Manchanda (2001) "Where There Are No Men: Women in the Maoist Insurgency in Nepal," in R. Manchanda (ed.) *Women, War and Peace in South Asia,* New Delhi: Sage.

Harmer, A. and L. Cotterrell (2005) *Diversity in Donorship: The Changing Landscape of Official Humanitarian Aid,* Humanitarian Policy Group Report 20, London: Overseas Development Institute.

Harmer, A. and J. Macrae (eds.) (2004) *Beyond the Continuum: The Changing Role of Aid Policy in Protracted Crises,* Humanitarian Policy Group Briefing Paper 16, London: Overseas Development Institute.

Human Rights Watch (2002) *The War within the War, Sexual Violence against Women and Girls in the Eastern Congo,* New York: Human Rights Watch.

Human Rights Watch (2003) *"We'll Kill You If You Cry": Sexual Violence in Sierra Leone,* New York: Human Rights Watch.

Huntington, S. (1998) *The Clash of Civilizations and the Remaking of World Order,* New York: Simon & Schuster.

Hyndman, J. (2001) *Managing Displacement: Refugees and the Politics of Humanitarianism,* Minneapolis, MN: University of Minnesota Press.

Jacobson, R. (2005) "Gender, War and Peace in Mozambique and Angola: Advances and Absences" in D. Mazurana, A. Raven Roberts, and J. Parpart (eds.) *Gender, Conflict, and Peacekeeping,* Boulder, CO: Rowman & Littlefield.

Kampwirth, K. (2002) *Women and Guerrilla Movements: Nicaragua, El Salvador, Chiapas and Cuba,* Philadelphia, PA: Pennsylvania State University Press.

Kaplan, R. (1994) "The Coming Anarchy," *The Atlantic Monthly,* February: 44–76.

Keen, D. (2000) "Incentives and Disincentives for Violence" in D.M. Malone (ed.) *Greed and Grievance,* International Peace Academy, Boulder CO: Lynne Rienner.

Klein, E. (2004) "The Gendered Impact of Multilateralism in the Post Yugoslav States," in W. Giles and J. Hyndman (eds.) *Sites of Violence: Gender and Conflict Zones,* Berkeley, CA: University of California Press.

Korac, M. (2004) "War, Flight and Exile; Gendered Violence among Refugee Women from Post-Yugoslav States," in W. Giles and J. Hyndman (eds.) *Sites of Violence: Gender and Conflict Zones,* Berkeley, CA: University of California Press.

Le Billon, P. (2000) *The Political Economy of War: What Relief Agencies Need to Know,* Humanitarian Practice Network Paper 33, London: Overseas Development Institute.

Lorentzen, L. and J. Turpin (1998) *The Women and War Reader,* New York: New York University Press.

Macklin, A. (2004) "Like Oil and Water, with a <atch; Militarized Commerce, Armed Conflict and Human Security in Sudan," in W. Giles and J. Hyndman (eds.) *Sites of Violence: Gender and Conflict Zones,* Berkeley, CA: University of California Press.

Macrae, J. (ed.) (2002) *The New Humanitarianisms: a Review of Trends in Global Humanitarian Action,* Humanitarian Policy Group Report 11, London: Overseas Development Institute.

Macrae, J., S. Collinson, M. Buchanan-Smith, N. Reindorp, A. Schmidt, T. Mowjee, and A. Harmer (2002) *Uncertain Power: The Changing Role of Official Donors in Humanitarian Action,* Humanitarian Policy Group Report 12, London: Overseas Development Institute.

Manchanda, R. (ed.) (2001) *Women, War and Peace in South Asia,* New Delhi: Sage.

Mazurana, D. and Carlson, K. (2004) *From Combat to Community: Women and Girls in Sierra Leone,* Cambridge, MA: Women's Policy Commission, Harvard University.

Mazurana, D., A. Raven-Roberts, and J. Parpart (eds.) (2005) *Gender, Conflict, and Peacekeeping,* Boulder, CO: Rowman & Littlefield.

Mertus, J. (2000) *War's Offensive on Women,* West Hartford, CT: Kumarian Press.

Nordstrom, C. (2004) *The Shadows of War: Violence, Power and International Profiteering in the Twenty-first Century,* Berkeley, CA: University of California Press.

Pain, A. and S. Lautze (2002) *Addressing Livelihoods in Afghanistan,* Afghanistan Research and Evaluation Unit Issues Paper Series, Kabul: AREU.

Rees, M. (2002) "International Intervention in Bosnia-Herzegovina: The Cost of Ignoring Gender," in C. Cockburn and D. Zarkov (eds.) *The Postwar Moment: Militaries, Masculinities and International Peacekeeping,* London: Lawrence & Wishart.

Slim, H. (1998) "International Humanitarianism's Engagement with Civil War in the 1990s: A Glance at Evolving Practice and Theory,' a briefing paper for ActionAid UK, published in the *Journal of Humanitarian Assistance,* available at www.jha.ac/articles/a033.htm (retrieved August 29, 2005).

Turshan, M. and C. Twagiramariya (eds.) (1998) *What Women Do in Wartime: Gender and Conflict in Africa,* London: Zed Books.

de Waal, A. (2001) *Who Fights? Who Cares?,* Trenton, NJ: Africa World Press.

Whitworth, S. (1998) "Gender, Race and the Politics of Peacekeeping," in E. Moxon-Browne (ed.) *A Future for Peacekeeping?,* London: Macmillan.

Zur, J. (1998) *Violent Memories: Mayan War Widows in Guatemala,* Boulder, CO: Westview Press.

First published in *Development in Practice* 16(3&4): 342–353 in 2006.

THIRTEEN

Selected Resources on Contemporary Humanitarianism

DEBORAH EADE

As Tony Vaux points out in his introductory essay, the concept of humanitarianism applies to both war and general disaster, and is based on the principle that "in extreme cases of human suffering external agents may offer assistance to people in need, and in doing so should be accorded respect and even 'rights' in carrying out their functions." However, policymakers in humanitarian agencies and aid workers on the ground face a bewilderingly complex set of challenges in determining such rights. Gone are any comfortable certainties about what is known in the commercial sector as "the license to operate," and claims to the moral high ground of neutrality have an increasingly hollow ring. Perhaps more to the point, such assumptions are of little practical use to frontline workers who may risk ambush, abduction, deportation, injury, accidental death, or assassination as the result of their professional activities; nor do outdated road maps help relief agencies to orient their decisions on whether to withdraw or continue providing material assistance even in the knowledge that a proportion of this assistance is fueling the violence or lining the pockets of conflict profiteers. There are no standard "off-the-peg" answers because each situation has to be considered on its own merits. And of course no two aid agencies share an identical mandate or have precisely the same expertise or history of involvement with the affected population—all factors that must be weighed in deciding the appropriate course of action.

Early warning, prevention, mitigation, and other more technical
issues associated with natural disasters are not covered here for reasons
of space. Because catastrophic events disproportionately affect the poor
and marginalized, however, they expose and may intensify existing
political crises, social cleavages, and structural injustice, as became
clear in wake of the Asian tsunami in areas such as Aceh and Sri Lanka.
For instance, in his seminal work on the 1943 Bengal famine, *Poverty
and Famines: An Essay on Entitlement and Deprivation* (Oxford
University Press 1984) Amartya K Sen argued that famines do not occur
in functioning democracies. Similarly, in *Guatemala: Unnatural Disaster*
(Latin America Bureau 1978) Roger Plant showed how the 1974 earthquake triggered the brutal intensification of state violence that resulted
in the death or disappearance of 200,000 Guatemalans and created "a
nation of widows and orphans." The events surrounding Hurricane Katrina
underscore the point.

In keeping with the focus of this collection, we have given priority
to publications and organizations reflecting on some direct involvement
in humanitarian endeavor rather than more policy-oriented or scholarly
works or academic institutions. We have highlighted literature on the
1994 genocide in Rwanda because this was such a defining event for
contemporary humanitarianism, and some recent publications concerning the US-led invasions of Afghanistan in October 2001 and of Iraq in
March 2003 because these have significantly redefined the global policy and practice landscape within which humanitarian agencies operate.
Inevitably this selection represents only a glimpse of the burgeoning literature in these fields, but we trust that this will encourage readers, and
particularly those directly involved in humanitarian endeavors, to explore
the issues further.

SECTION 1: PUBLICATIONS

1.1 BOOKS AND REPORTS

Adebajo, Adekeye, and Ismail Rashid (eds.). *West Africa's Security Challenges:
Building Peace in a Troubled Region.* Boulder, CO: Lynne Rienner, 2004,
ISBN: 1 5882 6284 7, 449 pp.

> Contributors examine the internal factors leading to violent con-
> flict in West Africa through the 1990s and ways in which regional
> and external actors tried to mitigate or fuel it. Topics addressed
> include civil–military relations' the political economy of conflict,

small arms and light weapons' the roles of France, the United Kingdom, the United States, and the UN' and the security challenges facing West Africa. See also Adekeye Adebajo *Building Peace in West Africa: Liberia, Sierra Leone, and Guinea-Bissau* (Lynne Rienner 2002) and *Liberia's Civil War* (Lynne Rienner 2002), and Adekeye Adebajo and Chandra Lekha Sriram (eds.) *Managing Armed Conflicts in the 21st Century* (Routledge 2001).

Afshar, Haleh, and Deborah Eade (eds.). *Development, Women, and War: Feminist Perspectives.* Oxford: Oxfam GB, 2004, ISBN: 0 8559 8487 2, 385 pp.

This volume presents different feminist approaches to humanitarian assistance, peacebuilding, and conflict resolution, ranging from high-level international interventions to grassroots work for peaceful solutions to war and political violence. Focusing on conflicts in Africa, the Balkans, Central America, and the Middle East, contributors underline the need to comprehend the underlying gendered power relations and the dynamics of social change during and after violent conflict. Available free online at www.developmentinpractice.org.

Baksh, Rawwida, Linda Etchart, Elsie Onubogu, and Tina Johnson (eds.). *Gender Mainstreaming in Conflict Transformation: Building Sustainable Peace.* London: Commonwealth Secretariat, 2005, ISBN: 0 8509 2754 4, 248 pp.

Designed as a capacity-building, advocacy, and policy tool, the first section addresses general issues such as how to apply a gender lens to an analysis of violent conflict and post-war reconstruction. Part II documents experiences of gender and conflict in Commonwealth countries and subregions, including Bangladesh, Cyprus, India, Jamaica, the Pacific, Papua New Guinea, Sierra Leone, and Sri Lanka.

Bais, Karolein, and Mijnd Huijser. *The Profit of Peace: Corporate Responsibility in Conflict Regions.* Sheffield: Greenleaf Publishing Ltd., 2005, ISBN: 1 874 719 90 X, 144 pp.

Many of the 60,000 multinational companies that work in conflict-affected regions profit by trading arms, taking advantage of the absence of the rule of law, or exploiting the availability of cheap labor. Extensive interviews with corporate managers working in countries such as Afghanistan, Burma, and Rwanda show that even if these managers observe high ethical standards, they understand that their investment inevitably influences the outcome of the conflict. The authors set out business practices that can help contribute to peace and stability.

Barakat, Sultan (ed.). *Reconstructing War-torn Societies: Afghanistan.* Basingstoke: Palgrave Macmillan, 2004, ISBN: 1 403 920 64 8, 212 pp.

Contributors examine the concepts underpinning the aims of post-war recovery and the strategies being used to achieve it, concluding that reconstruction is essentially a development challenge and that good governance and institutional development depend upon healthy collaboration between the state, the market, and civil society. It is argued that in Afghanistan, however, this understanding has largely failed to shape operational practice.

Barnett, Michael. *Eye-witness to a Genocide: The United Nations and Rwanda.* Ithaca, NY: Cornell University Press, 2002, ISBN: 0 8014 8867 2, 240 pp.

Barnett, who worked at the US Mission to the United Nations during the period of the Rwanda genocide, argues that, although it was rep-rehensible, the organization's inaction was rooted in a bureaucracy that saw its role in terms of neutrality, impartiality, and consent, and the observance of rules governing the pre-emptive use of peacekeeping forces. The author believes that the United Nations did violate its moral responsibilities, as did the entire international community, but that institutional cultures create their own moral universe within which perverse judgments seem both logical and ethical.

Bhatia, Michael. *War and Intervention: Issues for Contemporary Peace Operations.* Bloomfield, CT: Kumarian Press, 2003, ISBN: 1 5649 164 5, 240 pp.

This book addresses developments in the nature of war and international intervention, both political and military. Intrastate wars are increasingly conducted by irregular armed forces, whereas peace operations are also expanding in scope. Topics include the nature of UN and US intervention; armed movements and internal conflicts; peace operations and other forms of external intervention, such as sanctions and the use of force; and the military dimension.

Boyce, James K. *Investing in Peace: Aid and Conditionality after Civil Wars.* Adelphi Paper No. 351, Oxford: International Institute for Strategic Studies/ OUP, 2002, ISSN: 0 567-932 X, 96 pp.

Drawing on experiences from Bosnia, Cambodia, El Salvador, and Guatemala, the author makes the case for peace conditionality by linking aid to steps to implement accords and consolidate peace processes. In *Economic Policy for Building Peace: The Lessons of El Salvador* (Lynne Rienner 1996) Boyce argues that while macro-economic stability is important in post-conflict settings, political stability may depend upon resources to meet more immediate needs, such as the reintegration of ex-combatants and the strengthening of democratic institutions.

Brahimi, Lakhdar. *Report of the Panel on United Nations Peace Operations (Brahimi Report).* Report delivered to the UN General Assembly and Security Council, New York, August 2000

This report, prepared by a panel of eminent experts in the fields of peacekeeping, peacebuilding, development, and humanitarian assistance, reviews UN peace and security activities and makes practical recommendations for improving its performance in such activities. The report also addresses the many issues entailed in implementing them, including additional resources, the involvement of civil society, and staffing. The report and related documents are available free of charge at www.un.org/Depts/dpko/lessons/.

Cahill, Kevin (ed.). *Traditions, Values and Humanitarian Action: Foundations, Fault Lines and Corrections.* New York: Fordham University Press and the Center for International Health Cooperation, 2003, ISBN: 0 8232 2288 8, 466 pp.

This volume in the International Humanitarian Affairs series addresses how different religious, cultural, and social systems and values shape humanitarian action; discusses what makes for a "caring society"; and asks whether there are universal values for human well-being. Contributors discuss how best to respond to both acute and structural threats to human welfare from a range of perspectives, from the military and the medical profession to the media and specialists in gender studies.

Cosgrave, John. *The Impact of the War on Terror on Aid Flows.* London: Action Aid, 2004, No ISBN, 35 pp.

The author argues that the "global war on terror" (GWOT) resembles the Cold War in that all other considerations, including humanitarian and development assistance, are subordinated to a single purpose. Development is increasingly replaced by questions of security; and Northern countries that restrict basic liberties or that violate human rights and flout international humanitarian law in the name of combating terrorism are poorly placed to promote human rights elsewhere. Aid agencies and civil society organizations that do not share the prevailing views on global security may face constraints on their operations and cuts in official funding, and even be accused of supporting international terrorism.

Cramer, Christopher. *Civil War Is Not a Stupid Thing: Accounting for Violence in Developing Countries.* London: C. Hurst & Co., 2006, ISBN: 1 8506 5821 8, 329 pp.

Civil war is conventionally regarded as both inherently negative and "the reverse of development," in the words of the World Bank. Cramer argues that such assumptions are ahistorical in ignoring the extent to which Western democracies have their roots in violent contestation and subsequent reconstruction. In policy terms, the view that war can only have negative outcomes leads to the now familiar neoliberal mantras of democratization and free trade as the solution. The alternative view of violence as a benign form of resistance to forces that are deemed oppressive, however, is romantic and utopian in the contemporary world. The author takes a comparative approach to war and reconstruction, setting these in the context of transition to capitalism and a global economy.

Dallaire, Roméo. *Shake Hands with the Devil: The Failure of Humanity in Rwanda.* Toronto: Vintage Canada, 2004, ISBN: 0 6793 1172 6, 592 pp.

Written by the head of the UN peacekeeping mission in Rwanda at the time of the 1994 genocide, this book documents the failure of the rich nations and of the UN system to preempt the tragedy, or to respond promptly and adequately once it began to unfold, despite Dallaire's repeated appeals for engagement and support. Dallaire argues that this inaction cannot be attributed to individual persons or organizations, but was systemic; and that although humanitarian agencies were squeamish about cooperating with peacekeepers, their relief assistance was directly sustaining the war effort.

Donini, Antonio, Norah Niland, and Karin Wermester (eds.). *Nation-Building Unravelled? Aid, Peace and Justice in Afghanistan.* Bloomfield, CT: Kumarian Press, 2003, ISBN: 1 5654 9180 7, 256 pp.

This book asks whether external, and specifically Western, military strength and technology can indeed foster stability and democracy. Practitioners engaged in Afghanistan analyze the challenges and opportunities involved in responding to conflict, injustice, and insecurity, and argue that emerging international "ordering" practices are affecting the role and policy of international organizations, their interaction with national authorities and local communities, and their ability to generate just and sustainable social outcomes.

Dress, Tobi P. *Designing a Peacebuilding Infrastructure: Taking a System Approach to the Prevention of Deadly Conflict.* Geneva: UN NGLS, 2005, UNCTAD/NGLS/2005/1, 234 pp.

This volume focuses on the linkages between and among conflict prevention, governance and human rights, regional mechanisms and early warning systems, macroeconomic factors such as corruption and illicit trade, and the role of NGOs in these fields. Designed as a resource for policymakers and practitioners, the book includes appendices on the Global Partnership for the Prevention of Armed Conflict and on initiatives undertaken by subregional intergovernmental organizations.

Duffield, Mark. *Global Governance and the New Wars: The Merging of Development and Security.* London: Zed Books, 2001, ISBN: 1 8564 9749 6, 304 pp.

Development agencies are increasingly involved not only in providing humanitarian assistance but also in conflict resolution and post-war reconstruction. Duffield argues that contemporary global governance lies in networks among states, intergovernmental organizations, NGOs, and private companies. The various forms of delegation and subcontracting in situations of armed conflict and the preoccupation with "crisis management" have resulted in international humanitarian agencies' accommodation and de facto complicity with "network wars." See also "Complex Emergencies and the Crisis of Developmentalism," *IDS Bulletin* 25(4):37–45; and "The Symphony of the Damned: Racial Discourse, Complex Political Emergences and Humanitarian Aid," *Disasters* 20(3): 173–193.

Fisher, Simon, Dekha Ibrahim Abdi, Jawed Ludin, Richard Smith, Sue Williams, and Steve Williams. *Working with Conflict: Skills and Strategies for Action.* London: Zed Books in association with Responding to Conflict, 2000, ISBN: 1 8564 9837 9, 224 pp.

This handbook reflects the experiences and insights of some 3,000 practitioners from over seventy countries who adapted their methods to suit a wide range of situations. Examples are drawn from Afghanistan, Cambodia, Colombia, Kenya, Northern Ireland, and South Africa. The book highlights the options available to individuals and organizations and seeks to provide a basis on which they can plan sound responses. The handbook is also available in Bahasa (Indonesia), French, Georgian, and Spanish.

Forman, Shepard, and Stewart Patrick. *Good Intentions: Pledges of Aid for Post-conflict Recovery.* Boulder, CO: Lynne Rienner, 2000, ISBN: 1 5558 7879 2, 423 pp.

This comparative study is based on six case studies of multilateral efforts to support sustainable peacebuilding, covering issues that range from the timing, composition, and objectives of pledged assistance, to conditionality and the impact of international aid on reconstruction. The authors conclude that, despite donors' good intentions, inadequate preparation, poor coordination, and lack of perseverance can threaten the recovery of vulnerable societies, and draw lessons for improving the design, mobilization, and coordination of future assistance.

Galtung, Johan. *Transcend and Transform: An Introduction to Conflict Work.* London, Pluto Press, 2004, ISBN: 0 7453 2254 9, 216 pp.

This handbook draws out the interconnections between all expressions of conflict, from the personal or domestic to struggles relating to race, class, or gender, and to interstate conflicts or international divides along economic and religious lines. Founder of the world's first peace research institute (PRIO, see entry) and currently director of TRANSCEND, an international Peace and Development Network, details of Galtung's prodigious output can be found at www.transcend.org.

Holzgrefe, J.L., and Robert O. Keohane (eds.). *Humanitarian Intervention: Ethical, Legal and Political Dilemmas.* Cambridge: Cambridge University Press, 2003, ISBN: 0 521 52928 X, 350 pp.

> Contributors discuss dilemmas concerning the use of force in order to preempt or relieve extreme suffering from the perspectives of international human rights law and international humanitarian law as well as international relations, politics, governance, and ethics. In particular, the book seeks to identify strategies to address the tension between human rights and state sovereignty.

Ignatieff, Michael. *Empire Lite: Nation Building in Bosnia, Kosovo, Afghanistan.* New York: Minerva, 2003, ISBN: 0099455439, 96 pp.

> Ignatieff explores the imperial and the humanitarian sides of "the new global empire," arguing that the international community has failed to engage intelligently with the problems of nation-building in the aftermath of "apocalyptic events." Western powers, led by the United States, are making global stability and security the cornerstone of international relations. Aid agencies have largely reached an accommodation within this framework, recognizing that external military engagement in Bosnia, Kosovo, and Afghanistan made it possible to undertake humanitarian operations there. To this extent, humanitarianism has been co-opted into the US imperial project. Ignatieff looks at the obstacles to genuine international solidarity and at how to assist people in war-torn societies to realize the right to self-rule.

International Federation of Red Cross and Red Crescent Societies. *World Disasters Report 2005: Focus on Information in Disasters.* Bloomfield, CT: Kumarian Press, 2005, ISBN: 92 9139 109 3, 246 pp.

> Published annually since 1993, the 2005 issue explores the importance of information in emergencies and in early warning systems, most crucially for those affected, but also for national and international aid efforts. Timely and reliable information can save lives, whereas actions based on inadequate knowledge and understanding can be dangerous. The report calls on aid agencies to focus less on gathering information for their own needs, and more on exchanging information with those they seek to support. See also the *Code of Conduct for The International Red Cross and Red Crescent Movement and NGOs in Disaster Relief* (1994), Geneva: IFRC, available at www.ifrc.org.

Ismael, Tareq Y., and Jacqueline S. Ismael. *The Iraqi Predicament: People in the Quagmire of Power Politics.* London: Pluto Press, 2004, ISBN: 0 7453 2149 6, 271 pp.

> The authors examine the role of Iraq in world politics, the influence of the regime of Saddam Hussein in Iraq and the Middle

East, and the impact that the United Nations, economic sanctions, and war had on the Iraqi population and on related humanitarian issues.

Junne, Gerd, and Willem Verkoren. *Postconflict Development: Meeting New Challenges.* Boulder, CO: Lynne Rienner, 2004, ISBN: 1 5882 6303 7, 350 pp.

Focusing on the need to move beyond emergency relief to the social and economic structures that will underpin a lasting peace, the authors examine post-war reconstruction in sectors such as security, justice, and economic policy. They argue that, although prosperity does not guarantee peace, a lack of economic development is likely to lead to renewed violence. This view informs their discussion of the policy dilemmas that confront both affected societies and international actors, and their analysis of how to address them.

Juma, Monica Kathina, and Astri Suhrke (eds.). *Eroding Local Capacity: International Humanitarian Action in Africa.* Uppsala: The Nordic Africa Institute, 2003, ISBN: 9 1710 6502 4, 205 pp.

This book examines the interplay among international and local actors involved in humanitarian action in Africa. Despite the consensus that local capacity for humanitarian action needs to be strengthened, the results have been poor, and in some cases local capacity is overwhelmed by international aid. Drawing on cases from East Africa and the Horn, the book looks at institutional capacity in the public and private sectors, as well as at the legal and social norms of humanitarian action.

Livingstone, Grace. *Inside Colombia: Drugs, Democracy and War.* London: Làtin America Bureau, 2002, ISBN: 1 8993 6558 3, 216 pp.

The author draws on a range of academic and media sources on the war in Colombia, its impact on society, and prospects for peace. The book sets out the crisis regarding human rights violations and internal refugees, showing how Colombia fits into US and European foreign policy, discusses the ways in which drugs fuel the economy and the politics of the conflict, and provides a historical overview of key moments in the forty-year war.

Lederach, John Paul. *The Moral Imagination: The Art and Soul of Building Peace.* New York: OUP, 2005, ISBN: 0 1951 7454 2, 200 pp.

An influential thinker and practitioner in the field of conflict mediation and conciliation who has been involved in this capacity in Nicaragua, Northern Ireland, the Philippines, Somalia, and Spain, Lederach's *Building Peace: Sustainable Reconciliation in Divided Societies* (USIP 1998) is regarded as a classic in the discipline. In the present volume, Lederach explores the evolution of his own understanding of peacebuilding, concluding that it is both a learned skill and an art that requires "conflict professionals" to exercise "moral imagination." See also John Paul Lederach and

Moomaw Jenner (eds.) *A Handbook of International Peacebuilding: Into the Eye of the Storm* (Jossey-Bass 2002).

Mahajan, Rahul. *The New Crusade: America's War on Terrorism.* New York: Monthly Review Press, 2003, ISBN: 1 5836 7070 X, 160 pp.

> The author, an anti-war activist, exposes some of the myths about the "global war on terror" (GWOT), and shows discrepancies between the public reasons given for the US-led invasion of Afghanistan and the conduct and ultimate consequences of the war. He argues that the invocation of the GWOT has served to mask the financial and other benefits it has provided to powerful elites and has contributed to the redefinition of global power.

Marriage, Zöe. *Not Breaking the Rules, Not Playing the Game: International Assistance to Countries at War.* London: C. Hurst & Co., ISBN: 1 8506 5813 7, 265 pp.

> In the context of war, humanitarian principles, human rights, and other "rules" do not greatly influence how assistance is delivered and vice versa. Drawing on international aid programs in Democratic Republic of Congo, Rwanda, Sierra Leone, and southern Sudan, Marriage argues that the invocation of moral rights and principles allows aid agencies to justify their own operational weaknesses by blaming or discrediting others. She concludes that people in countries at war are not "breaking the rules" of assistance because assistance is not meaningfully "ruled" by rights or principles: rather, she says, they are "not playing the game." See also *Challenging Aid in Africa: Principles, Implementation and Impact* (Palgrave Macmillan 2006).

Martín Beristain, Carlos. *Humanitarian Aid Work.* Philadelphia, PA: University of Pennsylvania Press, ISBN: 0-8122-3943-1, 316 pp.

> Based mainly on the author's extensive experience in psychosocial health work in Central and South America, this book aims to show how people respond to civil war, political violence, and other traumatic experiences, and to appreciate the social and cultural context in which these responses occur. Beristain puts forward practical ideas for social reconstruction in such areas as prevention, care of victims, collective memory, respect for human rights, and help to the helpers. See also C. Martín Beristain and F. Riera, *Afirmación y Resistencia: La Comunidad como Apoyo,* UNAM 2002).

Mazurana, Dyan, Angela Raven- Roberts, and Jane Parpart (eds.). *Gender, Conflict, and Peacekeeping.* Lanham, MD: Rowman & Littlefield, 2005, ISBN: 0 7425 3633 5, 320 pp.

> Gender is a central factor in shaping current thinking about the causes and consequences of armed conflict, complex emergencies, and reconstruction. Drawing on expertise ranging from international policymaking to the daily struggle to implement peacekeeping

operations, this work spans a wide range of knowledge and experience about international intervention in local crises and reconstruction.

Médecins Sans Frontières (ed.). *In the Shadow of "Just Wars": Violence, Politics, and Humanitarian Action* (trans. Fabrice Weissman and Doctors without Borders). Ithaca, NY: Cornell University Press, 2004, ISBN: 0 80148911 3, 372 pp.

In the preparations for the US-led invasion of Iraq, as in earlier "humanitarian interventions" in the Balkans and Afghanistan, Sierra Leone, and Timor Leste, humanitarian NGOs were offered US government funds to participate in Operation Iraqi Freedom. Many accepted. Arguing that humanitarianism is "peaceful by nature but not pacifist," contributors from Médecins Sans Frontières and other international experts examine recent crises, contrasting those that command little or no international attention and less assistance against those that are of greater importance to the major powers. They call for a renewed commitment to the ideal of "humanitarianism that defies the politics of expendable lives." See also Fabrice Weissman, *Military Humanitarianism: A Deadly Confusion* (MSF 2005).

Melvern, Linda. *Conspiracy to Murder: The Rwanda Genocide and the International Community.* London: Verso, 2004, ISBN: 1 8598 4588 6, 256 pp.

Melvern, an investigative journalist, draws on material gathered in Kigali and major Western capitals, including documents abandoned when the conspirators fled Rwanda and the full confession of the prime minister who presided over the genocide. Detailing the roles played by prominent members of the international community, she shows that the killers, who had been trained by the French military, outmaneuvered the UN Security Council and UN peacekeepers; that the Conservative government in the United Kingdom ignored warnings and misled Parliament about what was really happening, and that the US government is still withholding evidence showing that the genocide had begun. See also *A People Betrayed: The Role of the West in the Rwanda Genocide* (Zed Books 2001).

Minear, Larry. *The Humanitarian Enterprise: Dilemmas and Discoveries.* Bloomfield, CT: Kumarian Press, 2002, ISBN: 1 56549 150 5, 304 pp.

The expansion of international humanitarian efforts in post–Cold War conflicts has underlined the uneasy relations between humanitarian assistance, military intervention, and politico-diplomatic concerns. The author, former director of the Humanitarianism and War Project (see entry) addresses issues such as neutrality, the use of military force for international peace and security as well as in humanitarian operations, the erosion of national sovereignty, and the role of local organizations. The book draws on the diverse experiences of aid workers, Red Cross officials, NGOs, and government bodies in these areas.

Montgomery, John D., and Dennis A. Rondinelli (eds.). *Beyond Reconstruction in Afghanistan: Lessons from Development Experience.* Basingstoke: Palgrave Macmillan, 2004, ISBN: 1 4039 6511 0, 240 pp.

> Placing the current situation in Afghanistan in its historical context, contributors highlight the limitations embedded in ambitious state-building projects, focusing on the interaction of the goals of external and domestic actors, and the importance of having a deep understanding of the internal environment and of the needs of the society receiving assistance.

Nordstrom, Carolyn. *Shadows of War: Violence, Power, and International Profiteering in the Twenty-first Century.* Berkeley, CA: University of California Press, 2004, ISBN: 978 0 520 24241 8, 306 pp.

> The author examines the complex and vastly profitable web of dealings in pharmaceuticals, illegal drugs, food, precious gems, and weapons that comprise the international economy of war, and the intense interests these dealings create in continuing to fuel violent conflict. Although there may be an appearance of conventional military objectives, these networks are motivated by profit and power rather than by territorial ambitions. Nordstrom's focus, however, is on the civilians who are often tangled up in these networks as a means of surviving the violence.

Price, Richard, and Mark W. Zacher. *United Nations and Global Security.* Basingstoke: Palgrave Macmillan, 2004, ISBN: 1 403 96391 6, 297 pp.

> This book examines global security in the wake of the September 11, 2001, attacks in the United States, focusing on the various roles played by the United Nations in relation to arms control, the prevention and mitigation of civil violence, attempts to deter acts of aggression, peace-keeping operations, and humanitarian assistance. Divergence about such issues within the United Nations and among member states illustrates the potential and limitations of multilateralism.

Rieff, David. *A Bed for the Night: Humanitarianism in Crisis.* New York: Simon & Schuster, 2002, ISBN: 0 684 8097 7 X, 384 pp.

> Rieff argues that humanitarian organizations work in a violent world governed by geopolitical concerns and are increasingly losing sight of their purpose. The civil wars and ethnic cleansing of the 1990s demonstrated that humanitarian aid has only a limited capacity to alleviate suffering and that it may do more harm than good. The author maintains that the principle of political neutrality has been eroded and that the independence of humanitarian agencies is now fatally compromised. In *At the Point of a Gun: Democratic Dreams and Armed Intervention* (Simon & Schuster 2005), Rieff

holds that international intervention in any form, military or humanitarian, should be pursued only as a last resort. Similar arguments are made by David Kennedy in *The Dark Side of Virtue: Reassessing International Humanitarianism* (Princeton University Press 2004).

Sánchez Rubio, David (ed.). *Interventions humanitaires?* Collection *Alternatives Sud*. Paris: Centre Tricontinental and Syllepse, 2004, ISBN: 2 84950 028 3, 178 pp.

Originally published as Volume 11(3) of the quarterly *Alternatives Sud,* which gathers Southern views on a topical debate, this collection examines controversies surrounding the "right" or the "duty" to intervene to relieve human suffering, and how these obligations have been redefined in the context of "humanitarian crises" and "preventive wars." Humanitarian agencies now operate in an ambiguous politico-military terrain, which raises the questions of whether charity has replaced development, and whether humanitarian interventions serve to mask its failure. Contributors cover drought in Rajasthan, the dumping of genetically modified crops as emergency food aid, ways in which emergency relief allows national governments to evade their responsibilities, military intervention in Haiti, and foreign relief programs in Chad, Mozambique, and Sudan. Some items are published in Spanish by Centro Investigación Para la Paz (CIP) (see entry).

Save the Children (UK). *Children's Feedback Committees in Zimbabwe: An Experiment in Humanitarian Accountability.* Harare: SCF (UK), 2005, ISBN: 0-7974-2933-6, 60 pp.

This report draws on children's feedback committees that were established by SCF during food aid programs in Zimbabwe during 2003–2004, which sought to show how children are affected by food distributions. The process of working with communities, establishing children's committees, and responding to inefficient or inequitable processes in the delivery of emergency assistance are all examined in light of this initiative.

Smillie, Ian, and Larry Minear. *The Charity of Nations: Humanitarian Action in a Calculating World.* Bloomfield, CT: Kumarian Press, 2004, ISBN: 1 56549 190 4, 288 pp.

Since the declaration of the "global war on terror" (GWOT), international humanitarianism has been increasingly influenced by geopolitics and commercial interests. As a result, some crises command more international attention and resources than other equally urgent situations. The authors call for a renewed commitment to multilateralism, accountability, and trust. See also Ian Smillie (ed.) *Patronage or Partnership: Local Capacity Building in Humanitarian Crises* (Kumarian 2001).

The Sphere Project. *The Sphere Handbook: Humanitarian Charter and Minimum Standards in Disaster Response.* Geneva: The Sphere Project, 2004 (2nd revised edition), ISBN: 9 2913 9059 3, 322 pp.

An international initiative aimed at improving the effectiveness and accountability of disaster response, the *Handbook* sets out the rights and minimum standards that organizations providing humanitarian assistance should guarantee to affected populations and aid recipients. The Charter is based on the principles and provisions of international humanitarian, human rights, and refugee law, and of the 1994 Red Cross Code of Conduct (see entry for IFRC). The *Handbook* covers five core sectors: water supply and sanitation; nutrition; food aid; shelter and site planning; and health services. It is also published in Arabic, French, Russian, and Spanish.

Sweetman, Caroline (ed.). *Gender, Development, and Humanitarian Work,* Focus on Gender Series. Oxford: Oxfam GB, 2001, ISBN: 0 85598 457 0, 88 pp.

Contributors focus on humanitarian activity during natural disasters and in response to violent conflict, and draw lessons and recommendations for conflict resolution and peacebuilding.

Terry, Fiona. *Condemned to Repeat: The Paradox of Humanitarian Action.* Ithaca, NY: Cornell University Press, 2002, ISBN: 0 80148796 X, 282 pp.

Head of the French section of Médicins Sans Frontières (MSF) when it withdrew from Rwandan refugee camps because the aid was reaching the *génocidaires,* Terry argues that international humanitarian agencies largely ignore wider political contexts in the rush to offer relief assistance. Rather than alleviating suffering, ill-judged aid can end up in the hands of those responsible for causing suffering, an argument the author supports by reference to refugees from Afghanistan, Cambodia, El Salvador, Nicaragua, and Rwanda.

Uvin, Peter. *Human Rights and Development.* Bloomfield, CT: Kumarian Press, 2004, ISBN: 1 56549 186 6, 256 pp.

Building on his acclaimed work on the 1994 Rwandan genocide, *Aiding Violence: The Development Enterprise in Rwanda* (Kumarian 1998), the author argues that development and human rights organizations must recognize and actively engage with the ethical issues implicit in their endeavors, however complex or intransigent, in order to surmount these problems in ways that reduce the propensity to conflict and contribute to sustainable peaceful outcomes. The failure to ground aid interventions in a rights-based framework can have profoundly perverse effects.

Vaux, Tony. *The Selfish Altruist: Relief Work in Famine and War.* London: Earthscan, 2002, ISBN: 1 85383 879 9, 256 pp.

> Famine and war evoke strong emotional reactions, which relief workers must convert into practical action, including choices about who they can help and how. The line between subjective impulses and objective judgments is seldom easily discerned, and aid workers' personal motivations are never far beneath the surface. The author draws on his own experience of emergency relief programs in the Balkans, central Asia, the Horn, and central and southern Africa.

Waters, Tony. *Bureaucratizing the Good Samaritan.* Boulder, CO: Westview Press, 2001, ISBN: 0813367905, 325 pp.

> This book describes the practical, political, and moral assumptions of the "international refugee relief regime," in which the values motivating the aid agencies are governed by their own bureaucracies, while the mass media also portray assistance in terms of "victims" and "saviors." Because the demands of the bureaucratized organization and the need of relief agencies to generate the emotional publicity to sustain donor interest affect decisions, the connections need to be acknowledged and addressed more honestly.

Wheeler, Nicholas J. *Saving Strangers: Humanitarian Intervention in International Society.* Oxford: Oxford University Press, 2000, ISBN: 13: 978-0-19-829621-8, 352 pp.

> This book compares the international response to humanitarian interventions during and since the Cold War, and the ways in which these interventions have been legitimized as an exception to the rules of sovereignty and non-intervention and non-use of force. The cases of Bosnia, Cambodia, East Pakistan, Iraq, Kosovo, Rwanda, and Somalia are used to illustrate pluralist and solidarist critiques of humanitarian intervention. Accepting that state actions will be constrained if they cannot be legitimated, Wheeler asks how far contemporary practices of humanitarian intervention resolve the conflict between order and justice in international society.

Wood, Adrian, Raymond Apthorpe, and John Borton (eds.). *Evaluating International Humanitarian Action: Reflections from Practitioners.* London and New Jersey: Zed Books, 2001, ISBN: 1 85649 976 6, 224 pp.

> This book analyzes humanitarian assistance both in terms of how it is and should be delivered and in terms of how it is and should be evaluated, and draws on the experiences and lessons of those engaged in humanitarian program evaluations. Compiled by the Active Learning Network for Accountability

and Performance in Humanitarian Assistance (ALNAP) (see entry), case studies illustrate different kinds of post–Cold War emergency.

1.2 JOURNALS

Accord: An International Review of Peace Initiatives. Published twice yearly by Conciliation Resources. Editor: Andy Carl. ISSN: 1365 0742

> *www.c-r.org/accord/index.shtml*

> This journal analyzes peacebuilding processes, with each issue focuses on a specific country or process andusually including articles exploring the challenges of post-conflict reconstruction. Recent issues include *From Military Peace to Social Justice? The Angolan Peace Process, Alternatives to War: Colombia's Peace Processes,* and *Engaging Armed Groups in Peace* Processes. Contents are free online.

Conflict, Security and Development. Published three times a year by Routledge Editors: Mats Berdal, Michael Clarke and Keith Britto. ISSN: 1467 8802

> *www.tandf.co.uk/journals/titles/14678802.asp*

> Focusing on the economic and political changes taking place at the global level, and their impact on developing and transitional countries (including those emerging from civil war or international conflict), the journal promotes more integrated international responses to such problems through intellectually provocative research and analysis. It encourages the exchange of ideas and debate between the academic and policy communities, North and South.

Development in Practice. Published six times a year by Routledge, on behalf of Oxfam GB. Editor-in-Chief: Deborah Eade. ISSN: 0961-4524 (print)

> *http://www.tandf.co.uk/journals/carfax/09614524.html*
> *www.developmentinpractice.org*

> A multidisciplinary forum for development professionals and academics to exchange ideas and analysis, the journal regularly publishes articles, viewpoints, practical notes, and book reviews that are relevant to humanitarian policy and practice. The November 2005 issue was dedicated to post-war reconstruction and peacebuilding. Summaries of all articles in English, French, Portuguese, and Spanish are available on the Web site.

Disasters: The Journal of Disaster Studies, Policy and Management. Published quarterly by Blackwell, on behalf of the Overseas Development Institute (ODI). Editors: Paul Harvey, Helen Young, and David Alexander. ISSN: 0361-3666

> *http://www.blackwellpublishing.com/journal.asp?ref=0361-3666*

A forum for academics, policymakers, and practitioners to exchange research and practice related to natural disasters and complex political emergencies around the world, the journal includes a mix of field reports, case studies, academic papers, and book reviews.

Humanitarian Affairs Review. Published quarterly in English and in French by Humanitarian Affairs Review ASBL. Editor: Giles Merritt. No ISSN.

www.humanitarian-review.org

Aimed mainly at readers with only an indirect involvement in humanitarian issues, such as journalists and business managers, the journal covers topics ranging from the need for better prevention and management of human-made and natural disasters to the ethical and moral issues that confront the organizations and individuals who provide humanitarian aid.

Journal of Humanitarian Assistance. Published by the Feinstein International Center; updated continuously. Editor: Daniel Maxwell (Founding editor: Jim Whitman). ISSN: 1360 0222

http://jha.ac

This open-access online journal encompasses all aspects of humanitarian assistance, from early warning and emergency provision to post-conflict peacebuilding and the transition to development. Topics covered include law, politics, the military, logistics, and the work of national and international organizations. Established in 1995, it hosts more than 3,000 documents, composed of articles, reports, and book reviews.

Journal of Peacebuilding and Development. Published three times a year by the South North Centre for Peacebuilding and Development (SNCPD), Zimbabwe, and the Center for Global Peace, United States. Editors: Mohammed Abu-Nimer and Erin McCandless. ISSN: 1542-3166

http://american.edu/cgp/jpd/jpdhome.htm

This journal provides a forum for sharing experiences, critical thinking, and constructive action on issues at the intersections of conflict, development, and peace. Recent articles include Peter Uvin, "The Development/Peacebuilding Nexus: A Typology and History of Changing Paradigms," and Necla Tschirgi, "Making the Case for a Regional Approach to Peacebuilding."

International Peacekeeping. Published quarterly by Routledge. Editor: Michael Pugh. ISSN: 1353 3312

www.tandf.co.uk/journals/titles/13533312.asp

This journal examines the theory and practice of peacekeeping and reflects debates on issues ranging from the enforcement of sanctions and monitoring of agreements for the protection of aid to the relationship between peacekeepers, state authorities, rival factions, civilians, and NGOs in post-conflict reconstruction efforts.

The Online Journal of Peace and Conflict Resolution. Published by the Tabula Rasa Institute, Washington, DC, frequency varies. Editor-in-chief: Derek Sweetman. ISSN: 1522 211

> *www.trinstitute.org/ojpcr/*

> This open-access online journal is aimed at academics and practitioners working in fields relating to the reduction and eventual elimination of destructive conflict.

Peace, Conflict & Development. Published twice yearly by the Department of Peace Studies, University of Bradford. Editor: Department of Peace Studies

> *www.peacestudiesjournal.org.uk/*

> This open-access online journal addresses contemporary issues in peace, conflict, and development from an interdisciplinary perspective. Consisting primarily of academic papers and field reports, recent articles have covered democratic transition and consolidation in post-conflict Congo, the unfinished transition in East Timor, transitional justice in Guatemala and Peru, peace processes in Bosnia-Herzegovina, and governance and conflict in Burundi.

Security Dialogue. Published quarterly by Sage on behalf of the International Peace Research Institute (PRIO). Editor: J. Peter Burgess. ISSN: 0967 0106

> *http://www.sagepub.com/journal.aspx?pid=26*

> The journal provides a forum for analysis of the normative dimensions and conventional policy assumptions and practices concerning security, its gender aspects, and the theoretical and practical aspects of identity and identity-based conflict. It also explores new and traditional security issues such as globalization, nationalism, ethnic conflict and civil war, biological and chemical warfare, and environmental and human security.

SECTION 2: ORGANIZATIONS, NETWORKS, AND WEB SITES

Active Learning Network for Accountability and Performance in Humanitarian Action (ALNAP), ALNAP Secretariat, Overseas Development Institute, 111 Westminster Bridge Street, London SE1 7JD, United Kingdom

> *www.alnap.org*

> Established in 1997, ALNAP is one of several quality and accountability initiatives in the humanitarian sector, distinguished by being

an international membership network of development organizations and practitioners committed to active learning. Its *Review of Humanitarian Action in 2004* is available in English, French, and Spanish. The latest in its series of practical guides for humanitarian agencies is Hugo Slim and Andrew Bonwick's *Protection: The ALNAP Guide for Humanitarian Agencies* (2005).

Centre for Humanitarian Dialogue (HD Centre), 114 rue de Lausanne, CH-1202, Geneva, Switzerland

www.hdcentre.org

The HD Centre mediates and facilitates the resolution of armed conflict in order to reduce the suffering of civilians directly and indirectly affected by fighting. It has played a role in many recent and ongoing conflicts, including Aceh, Burma (Myanmar), Darfur, the Geneva Initiative, which supports negotiations between the two parties to the Middle East conflict, Nepal, and Uganda. Titles by Hugo Slim include *Politicizing Humanitarian Action according to Need* (2004); *How We Look: Hostile Perceptions of Humanitarian Action* (2004); and *With or Against: Humanitarian Agencies and Coalition Counter-insurgencies* (2004). Other recent publications include Cate Buchanan and Robert Muggah, *No Relief: Surveying the effects of Gun Violence on Humanitarian and Development Personnel* (2005) and Antonia Potter, *We the Women: Why Conflict Mediation Is Not Just a Job for Men* (2005).

Centro de Investigación para la Paz (CIP) [Peace Research Centre] Calle Duque de Sesto 40, 28009 Madrid, Spain

www.cipresearch.fuhem.es

Conducting multidisciplinary research on international issues, CIP focuses on armed conflicts, the multilateral system, indigenous peoples, gender, and international justice. It maintains an extensive documentation center on these issues. Recent publications include: José Antonio Sanahuja, *Comercio, ayuda y desarrollo en tiempos de guerra* (2004); Francisco Rey Marcos, *La financiación de la asistencia humanitaria* (2004); Gérard Pierre-Charles, *Crisis del Estado e intervención internacional en Haití* (2005); and Ali Zakaria Moussa, *La acción humanitaria en Chad y Darfur* (2005).

Christian Michelsen Institute (CMI)—Development Studies and Human Rights PO Box 6033 Postterminalen, N-5892 Bergen, Norway

www.cmi.no

CMI is a development research center with a focus on policy-related and applied research. Its program on peacebuilding addresses issues such as international assistance and multilateral peace-keeping operations, state formation, democratization, the rule of law, and economic reconstruction in countries such as Angola, Afghanistan, East Timor, Kosovo, and Sri Lanka. Information about its extensive publishing program is available online.

Clingendael Institute, Conflict Research Unit (CRU), PO Box 93080, 2509 AB The Hague, the Netherlands

www.cliengendael.nl

CRU focuses on ways to prevent and address intrastate conflict through translating research into practical policy recommendations, and developing tools for decision makers in official aid agencies and NGOs. The Institute produces a range of publications on topics related to peacebuilding and post-conflict reconstruction, many of which are free online.

Conflict Prevention and Post-Conflict Reconstruction Network

http://cpr.web.cern.ch/cpr/

This network comprises an informal group of twenty-nine donor countries and UN agencies dealing with conflict management in order to share knowledge and improve their operational effectiveness. The Network runs the CPR Network Web portal and produces practice-based materials such as the Compendium of Operational Tools, approaches to Peace and Conflict Impact Assessment, and an early warning response methodology.

CRInfo—the Conflict Resolution Information Source, c/o Conflict Research Consortium, University of Colorado, Campus Box 580, Boulder, CO 80309, United States

http://v4.crinfo.org/intro.jsp

CRInfo is an online clearinghouse that indexes more than 25,000 conflict-related Web pages, books, articles, audiovisual materials, organizational profiles, events, and news items. The site offers recommended readings and brief items on related topics and enables users to connect with an extensive global network.

Human Rights Watch, 350 5th Avenue, 34th floor, New York, NY 11018-3299, United States

www.hrw.org

Human Rights Watch (HRW) investigates and exposes violations of human rights and holds the perpetrators and their supporters accountable. Although it is not directly concerned with humanitarian relief, it consistently documents situations that are relevant to humanitarian agencies. Its Opportunism Watch documents restrictions of civil liberties in the name of the Global War on Terror. The Web site contains HRW publications and press releases and information on issues such as conventions relating to torture and the

International Criminal Court. Recent reports include *Off Target: The Conduct of the War and Civilian Casualties in Iraq* (2003), *Colombia: Displaced and Discarded—The Plight of Internally Displaced Persons in Bogotá and Cartagena* (2004), *Bloodstained Hands: Past Atrocities in Kabul and Afghanistan's Legacy of Impunity* (2005), and *Entrenching Impunity: Government Responsibility for International Crimes in Darfur* (2005). Its book *Genocide, War Crimes and Crimes against Humanity* looks at the tribunals for Rwanda and the former Yugoslavia.

Humanitarian Accountability Project International (HAP-I), International Environment House 2, ch Balexert 7-9, CH-1219, Geneva, Switzerland

www.hapinternational.org

HAP-I works to make humanitarian action accountable to its intended beneficiaries through self-regulation and compliance verification. It develops and promotes the principles of accountability through research, consultation, and collaboration; helps its members to establish such principles; monitors and reports on their performance; offers accreditation accordingly; and takes up concerns or complaints raised about member organizations.

Humanitarian Policy Group (HPG), Overseas Development Institute, 111 Westminster Bridge Street, London SE1 7JD, United Kingdom

www.odi.org.uk/hpg/

HPG is a team of researchers and information professionals working on humanitarian policy issues. They aim to improve humanitarian policy and practice through a combined research program, the Humanitarian Practice Network (HPN), and specific events. Recent HPG Reports include Joanna Macrae and Adele Harmer (eds.), *Humanitarian Action and the "Global War on Terror": A Review of Trends and Issues* (2003), Charles-Antoine Hofmann, *Measuring the Impact of Humanitarian Aid* (2004), Adele Harmer and Lin Cotterrell, *Diversity in Donorship: the Changing Landscape of Official Humanitarian Aid* (2005), and Paul Harvey and Jeremy Lind, *Dependency and Humanitarian Relief: A Critical Analysis* (2005). The HPN produces a magazine and occasional publications, such as guidelines and manuals, and also publishes the journal *Disasters* (see entry). Apart from the journal, HPG publications are available free online.

Humanitarianism and War Project, Feinstein International Famine Center, Tufts University, 150 Harrison Ave., Boston, MA 02111, United States

Although the HWP closed in 2006, its archives review the experience of the international community in responding to complex emergencies during the post–Cold War period, in particular the interplay between humanitarian action and political–military forces. HWP produced a prodigious number of publications, including books (see entries for Minear and Smillie), briefing papers, monographs, and both scholarly and newspaper articles. Many are available free online, some are also in French and Spanish.

International Alert, 346 Clapham Road, London SW9 9AP, United Kingdom

www.international-alert.org

International Alert works to build sustainable peace in areas threatened or affected by violent conflict. In addition to direct involvement in some twenty countries and an extensive advocacy program, it also publishes reports, briefing papers, manuals, and resource packs on issues such as the safe storage and disposal of ammunition, gender justice and accountability in peacekeeping operations, conflict and the corporate sector, and a series of country reports on small arms. Recent publications include *Aid, Conflict and Peacebuilding in Afghanistan. What Lessons Can Be Learned?* (2002); *Conflict, Humanitarian Assistance and Peacebuilding: Meeting the Challenges* (2003); *Inclusive Security, Sustainable Peace: A Toolkit for Advocacy and Action* (2004); and *Building Institutional Capacity for Conflict-Sensitive Practice: The Case of International NGOs* (2004). Many titles exist in French and Spanish; most are available free online.

International Committee of the Red Cross (ICRC), 19 Avenue de la Paix, CH 1202, Geneva, Switzerland

www.icrc.org

ICRC offers humanitarian protection and assistance for victims of war and armed violence. The Geneva Conventions give ICRC the legal mandate to visit prisoners, organize relief operations, reunite separated families, and perform similar humanitarian activities during armed conflicts. Its statutes encourage it to undertake similar work in situations of internal violence, where the conventions do not apply. The Geneva Conventions are binding instruments of international law, applicable worldwide, whereas the statutes have quasi-legal or "soft law" status. ICRC produces films, guides, and manuals for humanitarian personnel and journalists working in conflict areas, and information on matters of international humanitarian law. Recent publications and articles include *Hard Choices: Moral Dilemmas in Humanitarian Intervention* (1999); *Strengthening Protection in War* (2001); and *Protection of Detainees: ICRC's Action behind Bars* (2005). The Web site is in Arabic, English, French, Japanese, Portuguese, Spanish, and Russian.

International Crisis Group (ICG), 149 Avenue Louise, Level 24, B-1050, Brussels, Belgium

www.crisisgroup.org

ICG works to prevent and resolve violent conflict, focusing on field-based research and high-level advocacy, and regular analyses and recommendations aimed at international decision makers. Its reports are available online.

International Peace Academy (IPA), 777 United Nations Plaza, 4th floor, New York, NY, 10017-3521, United States

www.ipacademy.org

IPA promotes the prevention and settlement of armed conflicts between and within states through policy research and development and an extensive publishing program that covers both general topics and in-depth analyses of specific conflicts and regions. Many of its reports and occasional papers are available free online. Recent books include Karen Ballentine and Jake Sherman (eds.), *The Political Economy of Armed Conflict: Beyond Greed and Grievance* (Lynne Rienner 2003); Chandra Sriram and Zoe Nielsen (eds.), *Exploring Subregional Conflict: Opportunities for Conflict Prevention* (Lynne Rienner 2004); and David Keen, *Conflict and Collusion in Sierra Leone* (James Currey 2005).

International Peace Research Institute (PRIO), Hausmanns, Gate 7, NO-0186, Oslo, Norway

www.prio.no

PRIO researches and publishes on peace-related issues, in particular, communities affected by civil war, small arms, and landmines. PRIO also sponsors a project, Conflict Studies from a Gender Perspective, and publishes the *Journal of Peace Research* and *Security Dialogue* (see entry).

Integrated Regional Information Networks (IRIN)

www.IRINnews.org

Based in Nairobi, IRIN was founded by OCHA (see entry) in 1995 to improve the flow of vital information to those involved in relief efforts in the Great Lakes region following the 1994 Rwandan genocide. Its main role is to provide independent news and analysis about sixty-two countries in sub-Saharan Africa, the Middle East, and central Asia (plus Nepal) for the humanitarian community. It also provides a range of multimedia services including PlusNews, for people living with or working on HIV/AIDS issues, in both English and French (www.PlusNews.org and www.PlusNews.org.fr); IRIN radio, which works through local radio stations to reach an audience of tens of millions; IRIN film; and IRIN photo library. All IRIN materials, e-mail delivery services, and newsfeeds are free.

Life & Peace Institute (LPI), PO Box 1520, SE-751 45, Uppsala, Sweden

www.life-peace.org

LPI is an international and ecumenical center for peace research and action. Its publishing division includes *New Routes,* a journal of peace research and action; Tools for Peace; and two book series, *Transition to Democracy* and *Women and Nonviolence.*

Oxfam GB (OGB), John Smith Drive, Oxford OX4 2JY, United Kingdom

http//: publications.oxfam.org.uk/

OGB is extensively involved in humanitarian relief work on which it publishes advocacy briefings, books for humanitarian professionals, reports and case studies, and manuals and how-to guides. OGB also co-publishes campaign documents with Oxfam International, and with specialized agencies such as Amnesty International and coalitions such as the International Action Network on Small Arms. Recent publications include *The Impact of Guns on Women's Lives, Predictable Funding for Humanitarian Emergencies,* and *Transitional Settlement, Displaced Populations.* For information about OGB's humanitarian programs, visit www.oxfam.org.uk.

Refugees International, 1705 N Street NW, Washington, DC 20036, United States

www.refintl.org

Founded in 1979 in response to the forced repatriation of Indochinese refugees, RI has been involved in thirty missions concerning refugees and mass exodus worldwide. It undertakes low-profile diplomacy while using the power of the press to mobilize governments and engage the United Nations. Its Web site is a valuable source of information on refugee issues and includes online reports and publications. Titles published in 2005 include *Lives on Hold: The Human Cost of Statelessness; No Power to Protect: The African Union Mission in Sudan;* and *Must Boys Be Boys? Ending Sexual Exploitation in UN Peacekeeping Missions.*

ReliefWeb, ReliefWeb New York, OCHA, United Nations, New York, NY 10014, United States; ReliefWeb Geneva, OCHA, Palais des Nations, CH-1211, Geneva, Switzerland; ReliefWeb Kobe, OCHA, Hitomiraikan 5F, 1-5-2, Wakinohama-kaigan-dori, Chuo-ku, Kobe City, Hyogo 651-0073, Japan

www.reliefweb.int

Administered by OCHA (see entry), ReliefWeb is the leading global gateway to information on humanitarian issues, receiving an average of 3 million Web site visits per day. Designed to help the international humanitarian community to deliver emergency assistance, it provides information that is updated around the clock—made possible by working across three time zones— while also emphasizing "forgotten emergencies." The Web site contains over 300,000 documents and maps and provides profes- sional resources, reference materials on policy-related issues, and information about specific appeals and funding. ReliefWeb offers a newsfeed service and e-mail subscriptions for those with low- bandwidth Internet connections.

Stockholm International Peace Research Institute (SIPRI), Signalistgatan 9, SE-169 70, Solna, Sweden

www.sipri.org

SIPRI conducts research on conflict and cooperation in relation to international peace and security. The *SIPRI Yearbook: Armaments, Disarmament and International Security* (Oxford: OUP) is an annual compilation of studies on major armed conflicts and multi- lateral peace missions, developments in international courts, and the dynamics of external intervention.

UNDP Bureau for Crisis Prevention and Recovery (BCPR), One UN Plaza, New York, NY 10017, United States, and 11 Ch des Anemones, Châtelaine, CH-1219, Geneva, Switzerland

www.undp.org/bcpr/

Within the UN system, the BCPR strives to ensure that UNDP plays a pivotal role in transitions from relief to development; pro- motes linkages between UN peace and security and development objectives; and enhances governments' responsibilities and technical and national capacities to manage crisis and post-conflict situations. It focuses on promoting the rule of law and good governance; justice and security; demobilization; reducing the flow of small arms; supporting action on landmines; and pro- viding war-affected populations with alternative livelihoods. In relation to natural disasters, UNDP seeks to establish recovery initiatives that can be sustained by attention to disaster mitiga- tion and preparedness.

UN Office for the Coordination of Humanitarian Assistance (OCHA), UN Headquarters, First Avenue at 46th Street, New York, NY 10017, United States

http://ochaonline.un.org/index.asp

OCHA is responsible for promoting a coordinated approach to humanitarian assistance among UN specialized agencies and other bodies through the Common Humanitarian Action Plan (CHAP), and for establishing a clear division of responsibility regarding humanitarian needs. Specifically it oversees needs assessment and resource mobilization (through the Coordinated Appeals Process) and acts as the secretariat for interagency coordination. It administers ReliefWeb (see entry) and hosts the Integrated Regional Information Networks (IRIN) (see entry).

The World Bank Group Conflict Prevention and Reconstruction Unit (CPRU), 1818 H Street N.W., Washington, DC 20433, United States

http://lnweb18.worldbank.org/ESSD/sdvext.nsf/67ByDocName/ ConflictPreventionandReconstruction

Although the World Bank does not deal with humanitarian issues, the CPRU designs development strategies for conflict-affected countries and publishes regularly. Relevant works include Paul Collier and Nicholas Sambanis (2005) *Understanding Civil Wars* (2 volumes): Paul Collier and Anke Hoeffler (2002) *Aid, Policy and Growth in Post-Conflict Societies;* and Paul Collier (2000) *Policy for Post-Conflict Societies: Reducing the Risks of Renewed Conflict.*

About the Contributors

Gretchen Alther works with the Centre for Development and Population Activities (CEDPA) in Washington, DC and volunteered with the American Friends Service Committee (AFSC) in Colombia in 2003 and 2004.

Andrew Bonwick was, at the time of writing, Oxfam GB's Humanitarian Protection Adviser, and previously worked for ICRC and other NGOs. He is currently studying Public International Law at the London School of Economics.

Julia Buckmaster works with Astri Suhrke on the Christian Michelsen Institute's peacebuilding program (see below).

Deborah Eade became Editor of the international journal *Development in Practice* in 1991, and has published extensively on international development and humanitarian issues. She was Oxfam GB's Deputy Regional Representative for Mexico and Central America (1984–1991).

Udan Fernando is studying at the University of Amsterdam, focusing on Dutch donors and Sri Lankan NGOs.

Dorothea Hilhorst is a senior lecturer at Wageningen University, and specializes in natural disaster, conflict, and humanitarian assistance.

Jonathan Makuwira is a lecturer at Nulloo Yumbah, Central Queensland University's Indigenous Learning, Spirituality, and Research Centre.

Vanessa Pupavac lectures in the Department of Politics and International Relations in the Faculty of Law and Social Sciences at the University of Nottingham. She previously worked for the UN Criminal Tribunal for Former Yugoslavia and the OSCE, and has advised on international humanitarian missions and asylum cases.

Volker Schimmel works in the African Great Lakes region and was a spokes-person for the Office of the United Nations High Commissioner for Refugees (UNHCR) in Rwanda. He is currently Associate

Humanitarian Affairs Officer for the United Nations Office for the Coordination of Humanitarian Affairs (OCHA) in Burundi.

Astri Suhrke is a senior researcher at the Christian Michelsen Institute (CMI) and has written widely on the politics of international humanitarian policies. She is currently leading a project funded by the Research Council of Norway on aid strategies in post-war situations.

Frank James Tester teaches social and international development studies in the School of Social Work at the University of British Columbia, and has worked internationally for many years with various Canadian NGOs. He has published extensively on the history of colonial relations in the Canadian eastern Arctic.

Martha Thompson is a social scientist and community health professional. She worked in Central America for 16 years (1981–1995) before becoming Oxfam Canada's representative for Cuba and the Eastern Caribbean, based in Havana. She now lectures on conflict issues at Brandeis University and Tufts University and is responsible for post-tsunami work with the Unitarian Universalist Service Committee (UUSC).

Tony Vaux is the founding director of Humanitarian Initiatives, which promotes exchange on conflict-related issues among practitioners. He has been a consultant to DFID, UNDP, and Swiss Development Cooperation; and in 2005 led a UK Disasters Emergency Committee (DEC) team evaluating post-tsunami assistance. Previously he was responsible for Oxfam GB's programs in West India (1976–1980) and East India and Bhutan (1982–1984), coordinated its emergency response department (1984–1994), and managed its work in Eastern Europe and the Former Soviet Union (1994–1998).

Suzanne Williams is a social anthropologist and pioneered gender and development work in Oxfam GB, with which she worked for many years in Brazil, Namibia, and South Africa before becoming its Rights Policy Adviser. Author of *The Oxfam Gender Training Manual* (Oxfam GB, 1995), and co-author (with Deborah Eade, see above) of *The Oxfam Handbook of Development and Relief* (Oxfam GB, 1995), she is currently an artist and an independent consultant on gender and conflict.

Index

*Kumarian Press, located in Bloomfield, Connecticut, is a forward-looking,
scholarly press that promotes active international engagement and an
awareness jof global connectedness.*